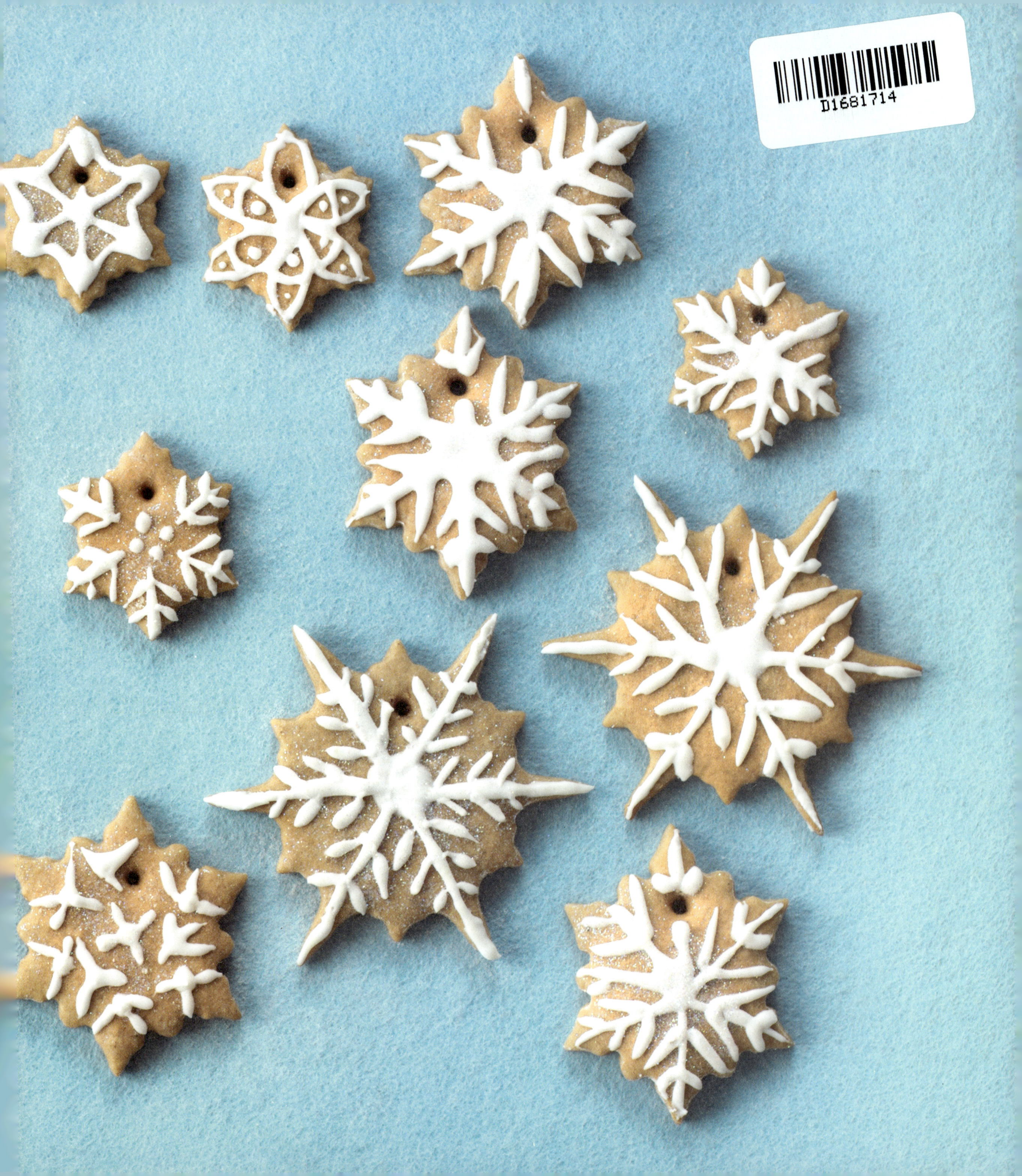

NIGELLA CHRISTMAS

Also by Nigella Lawson

HOW TO EAT
THE PLEASURES AND PRINCIPLES OF GOOD FOOD

HOW TO BE A DOMESTIC GODDESS
BAKING AND THE ART OF COMFORT COOKING

NIGELLA BITES
FROM FAMILY MEALS TO ELEGANT DINNERS—
EASY, DELECTABLE RECIPES FOR ANY OCCASION

FOREVER SUMMER

FEAST
FOOD TO CELEBRATE LIFE

NIGELLA EXPRESS
GOOD FOOD FAST

NIGELLA CHRISTMAS

FOOD ❄ FAMILY ❄ FRIENDS ❄ FESTIVITIES

NIGELLA LAWSON

PHOTOGRAPHS BY LIS PARSONS

HYPERION
NEW YORK

Copyright © 2008, 2009 Nigella Lawson
Photographs copyright © 2008, 2009 Lis Parsons

Design and Art Direction: Caz Hildebrand
Cookery Assistant: Hettie Potter
Editorial Assistant: Zoe Wales
Props: Rose Murray
Layout/Design: Julie Martin
Home Economics adviser: Moyra Fraser
Index: Vicki Robinson

All rights reserved. No part of this book may be used or reproduced in any manner whatsoever without the written permission of the Publisher. Printed in the United States of America. For information address Hyperion, 114 Fifth Avenue, New York, New York 10011.

First published in Great Britain in 2008 by Chatto & Windus

ISBN: 978-1-4013-2336-3

Hyperion books are available for special promotions and premiums. For details contact the HarperCollins Special Markets Department in the New York office at 212-207-7528, fax 212-207-7222, or email spsales@harpercollins.com.

First U.S. Edition

10 9 8 7 6 5 4 3 2 1

CONTENTS

INTRODUCTION — vi

🎄 **THE MORE THE MERRIER** — 1
COCKTAILS, CANAPÉS AND MANAGEABLE MASS CATERING

🎄 **SEASONAL SUPPORT** — 49
SOUPS, SALADS, SAUCES AND SERVE-LATER SIDES

🎄 **COME ON OVER...** — 69
STRESS-FREE SUPPERS

🎄 **THE MAIN EVENT** — 105

🎄 **JOY TO THE WORLD** — 171
CHRISTMAS BAKING AND SWEET TREATS

🎄 **ALL WRAPPED UP** — 219
EDIBLE PRESENTS AND PARTY PRESERVES

🎄 **A CHRISTMAS BRUNCH FOR 6–8** — 249

🎄 **A BEVY OF HOT DRINKS** — 258

🎄 **DR LAWSON PRESCRIBES...** — 264

SUPPLIERS — 267

ACKNOWLEDGMENTS — 268

INDEX — 270

INTRODUCTION

I'LL BE HONEST: I NEVER THOUGHT I'D WRITE A CHRISTMAS BOOK. But then, not so long ago, I never actually thought I'd become a food writer. I hadn't rejected either idea; it just never occurred to me. That's how life works, and so much the better for it. I accept – with gratitude – that what makes one happiest cannot be planned.

This is not to say I have anything against Christmas. Far from it: almost every book I've written has a chapter on Christmas. I wallow in it; I relish it. Everything I believe in – essentially, that warmth and contentment and welcome and friendship emanate from and are celebrated in the kitchen – finds most cogent expression for me at Christmas. But I can't deny that I am, simply put, a heathen. Although I have not been able to stop myself from writing piecemeal about the joys – and the stresses, I don't dispute – of cooking for Christmas, I felt a certain reserve at interjecting myself a little too presumptuously into other people's feast and faith.

But truth is, the Christmas we celebrate in our kitchens is not the Christmas that is celebrated in Church. Yes, of course, they coincide, and, for many, the latter corroborates and gives meaning to the former, but the Christmas feasting, the Christmas lights, the carousing and the gift-giving, these come from much further back than the birth of Christianity. Indeed, one of the great geniuses of Christianity has been its sage piggybacking of pre-existing feasts and festivals. If you want to encourage the heathens to adopt your faith, how very sensible to reassure them that their fun is not going to be taken away. This, anyway, is the frank explanation of what is more eruditely tagged syncretism. Biblical scholars generally tend to believe that Christ's birth probably fell about six months after Passover, which would make it nearer September than December. However, the Roman Festival of Saturnalia – a time of merrymaking, excess and misrule, precursor to the office party and much else besides – fell around the middle of December, and led up to the Sol Invictus – or unconquered sun – festival. Around this time mummers would go about carousing and entertaining people in their homes, which is what has led to our carol-singing now. The idea of the unconquered sun, or the rebirth of the sun, has been linked by Catholics to the notion of the birth of Christ, and links, too, with the pagan notion, the one I cling to most affectionately, of the winter solstice being about the promise of the return of light in the depth of the dark winter.

This isn't a history lesson, nor would I be qualified to give one, but this mesh, or rather mish-mash, of traditions and festivities, enthralls me as it speaks so pointedly to our customs now. Saturnalia – in other words, the celebration of Saturn, the Roman god of agriculture and plenty – began the tradition of gift-giving, in the sense that the rich were encouraged to give food and money to the poor, at what was an inhospitable time of year. And, taking advantage of all that, it was Pope Julius I who decreed that the birth of Christ be celebrated on December 25th, the better to bring recalcitrant Romans, still very much in the majority, into the fold. The day itself had other advantages, being as well, in Ancient Babylon, the Feast of the Son of Isis, Goddess of Nature, and a time, too, of hedonistic mayhem, gluttony, inebriation and the bestowing of monies and presents. Or so I believe, and want to believe. It's obvious that the day is intended to have pan-significance, and I embrace that joyfully. I like the sense of enjoying the legacy of partying down the ages.

But my greatest love, my deepest feelings, are for the pagan rituals that underpin the contemporary Christmas. In fact, I'd go further and say that my approach to the festival is ultimately pagan. We all know that the tree is a remnant (or adoption, if you wish) of the pagan celebration of the winter solstice, when a green bough would be brought into the house to serve as a reminder that the earth would renew itself again, and that the crops would return. But there is so much more to it than that. Christmas in my home really is about bringing light and fire and warmth into the chill darkness. I love the reminder of the cycle of the seasons, the belief in the beneficence of Mother Nature and the sense that the hearth and the home keep the light alive and provide sustenance and hope. For me, Christmas is not just a time when the Domestic Goddess comes into her own but a moment to conjure up the Domestic Druid as well. There are those within the fantastically named Pagan Federation, who still call the winter solstice, not Yule, as the Scandinavians did, but in the style of the Anglo-Saxons, Mother Night. When I was once on a radio program discussing Christmas rituals, a high priestess of a Wiccan coven and I discovered we celebrated the festival in much the same way; she felt that the lighting of the oven, the creating of the feast, was the human way of understanding, celebrating and enshrining the sustenance of Mother Nature. How could I object to that?

I feel the Christmas rituals of the home are, even if not based around faith, essentially an act of good faith. I see the argument against: the world is starving and we overeat and celebrate overeating; the world is poor and we spend money to give presents to people who don't truly need anything. I know how it seems – crassly commercial, tawdry, tacky and insincere. But I defend the exuberance and the lurch of excess as a kind act in a cruel world. It is about shining a light in the darkness, providing warmth in the coldness. I make no distinction between the glow from the fairy lights, the warmth of the oven, and the welcome in the home. And this is probably best symbolized by the act of bringing the flaming Christmas pudding to the table.

So, if I've found myself having written a Christmas book, it is all this – the belief in hearth and home, the fervent adherence to ritual and tradition when everything else in the world can make one feel unmoored, a faith in hospitality and fellow-feeling – that the book is about. And yes, it is also about indulgence, although I see festive indulgence not as a bad thing or an act of weakness, but a celebration of being alive – a positive source, if not for good, then for happiness. The book's subtitle – food, family, friends, festivities – is not just a frenetic exercise in alliteration but an affirmation of what I believe is important in life, and all – praise be – that Christmas celebrates.

That is my inspiration, but I aim, too, to mop up some of the perspiration. I am not by nature a calm person, and, much as I love Christmas, I can be kyboshed by it. I know from experience how easy it is to be overwhelmed by the sheer workload and the burden of expectations, one's own above all. Christmas has to be about plenty, and the last thing I'd ever advocate is a miserly, pared-down version, but there is abundant sense in finding a workable, enjoyable way through it. This, I hope, my book does. It is certainly the way I have found to save my own seasonal sanity.

I should, though, admit that my own shortcomings and temperamental failings ensure that there are many things this book is not. I have learned how to get maximum pleasure with minimum stress, but I am never going to be the sort of person who has cake and dessert made and presents bought before November, and this book does not presume that you are, either. If you want to get ahead, and really can pull that micro-management and super-organization off, then this book gives you plenty of scope for that, as there are make-ahead and freeze-ahead tips throughout; if you are not that way inclined, then I have a couple of Christmas cakes you can make at the very last minute and a pudding that is luscious enough without having the traditional year in which to mature. I do indeed own a book – Fanny and Johnnie Cradock's *Coping with Christmas* – that begins: "January 1st: Make Christmas pudding for next year." I don't find such an injunction inspiring; I find it discouraging.

Likewise, although I know that it is in the tradition of Christmas manuals to suggest clever ideas for making table decorations and suchlike, I just couldn't. I'd love to be able to, but I am the living embodiment of the term cack-handed. I can wrap up a book and it looks as though I'm giving a bottle of wine. Still, I did want to share some of my enthusiasms, and thus I give you these presents here (overleaf). Although I have a weakness for bulk-buying gift wrap online, I have a contrary addiction to recycling. I'm afraid my recycling doesn't take the form of good trash-can management or anything as civic minded as that, but I am always happier to wrap a present in brown paper and string, with a couple of cinnamon sticks, or old newspaper and ribbon, than hand over the sheeniest, shiniest beribboned and rosetted parcel. My prompt is aesthetic rather more than ecological, though you could argue the effect is the same.

But if I can't fashion wreaths or fold napkins, I am happy to say that there is a Christmas craft for the clumsy, and it has an important place in this book. I make relishes and chutney. Chutney is jam-making for the time-pressed.

When I say that you don't have to do anything except put all the ingredients needed into a pan, bring to a boil and cook for about 40 minutes, untended, I mean it. Moreover, I have quite a few recipes here, if such they can be called, for edible presents that involve no cooking whatsoever. And it is not some post-ironic, post-industrial, make-do-and-mend mentality (though there is every reason for heeding that) that makes me implore you to make your own presents, but a belief that what comes out of your kitchen means more than anything from a shop ever will, and that the satisfactions of the season can stem from the stove.

NOTE FOR THE READER

- all eggs are extra large, organic
- all butter is unsalted
- all herbs are fresh, unless stated
- all chocolate is bittersweet (min. 60% cocoa solids), unless stated
- all olive oil is regular (not extra virgin), unless stated
- cup measures are scooped
- heavy whipping cream can be used instead for heavy cream

THE MORE THE MERRIER

COCKTAILS, CANAPÉS AND MANAGEABLE MASS CATERING

THIS IS PROBABLY THE ONE TIME OF YEAR when people who aren't party-givers give parties. Sometimes, this is due to an uncharacteristic but nevertheless welcome burst of bonhomie and seasonal spirit; as often, it's a duty-date, the product of habit, pressure or other presumed or existing obligations. For as many people who feel a blood-rushing joyousness at the prospect of having their home overrun with people out to have a good time, there are perhaps more who are filled rather with dread, and lacerated by the anxiety that a good time will be neither provided nor had.

This may be a strange thing to say at the beginning of a cookbook, but if it's the cooking that makes you not enjoy giving a party, don't cook. Buy salami, get cheese (all chic Italians hand round roughly chunked shards of fresh Parmesan), put grissini in jars, and regular French breadsticks in vases. But know that, sometimes, the act of preparing for a feast, by cooking simple, low-effort food, can make you look forward to the party more. I love to wallow in the Christmas spirit as I get it all underway. I'm always happy in the kitchen with Christmas songs – Elvis singing "Silent Night," Wham with "Last Christmas" – a-playing, fairy lights a-twinkling, platters of food slowly covering every surface.

And, actually, I think that a Christmas party is the best sort to give. For one thing, everyone is predisposed to have a good time. They're out to enjoy themselves: they're not coming to carp at your canapés.

Of course, there are ways of making things easier on yourself. It is indeed my hope, my very aim to make things easier on you: I am too clumsy and time-squeezed to do anything elaborate, so I don't expect you to, either. You can make a lot of different bits and pieces, or keep the choice restricted. This is up to you, though I have always, with food, had my mantra: Better a lot of a few things, than a little of many. That's my own rule, but you should also bear in mind the professional caterer's rule, which is that the more people there are, the less they eat per head.

Not that it helps, I find, to get too mathematical about it. A certain amount of clipboard briskness is all well and good, but the only formula that really works is that the less stressed you are, the better the party will be. (I know that the two most irritating things someone can say to you are "Relax!" or "Calm down," but I am trying to help.) So: make sure all drinks that need to be are chilled on time; don't wear new or uncomfortable shoes; and invite everyone you can think of, as worrying about people being cross with you for not being invited is more anxiety-provoking than having too many people in the house.

"The more the merrier" might not be something you believe now, but the only way to enjoy Christmas fully is to act as if you do. And then you will.

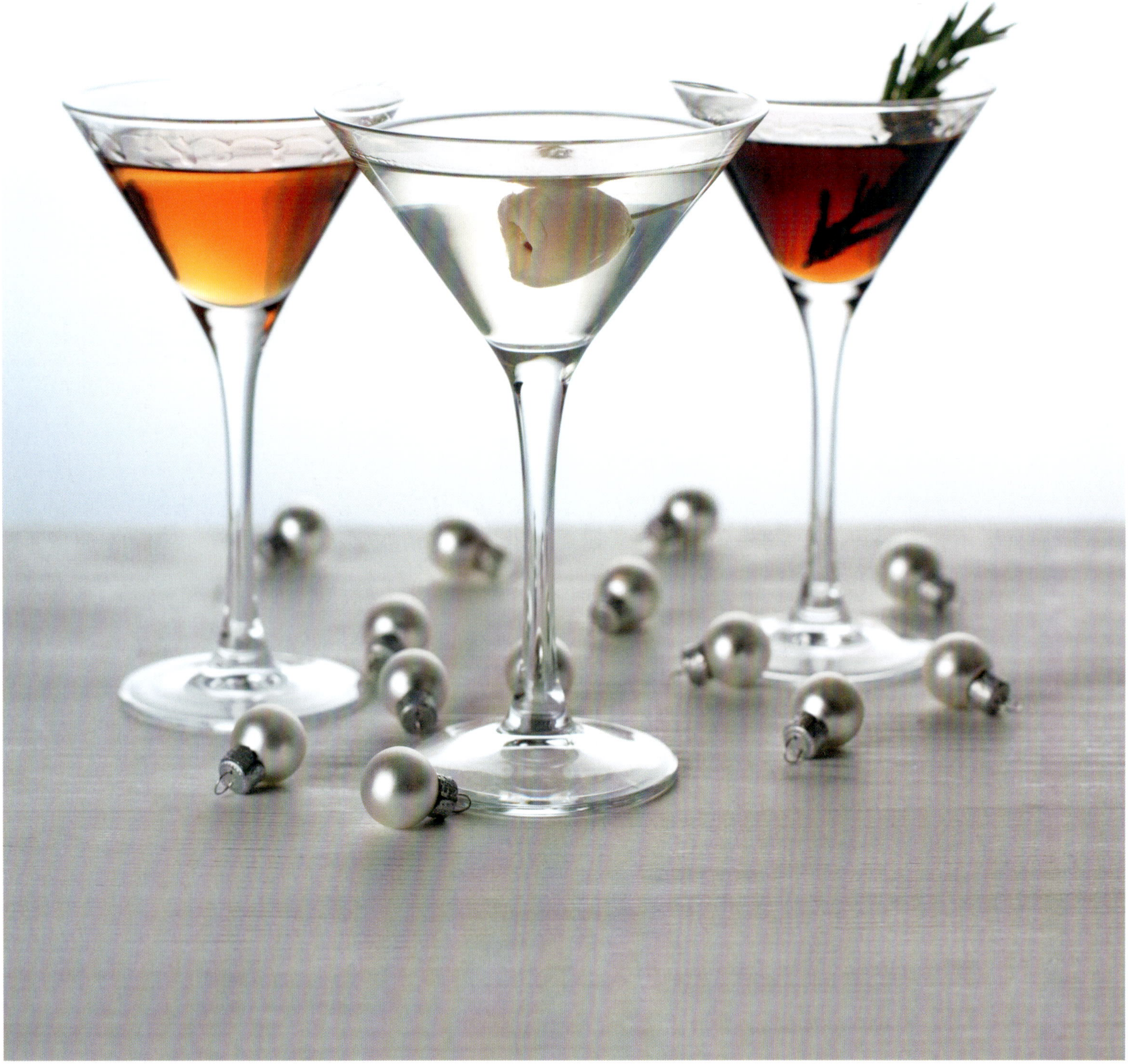

COCKTAILS

Believe me, you don't have to turn mixologist to throw a good party. I am more than happy to provide nothing but wine, for all that Kingsley Amis once said that the three most depressing words in the English language were "Red or White?" And fizz doesn't have to be champagne, either: my preference here is for Prosecco, which (and I think I have told you this before) is known in casa mia as "Prozacco," for its mood-enhancing qualities.

But a cocktail can be a wonderful thing – exuberant, extravagant, humdingingly uplifting – and a Christmas party is a good excuse for one.

POINSETTIA

This is probably the most serviceable, all-around Christmas cocktail: eminently refreshing; satisfyingly quaffable. Think of it as a juicily seasonal Buck's Fizz (a drink I normally find too acidically challenging at best and downright depressing at worst). This prettily pink – rather than authentically red – Poinsettia can be knocked back without a moment's thought. Whether this is entirely a good thing is another matter . . .

Makes 8–9 glasses

1 x 750ml bottle Prosecco or other fizzy dry wine, chilled

1/2 cup Cointreau or Grand Marnier or Triple Sec, chilled

2 cups cranberry juice, chilled

❊ Mix the Prosecco or other fizzy wine with the Cointreau (or Grand Marnier or Triple Sec) and cranberry juice in a large pitcher.

❊ Pour into wine glasses or champagne flutes.

MAKE AHEAD TIP:
Mix together the Cointreau and cranberry juice in a large pitcher, cover with plastic wrap and keep chilled for up to 24 hours. Just before serving, top up with the chilled fizz.

POMEGRANATE MARTINI

ice cubes
2 parts vodka
1 part Pama pomegranate liqueur
½ part Grenadine

I must confess, upfront, that I don't make a martini like a bartender, and don't expect you to either. Of course, if you're throwing an intimate party for two, a quick shimmy with a cocktail shaker is entirely possible, but it is inconceivable for a crowd so I don't bother. And not being a really proper drinker (despite the evidence of these pages) I don't mind diluting hard liquor with ice.

I find the simplest way to give measures for this sort of drink is by ratio, but if you prefer amounts, think of "1 part" as equivalent to a barman's 1-ounce shot. And a shot measure, or jigger, is easy enough to buy.

Although I keep my vodka in the freezer, I cannot overestimate how important extra ice is here. A martini has to be temple-achingly cold, and I can't be faffing about with straining, so let those cubes chink, and just drink up before the martini is turned to water.

If a gin martini is more to your taste, proceed and pour accordingly.

❊ To make 1 cocktail, put at least 3 ice cubes into a martini glass and pour the alcohol over, using a 1-ounce measure per part. I like a small (4-ounce) martini glass rather than one of those vast, gaping upended triangles on stems.

❊ To make a big batch, chill a pitcher and cram it with ice, then use a 1-cup measure per part, to make 3½ cups, enough for 10 cocktails, or maybe 8 if each waiting martini glass hasn't got ice to bulk up the drink.

If you'd prefer to stick to my pomegranate theme, but dispense with the vodka (or bear this in mind as an add-on rather than a substitution), make my Christmas Fizz by adding a glug or two of the Pama pomegranate liqueur to a glass of champagne or fizzy wine. Or you can branch out and add viscous, fragrant drops of flavoured Monin syrups – think gingerbread, cranberry, spiced winter fruits (see Suppliers p.267) – to fizzy wine for party pizazz.

MAKE AHEAD TIP:
Make in a pitcher just before guests arrive and keep chilled by sitting the pitcher in a large bowl of ice and water, or stash in the refrigerator.

LYCHEENI

After a pomegranate, the lychee feels the most seasonally celebratory of fruits, and it didn't seem fair to leave it out of the Christmas canon, just because of its unfestive pallor. Plus, I stumbled across *the* most beautiful bottle, in the form of a French lychee liqueur (see Suppliers p.267) that begged to bought. I couldn't resist, and I love this lychee martini it was born to make.

And it's not just for the party scene that it gives seasonal succour: even a never-ending school concert is a little more manageable with a hit of this inside you; I have been known to empty out a small water bottle and pour in some of this clear and precious liquid instead. But then, I come to the conclusion that my motto has to be All Life Looks Up With a Lycheeni.

I can't peel a lychee without savaging it, so I feel fine about suggesting canned ones for adornment and a hint of pearly sweetness.

ice cubes
1 part white rum
1 part vodka
2 parts lychee liqueur
½–1 part syrup from canned lychees
canned lychees to garnish

❄ Chunk up a martini glass with ice, and add the rum, vodka and lychee liqueur, using a 1-ounce measure per part. If you want this a little sweeter, which all but real firewater-drinkers will, add some of the syrup from the can of lychees to taste.

❄ If in garnishing mood, pierce a lychee on a toothpick, and drop into the martini.

❄ To make a big batch, cram ice into a pitcher, and add the alcohol (and syrup, to taste), using a 1-cup measure per part. You will have about 1 quart, more than enough for 10 drinks. This is strong stuff!

As with the Pomegranate Martini, opposite, you can simply add a splosh of this creamily fruity liqueur straight into a glass of fizzy wine – my Lychee Fizz. Or, for those who like sweeter drinks with less kick, look out for lychee purée in foil pouches and add it to sparkling wine, about 1 part purée to 2 parts wine.

MAKE AHEAD TIP:
Make in a pitcher just before guests arrive and keep chilled by sitting the pitcher in a large bowl of ice and water, or stash in the refrigerator.

BLACK FOREST MARTINI

ice cubes
1 part vodka
1 part cherry brandy (the red stuff, not kirsch)
½ part crème de cacao
rosemary sprigs

Humor me here. I couldn't help myself, and I'm not sure I'd have wanted to. There is something undeniably Germanic and kitsch in the evolution of the contemporary Christmas and this drink recognizes and marries the two in a fabulous fusion. And the taste – well, it's heaven. Not too sweet, not at all sickly, but with a rounded, hint of dessert that makes it a perfect after-dinner cocktail as well as a bolstering early evening mood-lifter.

The rosemary, flavorwise, is a tiny deviation from our walk through the Black Forest, but its scent is beautiful, and the sprig, peeking out from the martini glass, has the right hint of festive fir and woodsy warmth about it.

❊ To make 1 cocktail, put at least 3 ice cubes in a martini glass and build your drink over them, using a 1-ounce measure per part.

❊ To make a party pitcher, use a 1-cup measure per part; you will have 2½ cups, enough for 10 cocktails, but cram the pitcher with ice, and lay a rosemary sprig in each waiting martini glass.

MAKE AHEAD TIP:
Make in a pitcher just before guests arrive and keep chilled by sitting the pitcher in a large bowl of ice and water, or stash in the refrigerator.

SANTA'S LITTLE HELPER

ice cubes (optional)
1 part brandy
½ part amaretto liqueur
½ part Cointreau, Grand Marnier or Triple Sec

I'm not even going to broach the possibility of a pitcher of this; it would be irresponsible in the extreme. But it's probably just what you need on Christmas Eve, when you've got to fill the stockings, wrap the presents, get out the Christmas china and do everything else on your overburdened plate. Bottoms up!

❊ To make 1 stiffener, over ice (my choice) or straight up if preferred, pour the alcohol into your glass, using a 1-ounce measure per part.

AMARETTO SOUR

I was once a whiskey sour drinker, inasmuch as I – an eater rather more than a bevver – drank any spirits at all, but that was a lifetime ago when I felt I had to come up with a request in bars and knew that a Brandy Alexander was probably best avoided, on grounds of coolth and calories. Now, what do I care? But whereas I'd be happy to order something naff and creamy, I wouldn't honestly want to drink it. This is my perfect compromise: sweet, sharp, rich and seasonally aromatic. It gives you the warmth of a mulled something or other, without having to go near a stove.

❊ To make 1 cocktail, part-fill a tumbler with ice (unless you prefer to drink this straight up) and build your cocktail over this, using a 1-ounce measure per part.

❊ Mix together with a swizzle stick or your finger, then plop in a maraschino cherry and, using a vegetable peeler, shave off a curl of orange peel.

❊ To make a pitcher, use a 1-cup measure per part; you'll have 5 cups of amaretto sour. I'd chill the pitcher in the refrigerator and have a cherry and some orange peel in each waiting glass. Since it's chilled, you won't need ice, so I'd serve in small, squat tumblers, nothing too roomy.

ice cubes (optional)
3 parts amaretto liqueur
2 parts lemon juice

FOR THE GARNISH:
1 orange for peeling
maraschino cherries

MAKE AHEAD TIP:
If you have no space in the refrigerator to chill the pitcher, drop a couple of handfuls of ice into the empty pitcher about half an hour before guests are due to arrive. When ready to serve, empty the (now chilled) jug of any remaining ice and water and mix the cocktail.

CORNISH CHAMPAGNE COCKTAIL

Serving: Each 750ml bottle of champagne should require 6 sugar cubes and approx. 1/3 of a cup liqueur to make 6 cocktails

approx. 6 tablespoons quince eau de vie, or Calvados or liqueur of your choice
6 La Perruche pure cane rough-cut cubes, or other sugar cubes of your choice
1 x 750ml bottle fizzy dry white wine of your choice, chilled

MAKE AHEAD TIP:
About half an hour before your guests are due to arrive, pop the sugar cubes in the glasses and pour the liqueur over. Just before serving, top up with the chilled fizz.

A champagne cocktail is a classic that needs no fiddling with, so I should defend my apparent lack of reverence here. When my friend Justine Picardie launched her book *Daphne* recently, I wanted to give her a pre-party party featuring a drink made in her and du Maurier's honor. Justine is a champagne cocktail girl, so replacing the champagne with Cornish fizz, and drenching the sugar cube with a gorgeous West Country quince liqueur instead of cognac seemed right all round. And I am now a convert to the Cornish sparkle even for occasions without the geo-literary justification. You can substitute any fizzy wine or liqueur, so those far away from the wilder shores of Cornwall need not worry.

I also make a version – my Tuscan Champagne Cocktail – redolent of Panettone and Italian Christmases which is simply Prosecco with a shot of Tuaca (and see Suppliers on p.267), a liqueur that also merits solo attention.

❋ Put 1 sugar cube into each champagne glass; I like a saucer not a flute and I reckon one bottle of fizz provides enough for 6 glasses.

❋ Pour the quince liqueur or brandy (probably no more than a tablespoon) over each sugar cube to soak it, and then top up with sparkling wine.

❋ For my Tuscan Champagne Cocktail, dispense with the sugar cubes.

YULE MULE

ice cubes
2 parts chilled vodka
1 part chilled cranberry juice
Angostura bitters or lime juice (optional)
5 parts chilled ginger beer (see Suppliers on p.267)

MAKE AHEAD TIP:
Measure the vodka, bitters (if using), and cranberry juice into a large pitcher. Keep chilled over ice, then top up with ginger beer to serve.

OPPOSITE:
Cornish Champagne Cocktail (back left); Yule Mule (back right); Amaretto Sour (front), next to a bowl of Seasonally Spiced Nuts (p.21)

I've always loved a Moscow Mule – vodka, bitters, lime juice and savagely peppery ginger beer – and this is no more than my seasonal slant on that. Very joyous it is, too. I find the tooth-roughening sharpness of the cranberry juice replaces not only the need for lime juice, but also the bitters, but if you wish to squirt in a little lime or drop in some Angostura, then I won't stop you.

❋ To make 1 cocktail, plonk some ice in a highball glass then build your drink over it, using a 1-ounce measure per part. Add 3 drops of Angostura bitters (or lime juice), if using.

❋ To make a pitcherful, use a 1-cup measure per part and you will have 2 quarts (about 10 glasses), so it may be wiser to have 2 pitchers crammed with ice.

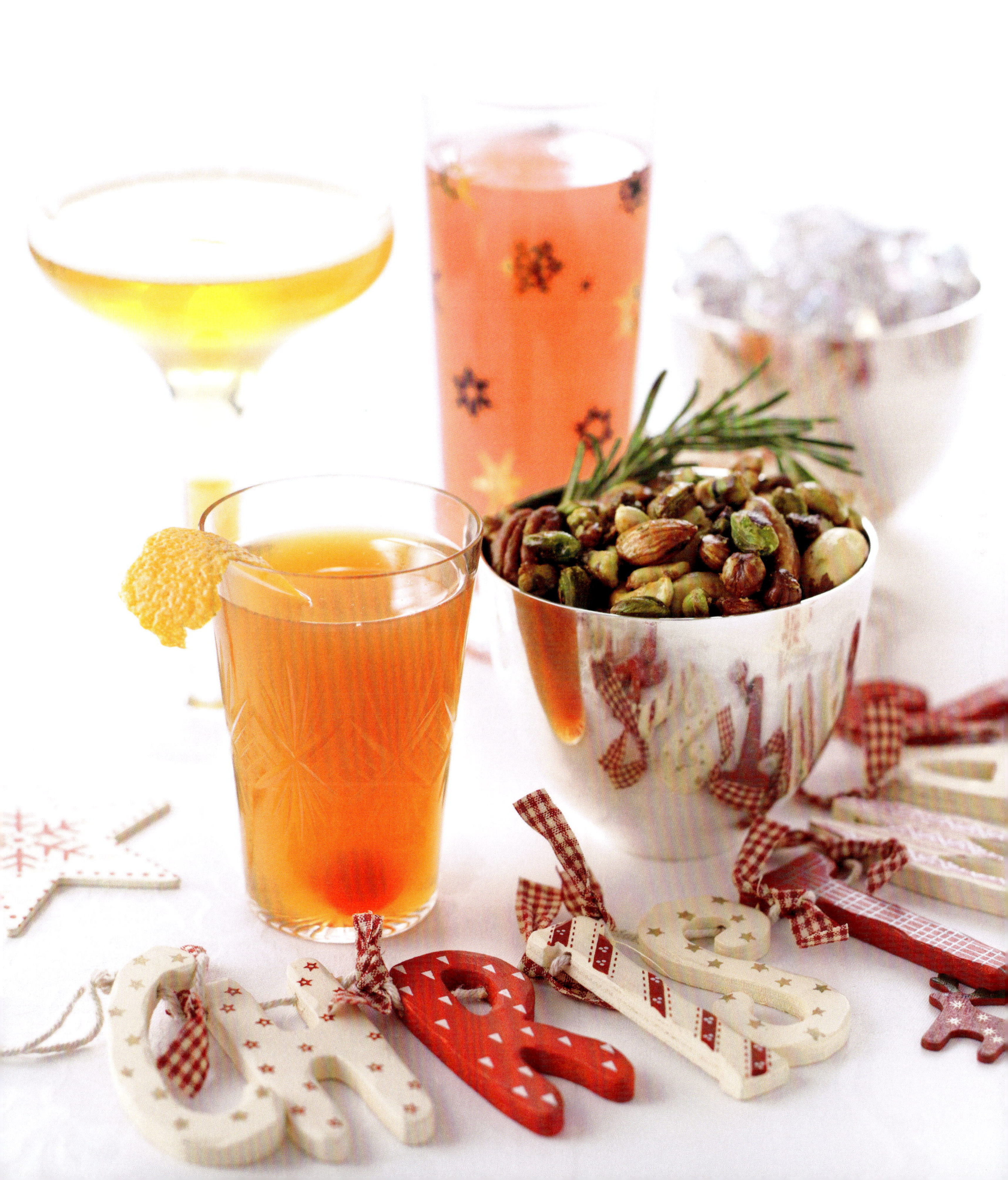

A SEASONAL MEDLEY OF MOCKTAILS

Before the pile up of over-the-top cocktail recipes begins to look like the diary entries of a déclassé dipsomaniac – or have we passed that stage? – I offer a barman's splayed handful of cocktails for those who might not want alcohol, but still want to join the party. As a self-confessed, pronounced aquaholic, I feel that any non-alcoholic drink must be well-balanced, finely tuned perfection in order to beat the simple perfection of water. Still, I concede that a night that offers no more drinking choice than still or sparkling could seem slightly lacking in festive spirit. And I certainly wouldn't want that. So the following, I hope, will allow the abstemious to raise a garish glass with the rest of us.

LEFT TO RIGHT:
Seasonal Breeze, Pussyfoot, Blissful Blueberry, Mistletoe, Xmas Xinger

SEASONAL BREEZE

I've written a recipe with this title before, I admit, but it seems fair to plagiarize oneself. Besides, the title conveys what the drink is about: a Christmassy hit of cranberry in a long drink that is vaguely reminiscent of a sea breeze. You could take the "vaguely" away by squeezing in pink grapefruit juice in place of the orange juice. And while you could use carton orange juice, as I have done in the Pussyfoot, overleaf (and I would if making a big pitcher), I like the pure sharpness that comes from squeezing the fruit proper. Look out, when shopping, for a clear, pressed apple juice – which tends to have a better modulated, less sugary appleyness, whether from a bottle or a carton.

1 part chilled cranberry juice
1 part chilled clear apple juice
1 part chilled freshly squeezed orange juice
ice cubes (optional)

❉ To make 1 cocktail, pour all the juices (over ice if desired) into a glass, using a 3-ounce measure per part.

❉ To make a big batch, chill a pitcher and cram it with ice, then use 3 cups per part to make 9 cups, enough for 10 cocktails.

MAKE AHEAD TIP:
Mix all the juices together in a large pitcher and keep covered in a cool place, or in a bucket of ice, if space allows, for up to 3 hours. Stir in 2 or 3 handfuls of ice when ready to serve.

PUSSYFOOT

FOR 1 GLASS:
2/3 cup chilled pink grapefruit juice
2/3 cup chilled freshly squeezed orange juice
1/2 teaspoon fresh lime juice
1–2 drops Grenadine
ice cubes (optional)

FOR A PITCHER:
3 cups chilled pink grapefruit juice
3 cups chilled freshly squeezed orange juice
2 tablespoons Grenadine
2 tablespoons fresh lime juice
ice cubes

MAKE AHEAD TIP:
Mix all the liquids together in a large pitcher and keep covered in cool place, or in a bucket of ice, if space allows, for up to 3 hours. Stir in 2 or 3 handfuls of ice when ready to serve.

I wish I could lay claim to this title, but it is the brainchild of a presumably hard-drinking bartender with as much condescension as goodwill towards his abstemious clientele. I have added some lime juice to the sweeter original; a more generous squeeze of lemon would also add a note of necessary, balancing, sharpness. There is nothing fancy about this, which is part of its charm, but a colorful pitcherful of the stuff gives a party a cheery boost, and it tends to be gulped down with brio. (And there is nothing to stop you leaving a bottle of vodka nearby for those who don't want to pussyfoot around.)

The basic ratio is 1 part pink grapefruit juice to 1 part orange juice, but my maths isn't good enough to work out what fraction of a part the Grenadine and lime constitute, which is why I write the quantities out twice.

❉ To make 1 cocktail, pour the grapefruit and orange juices into a tall glass (with ice if you like), add the lime juice and Grenadine and watch it fire up like a tequila sunrise and – if you can bear to – stir to mix.

❉ To make a big batch, chill a pitcher and fill it with ice, then proceed as above, to make enough for approx. 10 cocktails.

BLISSFUL BLUEBERRY

1 part chilled blueberry juice (sometimes labeled blueberry juice drink)
1 part chilled bitter lemon, or other sparkling lemony drink (see Suppliers on p.267)
fresh lemon juice
ice cubes (optional)

I'm not sure I could mount a convincing case for the essential Christmassyness of a blueberry, but the festive spirit is supplied by the treat of the, relatively speaking, exotic. It seems strange to me that you can actually buy cartons of blueberry juice at the supermarket now; I am showing my age, but I can remember when we couldn't even buy blueberries. So this, for me, has the out-of-the-ordinariness that is what makes a feast. Plus, there is something regally celebratory about its gorgeous hue. If you'd prefer to use Sprite in place of the bitter lemon do, but squeeze in a little fresh lemon juice at the same time.

❉ To make 1 cocktail, pour the juices into a glass (with ice if desired), using a 3-ounce measure per part. Stir gently to combine, adding a spritz of fresh lemon juice to taste.

❉ To make a big batch, chill a pitcher, then load it with ice and proceed as above, using 3 cups per part; this should make enough for 10 cocktails.

MISTLETOE

I love the mixture here of sweet lime cordial, peppery ginger beer and the uplifting sharpness of fresh lime. It's cool but warming at the same time, which makes it an entirely fitting drink for a fabulous Christmas party. (You could also, of course, consider a Virgin Version of the Yule Mule on p.8, by simply mixing ginger beer with cranberry juice.)

Again, as with the Pussyfoot, opposite, to avoid mind-numbing fractions, I am giving quantities for the Mistletoe twice, to cover glass and pitcher options. But, essentially, the drink is 1 part lime cordial to 3 parts ginger beer with a squeeze or so of fresh lime.

FOR 1 DRINK:
1 oz shot chilled lime cordial, such as Rose's
3 oz chilled ginger beer
**   (see Suppliers on p.267)**
½ teaspoon fresh lime juice

FOR A PITCHER:
1 cup chilled lime cordial
1 cup chilled ginger beer
1 oz shot fresh lime juice

❋ To make 1 cocktail, pour the lime cordial and ginger beer into a glass (over ice if required), spritz with fresh lime and stir gently.

❋ To make a big batch, chill a pitcher, cram it with ice, and proceed as above; this makes enough for 10 cocktails.

XMAS XINGER

This is simple and yet special, and a way of making those who have foresworn alcohol feel rewarded rather than punished. I've mentioned it before, a year or so ago, in an aside to a cocktail made with pomegranate liqueur, but this really does deserve stand-alone status.

The pomegranate juice (read the label and check it is pure pomegranate juice) is lusciously Christmassy and the ginger ale brings its own seasonal spiciness and sprightliness.

2 parts chilled pure pomegranate juice
1 part chilled ginger ale
ice cubes (optional)

❋ To make 1 cocktail, using a 3-ounce measure per part, pour the pomegranate juice into a glass (with ice if required), top up with ginger ale, and give a gentle stir just to combine.

❋ To make a big batch, chill a pitcher and cram it with ice, then proceed as above, using 3 cups per part, to make enough for 10 cocktails.

14 THE MORE THE MERRIER

CANAPÉS AND OTHER APPETIZERS

I am never going to be a canapé queen. I lack dexterity and patience and there is some small part of me that feels canapés really belong to the repertoire of the professional caterer, though I suspect the greater part of my reluctance is down to straightforward greed: small portions, little bites, make me panic. I can get over it: I simply produce a lot, but of only a few; in life as on the page, everything is in the edit. Choose about three you want to make for each party, and make plenty of each. It's not rocket science, but it works: your stress is lessened and your guests plentifully welcomed; now you've got a party . . .

DOUBLE-BLUE CROSTINI

I spent the year before last in a haze of Roquamole – my rich, dense and creamy blue cheese and avocado dip. And although I do, on occasion and out of greedy self-interest, bring it out for pre-dinner pickings at Christmas dinner parties, it is, alas, too volatile for appetizers; once the avocados start turning dark they may taste fine but, believe me, they lack plate appeal. So this is my seasonal substitute: a gorgeous, tangy blue cheese dip or spread, to be anointed – and here's the second of the two blues of my title – on thick, gritty, blue corn tortilla chips. I've mentioned before the joyous discovery that my favored appetizer, a plate of crostini, can be made with tortilla chips instead of toasted French stick slices, and in many ways the blue corn chip is the finest example of this labor-saving practice, as the chip itself is thicker (and so resists sogginess for longer) than its yellow corn counterparts, and the taste blander (an advantage in an appetizer). Don't worry if some of the chips are broken; I use shards of chips just as happily as whole, perfectly triangular ones. And by all means use the blue cheese spread as a dip, if you like, and simply provide the chips (or some raw vegetable sticks) as scooping tools.

Makes approx. 65 tortilla-chip crostini

1 cup crumbled blue cheese
4 oz cream cheese, at room temp.
½ cup sour cream
¼ cup sliced green jalapeños, from a jar or can
good grinding of white pepper
4 large handfuls (approx. 4 oz) blue corn tortilla chips
1 teaspoon very finely chopped chives

❊ Mash the blue cheese with the cream cheese and sour cream in a bowl; this is easier if the cream cheese has been out of the refrigerator for a while.

❊ Finely chop the sliced jalapeños and stir them in with the white pepper.

❊ Using a teaspoon, dollop the blue cheese mixture onto the chips.

❊ Delicately drop the chives over and serve.

MAKE AHEAD TIP:
Make the blue cheese mixture up to 6 hours ahead. Cover tightly with plastic wrap and store in the refrigerator. Remove from the refrigerator about 20 minutes before using to allow it to soften, then dollop over the tortilla chips just before the party.

16 THE MORE THE MERRIER

CRAB CROSTINI

I can eat crabmeat pretty much any way – as a fresh, chilefied and garlicky scattering over semolina-sweet linguine, mounded into a lightly but spicily dressed salad, wodged into cakes (and see p.24) – but this is probably the speediest and most effortless incarnation.

It's not so hard to chop scallions, cilantro and chile pepper by hand, but by all means get out the processor for the job if you prefer. However, be very cautious if you use it to mix in the crabmeat; any more than the most fleeting of pulses and the crabmeat loses its delicate shreds and turns to paste. It's not a disaster but neither is it entirely desirable.

I like to put chile into the crabmeat – I adore the Christmassy red flecks peeking out of the tender white flesh along with the green of the cilantro here – but if you prefer, leave out the chile and replace the plain tortilla chips with the fierier chile-flavored ones, as in the Chile Cheese Crostini, below.

❈ Finely chop the scallion and the chile (if using), then mix into the crabmeat along with the other ingredients, and dollop onto the tortilla chips.

Makes about 50 crab crostini

1 scallion
1 fresh red chile, seeded (optional)
2 cups white crabmeat
1/4 cup sour cream
handful of fresh cilantro leaves
1/4 teaspoon dried oregano
1 tablespoon lime juice
1 small packet plain tortilla chips (approx. 9oz)

MAKE AHEAD TIP:
About 3 hours before serving, stir the chopped scallion, chile, cilantro and oregano into the crabmeat. Cover with plastic wrap and store in the refrigerator. Just before assembling the crostini, stir in the sour cream and lime juice.

CHILE CHEESE CROSTINI

Yumbariba! The chile cheese is really just a lazy person's take on my longstanding family-favorite, liptauer (only with a Latino rather than Mitteleuropa flavor), and I ramp up the paprika punch by smearing it on hot chile tortilla chips.

I specify organic rather than regular cream cheese, as I like the rich texture and rounded flavor (and buy it easily from the supermarket) and it tastes like proper, old-fashioned homemade stuff, but the more familiar oblong-packaged packs of regular cream cheese would not be out of place here.

❈ Mix together the cream cheese and sour cream.

❈ Add the paprika, chopped jalapeños and Worcestershire sauce, combine well, and see the pale cheese turn a fetching coral.

❈ Just before your guests arrive, using a teaspoon, lightly dab the spread on a pile of chips and arrange on a platter or a couple of flat plates.

Makes about 100 chile cheese chips

1 1/2 x 8 oz packs cream cheese (preferably organic), at room temperature
1/2 cup sour cream
2 teaspoons sweet or mild paprika
2 tablespoons chopped red jalapeños (from a jar or can)
1/2 teaspoon Lea & Perrins Worcestershire sauce
1 x 8–9 oz bag chile tortilla chips

MAKE AHEAD TIP:
Make the chile cheese mixture the day before. Cover tightly with plastic wrap and store in the refrigerator. Remove about 20 minutes before using to allow to soften and spread just before serving.

SMOKED SALMON SODA BREADS

Makes approx. 30 salmon soda bread appetizers

1/3 cup crème fraîche or sour cream
1/4 cup hot horseradish sauce
approx. 10 slices brown soda bread, pumpernickel or rye bread
8 oz very thinly sliced smoked salmon
1/2 cup pickled red cabbage, from a jar, drained
5-6 stalks of fresh dill

The Irish have long known that the smooth richness of smoked salmon is gloriously partnered with the wheaten roughness of soda bread, and I aim to build on that borrowed alliance, drawing on my own Eastern European inheritance. Let me name the guilty parties: horseradish, for tang; pickled red cabbage, ditto, but also for the gloriously seasonal touch of its glistening dark-red tangle; the dill, too, looks fabulously firlike, but most of all, its delicate but resonant scent seals the deal with this flavor-packed mouthful.

Small rounds of pumpernickel, or regular squares of it quartered, or slices of rye bread can be substituted for the soda bread here.

❋ Mix together the crème fraîche and horseradish.

❋ You will need about 8–10 slices of bread. Cut each slice into 3 or 4 bits.

❋ Spread the bread with the horseradish–crème fraîche mixture and top with a snipped ribbon of smoked salmon.

❋ Fork a dark-red tangle of pickled red cabbage on each piece and top with a frond of dill.

MAKE AHEAD TIP:
The day before, cut the soda bread and store in a sealed bag. Make the horseradish–crème fraîche mixture, cover with plastic wrap and store in the refrigerator. Assemble the appetizers just before serving.

18 THE MORE THE MERRIER

THE MORE THE MERRIER **19**

PARTY PARMA HAM BUNDLES

Makes approx. 25 plumptious parcels

12 slices (approx. 14 oz) Parma ham or other cured prosciutto, not sliced ultra-thin
6 large or 12 small ready-to-eat dried figs
½ cup (approx. 5 oz) mild soft goat's cheese (chèvre)

Since I would find it hard to give a Christmas party without at least one plateful of these feast-time favorites of mine – salty pink prosciutto wrapped around sharp soft goat's cheese and sweet, grainy dried figs – it didn't seem fair to leave them out here, although they have had an outing in print with me before. They are positively *the* party perennial; their omission, for me, not to be countenanced.

❈ Cut or tear each slice of Parma ham into 2 or 3 strips.

❈ Scissor each fig in half or quarters, depending on their size, remove the woody stalks and spread a teaspoon of goat's cheese on the cut half of the fig.

❈ Place the piece of fig cheese side down on the center of a strip of ham and then roll or fold up to make a bundle.

❈ Sit each bulging pink parcel so that the darkness of the fig is hidden plate-side.

MAKE AHEAD TIP:
Make the parcels up to 6 hours ahead. Sit in a single layer on a plate and cover with plastic wrap. Keep chilled until ready to serve.

THE MORE THE MERRIER

SEASONALLY SPICED NUTS

There's something addictive about a bowl of warm, toasted bar nuts, and although I used to bring them out as a starter substitute at dinner parties, I have rejigged my usual seasonings to make these a little more spicily aromatic and find them just the thing to keep a crowd fed without too much commotion.

I don't pay particular attention to how many of each nut I put into the mix, but just go for those bags of mixed, unsalted nuts; my last bag contained (in the order listed on the bag) cashews, almonds, pecans, macadamias and pistachios. If you want to buy nuts in single bags and mix, I'd simply go for pecans, almonds, Brazils and pistachios. It's the spicing, and the warmth, that's key. Instead of the garam masala, you could use half a teaspoon each of ground ginger and ground cumin, and a pinch each of ground coriander, cloves and cinnamon. Indeed, it's the ginger and cloves in the garam masala that make these taste so Christmassy in the first place.

Makes enough to fill 2 small, not tiny, bowls

4 cups (approx. 1 lb) mixed nuts
1 1/2 teaspoons garam masala (usually found in the spice section of the supermarket)
1 teaspoon celery salt
2 tablespoons olive oil
2 tablespoons soft light brown sugar
3 sprigs rosemary, finely chopped to make about 3 teaspoons, plus 2 sprigs for garnish
sprinkle of kosher salt or pinch of table salt

❄ Put a large skillet on medium heat.

❄ Line a large cookie sheet or jelly roll pan with aluminum foil and put at a handy proximity to the stove.

❄ Tip the nuts into the now-warm skillet and toss or push about with a spatula for 3 minutes or so until they are lightly toasted.

❄ Add the garam masala and celery salt and push the nuts about in the pan again so that they are evenly coated.

❄ Add the oil, sugar and rosemary and stir about again to mix. When the nuts have darkened a little and are slicked with the sugary spice mix, tip them out briskly (before they burn) onto your prepared, lined sheet, and sprinkle with salt to taste.

❄ Preferably when still warm, arrange in small bowls, and tuck in a sprig of rosemary on top for a seasonal fir-tree flourish!

MAKE AHEAD TIP:
The day before, make the spiced nuts and tip them out onto an aluminum foil–lined baking sheet. Sprinkle with salt. Cover with foil and keep in a cool place. About 10 minutes before serving, pop the nuts into a moderate (350°F) oven to warm through.

DRUNKEN DEVILS ON HORSEBACK

Makes 24

24 ready-to-eat pitted dried prunes
1/3 cup Armagnac or any brandy
12 slices bacon

When I was a child, this is the sort of thing my parents would have eaten at cocktail parties, parties my mother would go to in her white patent boots, angora mini dress and false eyelashes – hairpiece, too – and lips slicked in pale, shimmery colors with names like Moist Madder Pink. It seemed ineffably glamorous – I can smell her wafting scent of face powder mixed with Guerlain's L'Heure Bleue now as I think about it – but also inexplicable: *how* could anyone want to eat a prune (the devil) or oyster (an angel) wrapped in bacon, and why they were on horseback was just as baffling. Now, I know (or think I do) that "on horseback" is a corruption of "hogsback," to indicate the bacon.

    Now, too, I'm happy – more than – to eat an angel-on-horseback, though less convinced that I want to make them; someone as clumsy as I am should not be let near an oyster shucker, ever. But a devil, which I like more, anyway – and mine are soused till sticky with Armagnac – is, if not child's food, then certainly child's play to make.

❋ The day before your party, soak the prunes in the Armagnac or brandy in a covered bowl.

❋ On the day of your party, preheat the oven to 400°F.

❋ On a board, spread out a slice of bacon and cut in half horizontally to give 2 shorter pieces of bacon. Then take a soaked prune from your bowl and roll it up in one of the half pieces of bacon, or a pancetta slice, securing it with a toothpick.

❋ Repeat this process with the remaining prunes, wrapping each one in bacon, and place them on a lined cookie sheet.

❋ Cook the drunken devils in the oven for 10–15 minutes, then let them cool a little, to avoid burnt fingers and mouths, before plating them up to serve.

MAKE AHEAD TIP:
Two days ahead, soak the prunes in the Armagnac. The day before, wrap in bacon and keep, covered, in the refrigerator. Allow 20 minutes at room temperature before cooking.

CRANBERRY AND SOY-GLAZED COCKTAIL SAUSAGES

I couldn't leave this out, even though you will probably have to follow round after with a packet of baby wipes. A party just isn't a party without a sticky sausage or three, and these are joyously seasonal. And nor do I stop here with this sweet, warm, sharp glaze: the ingredients can also be used as a marinade-cum-cook-in sauce for either 30 chicken wings or 20 small baby back ribs, with equally lip-smacking results.

❊ Preheat the oven to 400°F. Twist each sausage in the center to give two small sausages and snip the twist with scissors to separate.

❊ Put the cocktail sausages in an aluminum foil–lined roasting pan or, better still, a throwaway foil baking tray.

❊ Mix the chili, cranberry and soy sauces in a measuring cup and whisk in the sugar along with the clementine and lime juices.

❊ Pour the glaze over the sausages and turn them so they are evenly coated, before putting the pan in the oven for 30–40 minutes, with a gentle turnover after 20, by which time they should be hot, burnished and gorgeously sticky. (If you're cooking chicken wings or ribs, having marinated them overnight in the cranberry-chili-soy goo, you will have to up the cooking time: the wings should need about 45 minutes; the ribs an hour.)

❊ When serving, provide toothpticks and napkins, or make sure you have finger bowls or baby wipes to hand.

Makes 50

1/2 cup Thai or Chinese sweet chili sauce
1/4 cup cranberry sauce, from a jar or can
1/4 cup soy sauce
1 tablespoon dark brown sugar
juice of 1 clementine
juice of 1 lime
25 skinny breakfast sausage links (see Suppliers p.267)

MAKE AHEAD TIP:
Put all the sausages into a large, sealable bag (or glass bowl) and add all the other ingredients. Shake or stir everything together until the sausages are well coated and leave in the refrigerator for up to 1 day. When ready to use, just tip everything into the cooking pan and cook as directed.

FREEZE AHEAD TIP:
Make ahead as above and freeze for up to 3 months. Thaw overnight in the refrigerator.

WASABI CRAB CAKES

Makes approx. 45 crab cakes

1 lb fresh white crabmeat or frozen white crabmeat, thawed
4 scallions, very finely chopped
1 clove garlic, peeled and minced
2 teaspoons wasabi (Japanese horseradish) powder, or 3 teaspoons wasabi paste
2 teaspoons rice vinegar
3 teaspoons tamari or Japanese soy sauce
2 cups fresh breadcrumbs
canola or other vegetable oil for frying
lemon or lime wedges to serve

MAKE AHEAD TIP:
For previously frozen crabmeat, shape the crab cakes the day before and arrange on a plastic wrap–lined cookie sheet. Cover with plastic wrap and keep chilled overnight. Fry the chilled crab cakes as directed and keep warm in the oven for 20 minutes.

FREEZE AHEAD TIP:
For fresh, not previously frozen crabmeat only, make the crab cakes and freeze overnight until solid. Fry from frozen as above and keep warm in the oven. The crab cakes can also be stored in the freezer for up to 1 month before cooking.

I cook crab cakes so often, and tinker about with them to suit my mood, that I can offer up any number of variants on the recipe below. I will try and contain myself, though, as too much choice can be paralyzing rather than liberating. But feel free, if it suits you, to use $2/3$ cup brown rice flour in place of the breadcrumbs. If you can't find wasabi, use English mustard (powder or paste) as directed for the Japanese stuff and substitute lemon or lime juice for the rice vinegar.

❄ Press and drain any liquid from the crabmeat, and put the crabmeat in a large bowl. Add the scallions, garlic, wasabi, rice vinegar, soy sauce and breadcrumbs, and mix together to combine.

❄ Spoon or pinch out tablespoon-sized dollops, and press together tightly with wet hands or wearing vinyl disposable gloves, to form bite-sized crab cakes. Arrange the little crab cakes, on a plastic wrap–lined sheet that will fit into your refrigerator or freezer (don't freeze if using frozen crabmeat – see tips, below). You can have a double-decker arrangement if you put another layer of plastic wrap on top of the crab cakes. Cover with a final layer of plastic wrap and stash in the freezer overnight or for a few hours. If you're using thawed frozen crabmeat, do not refreeze, but just let the patties sit for about 30 minutes in the refrigerator to firm up.

❄ When party time comes around, preheat your oven to 250°F. Line a cookie sheet large enough to take all the crab cakes with parchment paper.

❄ Heat a skillet filled with oil about $1/4$ inch deep, take the frozen crab cakes out of the freezer, then fry the unthawed crab cakes until golden brown and crisp on both sides, which won't take long.

❄ As they brown, transfer the crab cakes to the parchment-lined cookie sheet and put in the oven for 20 minutes to heat through, holding them in the oven to keep warm before serving, if required. If you're using thawed crabmeat, fry the patties for a few minutes a side only, though you can hold them in the low oven if you want to keep them warm. The crab cakes will not be quite as crisp, but they will be scrumptious.

❄ Remove the crab cakes to a platter or pair of plates, scattering lemon or lime segment wedges among them. They are lovely, too, with sweet chili sauce. Use a good bottled one or, as I've done, mix a squirt of lime juice (to give extra sharpness and make it runnier) into the Chile Jam on p.241.

24 THE MORE THE MERRIER

SHORT AND SWEET

The fact that there are a mere trio of recipes for something sweet here is not meant to hint at restraint or austerity on my part. It's because there's a whole chapter you can draw on to strike a sweet note as well as a seasonal one (see Joy to the World, from p.171). You could add a trayful of bite-sized mince pies to hand around, or a nice fat Christmas cake standing proudly on display, with a knife for people to cut their own slices. The picture on p.26 illustrates just this point.

Indeed, add anything you want, or add nothing: the three recipes that follow are simple, no-bake, quick-assembly and low-effort sensations that will keep you, and your guests, sweet.

CHOCOLATE–PEANUT BUTTER CUPS

These are really a homespun version of the famous Reese's confection of the same name, embellished with gold to give a touch of seasonal glitz. I have on occasion used my children – their little fingers are better designed for the job – to press the peanut butter layer into the paper cups, but have generally lived to regret it. Anyway, this is not a hard job, just a boring one, and I find once I've accepted that, the mindless, repetitive activity can be positively therapeutic.

❊ Mix together the brown sugar, confectioners' sugar, butter and peanut butter either by hand, using a bowl and wooden spoon, or more easily with a free-standing mixer (my preference) or food processor to make a sandy paste.

❊ Use your hands to form scant 1-teaspoon discs to fill the base of about 48 mini baking cups placed in miniature tart pans or mini-muffin pans (each indentation about 3/4 inches in diameter). Press the sandy mixture as best you can to form a layer at the bottom of each paper case.

❊ Melt both chocolates very gently, either in a heat-proof bowl suspended over a pan of simmering water or, using a suitable bowl, in the microwave, according to the manufacturer's instructions.

❊ Stir the melted chocolates together and let cool *a little*, then spoon 1 teaspoonful into each baking cup, covering the sandy base.

❊ Decorate with edible gold decorations in the middle of each chocolate-covered, peanut-butter cup. Or sprinkle over any other decoration of your choice. Put in the refrigerator to set for 30 minutes or so before serving.

Makes approx. 48

FOR THE BASE:
1/4 cup packed dark brown sugar
1 3/4 cups confectioners' sugar
1/2 stick (4 tablespoons) soft butter
1 cup smooth peanut butter

FOR THE TOPPING:
1 cup (7 oz) milk chocolate, chopped, or chips
1/2 cup (3 oz) bittersweet chocolate, chopped, or chips
edible gold or other decorations e.g. red, white and green Christmassy sprinkles (see Suppliers p.267)
48–50 mini baking cups (preferably gold, see Suppliers p.267)

Don't use whole nut or other virtuous peanut butter here, only the regular sort. For what it's worth, I go for Skippy.

MAKE AHEAD TIP:
Make the cups up to 2 days ahead and keep, loosely covered, in a cool place.

FREEZE AHEAD TIP:
Make the cups and open freeze on a baking sheet. When frozen, pack into a rigid container. Thaw overnight in a cool place on a wire rack.

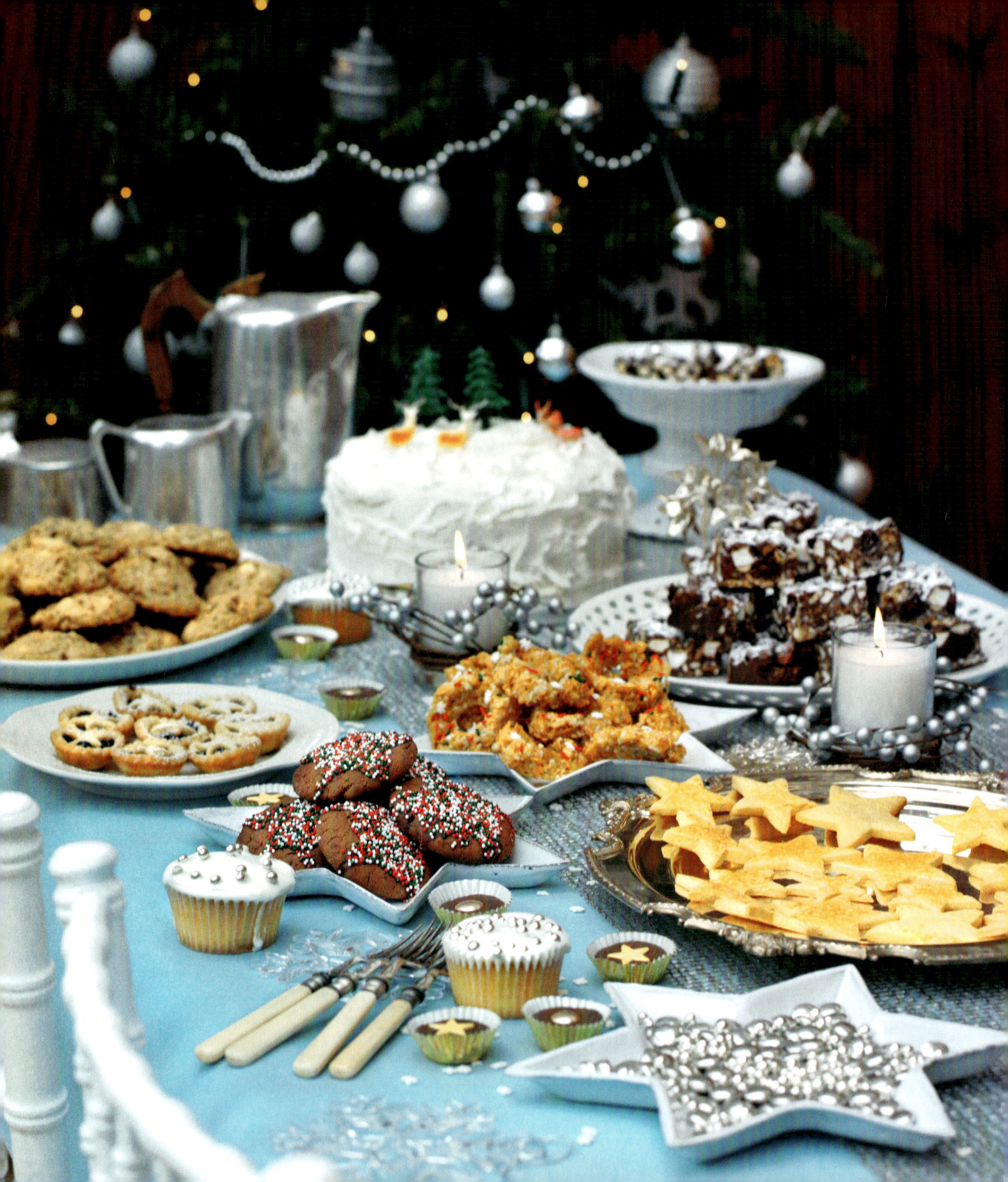

EGGNOG SYLLABUB

This is, in effect, an Anglo–American union: eggnog is *the* holiday tradition Stateside; and you could hardly get more quintessentially English than a syllabub. And actually, upping the Anglo-ante, I wouldn't mind it one bit in place of the whipped cream in the Boozy British Trifle on p.42. Though, it really would pack a killer punch.

Just as it is here, piled creamily, with celestial lightness into dinky espresso cups or shot glasses, it is, quite simply, exquisite. You can certainly taste the trio of tipples, but you don't feel as if you should avoid stepping near a naked flame after eating it.

❋ In a large bowl, crack the egg and add the vanilla, sugar, bourbon, rum and brandy, and grate in an exuberant amount of fresh nutmeg; you will be grating some more on the top of the syllabubs later, too. If you don't want to use all three drinks, then choose your preferred one and triple the single measure given.

❋ Whip together all the ingredients, except the alcohol, with an electric mixer; I use my free-standing mixer.

❋ Slowly whisk until the cream thickens, then trickle in the alcohol and continue whisking until the cream is softly whipped but will still hold its shape when the whisk is lifted out of the lightly bulging mass. Be patient: because the alcohol acts as a thinner, the cream will take a while to get desirably, floatily thick; this is why I suggest an electric mixer to do the work.

❋ Dollop moundingly into 15 espresso cups or shot glasses and grate a little more nutmeg over each one.

Makes 15 x 1/4-cup servings
(If you are having a bigger party and want more servings, it would be better to double the ingredients but make it in 2 batches)

1 egg (see note below)
2 teaspoons pure vanilla extract
1/3 cup superfine sugar
2 cups heavy cream
3 tablespoons bourbon
3 tablespoons dark rum
3 tablespoons brandy
good grating of fresh nutmeg (about a third of a nutmeg)

If you prefer not to give people raw egg to eat, then replace the egg with 1/4 cup of unflavored and unseasoned (check label on carton) egg replacer, such as Better'N' Eggs.

OPPOSITE:
The sweet delights of a dessert-dedicated welcome table.

CHRISTMAS ROCKY ROAD

Makes 24 big-bite-sized bars

1¼ cups (8 oz) bittersweet chocolate, chopped or chips

¾ cups (6 oz) milk chocolate, chopped or chips

1½ sticks (12 tablespoons) soft butter

¼ cup golden syrup, such as Lyle's, or light corn syrup

approx. 4 cups (7 oz) amaretti cookies (not the soft ones)

1 cup shelled Brazil nuts

⅔ cup candied or glazed cherries

2½ cups mini marshmallows

1 tablespoon confectioners' sugar

edible glitter (optional, see Suppliers p.267)

If you want to, there's nothing (except dexterity in my case) to stop you cutting these into tiny, petit four–size pieces, in which case you could almost double the number.

MAKE AHEAD TIP:
Make the Rocky Road and refrigerate to set. Don't add the confectioners' sugar yet, but cut into bars, then store in an airtight container in a cool place for up to 1 week. Decorate with confectioners' sugar and edible glitter about 1–2 hours before serving.

FREEZE AHEAD TIP:
Make the Rocky Road as above and freeze for up to 1 month. Thaw overnight in a cool place. Decorate as above.

It's not that I felt my usual Rocky Road Crunch Bars needed any improvement (though fiddling with recipes is one of life's pleasures) but I thought they would benefit from some seasonal adjustment. So, out go the plain cookies and in come amaretti cookies and – in the seasonal spirit – I've crammed in some Brazil nuts and candied cherries (as red as Rudolph's nose), along with snowy mini marshmallows. The fresh snowfall of confectioners' sugar on top might seem seasonal enough, but not for me. So I add some edible glitter in Disco Hologram White.

❅ Put both chocolates into a heavy-based pan to melt with the butter and syrup over a gentle heat.

❅ Put the cookies into a freezer bag and bash them with a rolling pin to get big- and little-sized crumbs; you want some pieces to crunch and some sandy rubble.

❅ Put the Brazil nuts into another freezer bag and also bash them so you get different-sized nut rubble.

❅ Take the pan off the heat, and add the crushed cookies and nuts, whole candied cherries and mini marshmallows. Turn carefully to coat everything with syrupy chocolate.

❅ Tip into an aluminum foil pan (I use one 9¼ x 12 inches), smoothing the top as best you can, although it will look bumpy.

❅ Refrigerate until firm enough to cut, which will take about 1½–2 hours. Then take the set block of Rocky Road out of the pan ready to cut.

❅ Push the confectioners' sugar through a small strainer to dust the top of the Rocky Road. Then, if you like, add a sprinkling of edible glitter for some festive sparkle.

❅ With the long side in front of you, cut it into 6 slices down and 4 across, so that you have 24 almost-squares.

THE MORE THE MERRIER **29**

THE WELCOME TABLE

You might be wondering what a "welcome table" is, and you'd be justified. I made it up. When I explain, I think you'll understand: it's the table loaded with food for people to plate up for themselves as they party. It could be called a buffet, I suppose, or a fork supper, but somehow both those terms make me feel I'm throwing a party on a cruise ship.

Besides, the essential element – the prerequisite of a party – is that mood of welcome and abundance, and this is what these recipes are all about. It really doesn't matter if the plates are paper, and there aren't enough chairs: this is food that's easy to make, easy to eat, and makes people know you want them there.

You could make just one or two of the recipes for the hard-core, inner circle who invariably stay behind at the end of a cocktail party, but I think of this, my welcome table, as the best way to feed a pile-up of friends at a warmly informal supper party to celebrate the season.

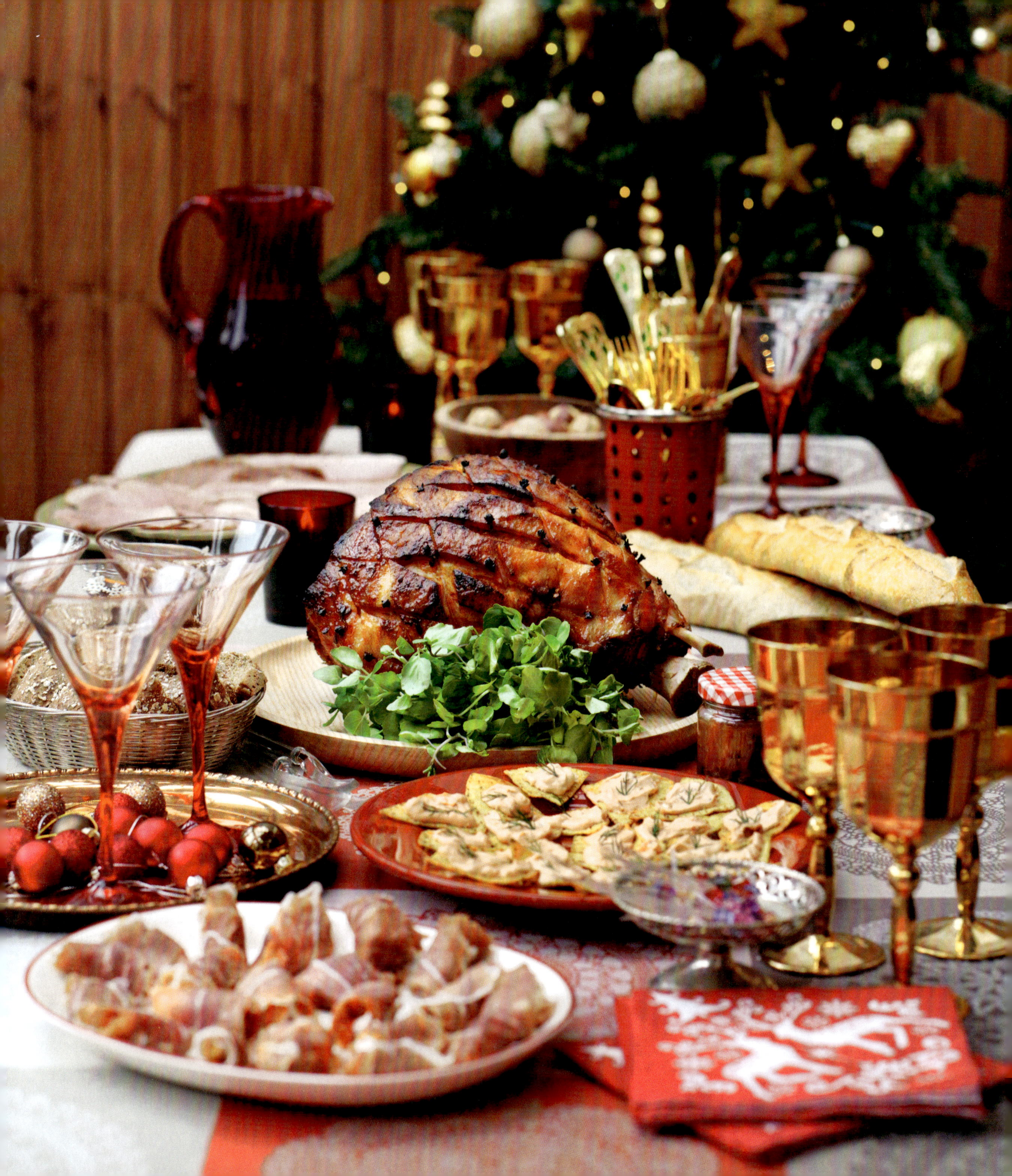

AROMATIC CHRISTMAS HAM

Serves approx. 10

14 lbs uncooked ham (see Suppliers p.267)
1 cup red wine
water to cover
1 large onion, halved
2 cloves garlic (unpeeled)
1 fennel bulb, halved
2 star anise
1 tablespoon coriander seed
1 tablespoon fennel seed
1 tablespoon mixed peppercorns

FOR THE GLAZE:
approx. 20 whole cloves
1/4 cup cranberry or red currant jelly
1/2 teaspoon ground cinnamon
1 teaspoon smoked paprika
1/2 teaspoon red wine vinegar

MAKE AHEAD TIP:
Cook the ham, loosely cover in a "tent" of aluminum foil and keep chilled for up to 1 week.

There's no absolute need to have a cold Christmas ham on a welcome table, but there are few sights more seasonally cheering. I like to have some of the sweet, salty pink meat carved, and some still clove-studded and gorgeously whole, as a joint, on a wooden board. Obviously, it is fabulous hot, too.

If you feel like adding the Christmas Chutney, by all means do (see p.235); I would. Though any number of other condiments in that chapter might also be a good match. Store-bought mango chutney is certainly not infra dig – or not in my house – and I definitely need English mustard with this. Those who like it less hot could turn to the Red Currant and Whole-grain Mustard Sauce (a quick stir-up, no cooking) on p.67, perhaps using cranberry jelly (if already using in the glaze) in place of the red currant.

❋ Soak the ham in cold water for 48 hours (or 24 hours if you like a saltier ham), changing the water every 8 hours. Put all the ingredients, except those for the glaze, into a large pan, on the stove but off the heat, adding fresh water until the ham is covered.

❋ Turn on the heat and bring to the boil, then turn down to a simmer and partially cover the pan. Cook for about 3½ hours. (This may not seem long for a big ham, but as it will carry on cooking as it cools, and this is going to be eaten cold, I don't want it overcooked. Nor do you.)

❋ Preheat the oven to 400°F. Lift the ham gently out of the hot liquid, sit it on a board and let it cool slightly, not too much but just so that you can touch it without burning yourself.

❋ With a sharp knife, strip off the rind, and a little of the fat layer if it's very thick, but leave a thin layer of fat. I love this work: it is peculiarly gratifying seeing the hot blubbery fat slither off. Use the same knife to score a diamond pattern in the remaining fat on the ham, in lines about ¾ inch apart. Stud the points of each diamond with a clove.

❋ Put the cranberry or red currant jelly, cinnamon, paprika and red wine vinegar into a little saucepan and whisk together over a high heat, bringing it to the boil. Let the pan bubble away, for about 5 minutes, so that the glaze reduces to a syrupy consistency that will coat the fat on the ham.

❋ Now sit the ham in a roasting pan lined with aluminum foil, as the sugar in the glaze will burn in the oven as it drips off. Pour the glaze over the diamond-studded ham, then put it in the oven for about 15 minutes, or until the glazed fat has caught and burnished. Take the ham out of the oven and sit it on a wooden board to cool (2–3 hours) before you carve it.

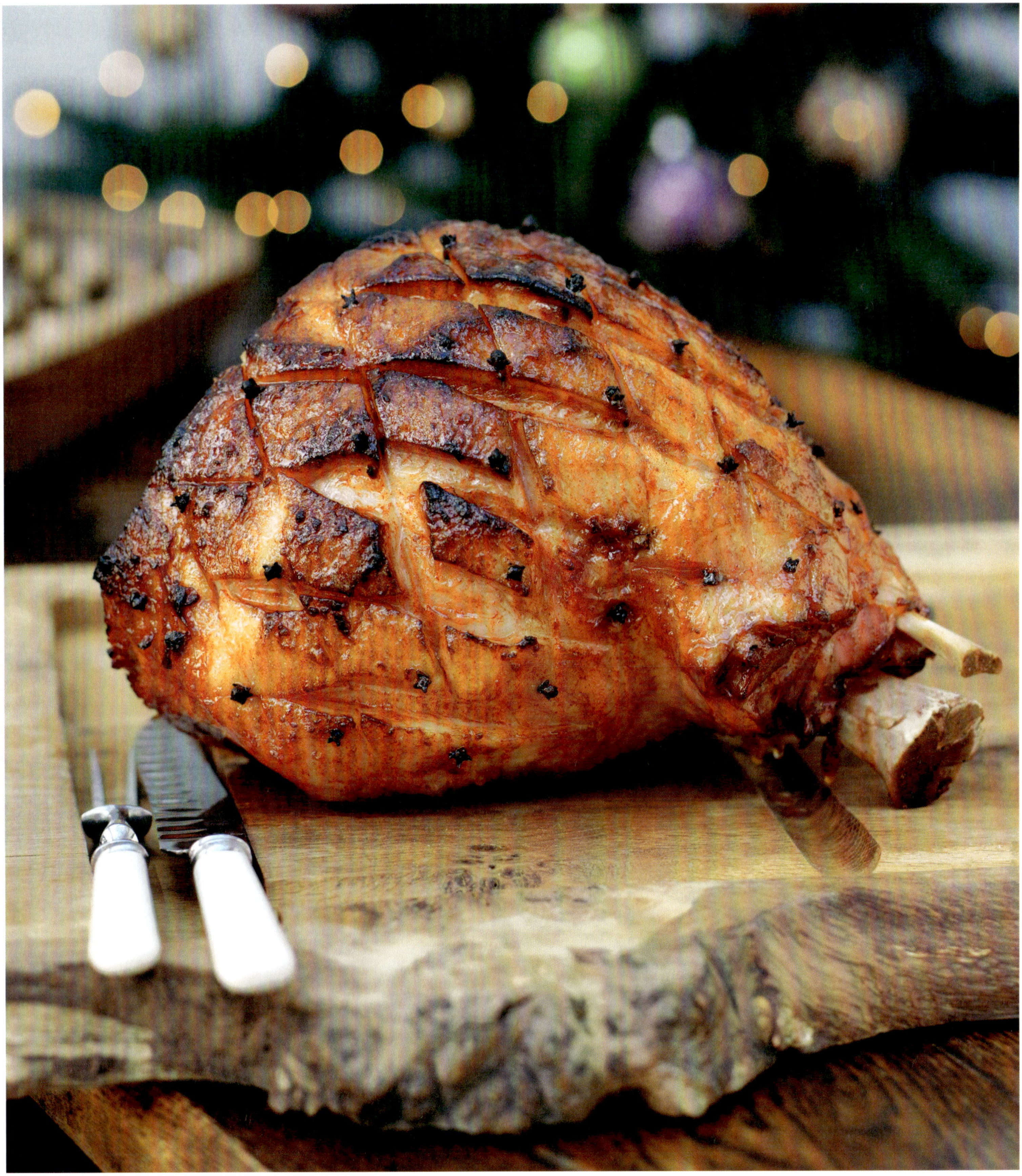

PUMPKIN AND GOAT'S CHEESE LASAGNE

Serves 12–15

FOR THE PUMPKIN FILLING:

- 2 tablespoons olive oil
- 2 tablespoons butter
- 8 sage leaves
- 2 onions, peeled and finely chopped
- 3 cloves garlic, peeled and minced
- 12 cups cubed pumpkin flesh (this is from a 5 lb pumpkin or about half a decent-sized pumpkin, a proper eating one not the Halloween kind, peeled, seeded and cut into 1-inch rough cubes)
- 1/3 cup dry vermouth or white wine
- 1/4 cup water
- 1 x 14 oz can diced tomatoes
- salt and pepper

FOR THE TOMATO SAUCE:

- 3 cups canned or bottled tomato sauce, pref. organic with no added salt
- 2 cups water
- 2 tablespoons sugar
- 2 tablespoons kosher salt or 1 tablespoon table salt
- good grinding of pepper

FOR THE CHEESE LAYER:

- 1 lb soft fresh goat's cheese (chèvre)
- 1 3/4 cups whole milk ricotta cheese
- 3 eggs
- good grating of fresh nutmeg
- 12 fresh lasagne sheets (approx. 1 1/4 lbs)
- 1/2 lb fresh mozzarella cheese
- 1 cup pine nuts, toasted in a hot dry pan
- salt and pepper

I use a soft goat's cheese log, often sold as chèvre, that has no skin and a texture more like that of a goat's curd cheese.

One of the questions I am asked most often is how do I come up with recipes? The answer is simple: greed. When I'm not eating, I'm thinking about what I might want to eat, and the notion of pumpkin lasagne came into my head when speculo-salivating, and it found its way from my head to my kitchen to my stomach with gratifying ease.

This is an easy lasagne to make in that, unlike a traditional meat one, there are not two sauces to do in advance. I simply cook the pumpkin earlier and layer it up with fresh lasagne sheets (bought from the supermarket) that don't need pre-cooking and an easy cheese and egg mixture.

Don't be put off by the length of the recipe that follows. It takes longer to explain than to do!

❉ **To make the pumpkin filling:** heat the oil and butter in a shallow Dutch oven or cast-iron braiser and fry the sage leaves over a gentle heat for about 2 minutes.

❉ Add the chopped onion and minced garlic to the pan and fry very gently for another 10 minutes or so.

❉ Add the pumpkin pieces, turn well in the oniony oil and, after about 5 minutes, add the vermouth (or wine), the water and diced tomatoes. Simmer, covered, for an hour, stirring occasionally so the pumpkin cooks evenly. Taste for seasoning – I tend to add quite a bit of salt here – and leave to cool.

❉ **For the tomato sauce:** simply pour the tomato sauce and water into a large jug or bowl, and stir in the sugar, salt and pepper, whisking it all together.

❉ **To make up the cheese layer:** in a separate bowl beat the goat's cheese and ricotta with the eggs, nutmeg, and salt and pepper to taste.

❉ Preheat the oven to 400°F, slipping in a large cookie sheet as you do.

❉ To assemble the lasagne, begin by putting 2 cups of the cold tomato sauce in the bottom of a roasting pan (measuring approx. 14 x 10 x 2 1/2 inches).

❉ Then layer with a third of the lasagne sheets, overlapping them well (Italians do it with the pan horizontal but the pasta vertical, if that makes sense, but I don't know that it truly matters …). Leave the rest of the tomato sauce aside for the time being.

THE MORE THE MERRIER **35**

MAKE AHEAD TIP:
Up to 2 days ahead, make the pumpkin filling, leave to cool and keep, covered, in the refrigerator. Make the cheese layer and keep, covered, in the refrigerator. When ready to use, assemble the lasagne and cook as directed.

FREEZE AHEAD TIP:
Cook, cool and freeze the cooked pumpkin for up to 1 week. Thaw overnight in the refrigerator. When ready to use, assemble the lasagne and cook as directed.

❋ Layer a third of the pumpkin filling over the lasagne, and dollop on a third of the cheese mixture, coaxing with a rubber spatula. It won't cover completely; think more of spreading blobs about. Then start again with a layer of lasagne, followed by pumpkin, then the cheese. Repeat once more – lasagne, pumpkin, and the last of the cheese mixture.

❋ Pour the remaining cold tomato sauce over, letting it sink down and be absorbed in the layers.

❋ Slice and chop the mozzarella and dot over the top.

❋ Bake in the oven, on the cookie sheet, for 1 hour. Once baked, take it out of the oven and let it stand for 15–30 minutes to make cutting and serving easier. (I love this when it's stood for an hour or so, too.) As you cut and slice, you will notice a shallow tomatoey cheesey pool at the bottom of the pan; bread dunked into this is gorgeous.

❋ Sprinkle the toasted pine nuts over the lasagne, and cut into squares to serve.

CHRISTMAS COLESLAW

For someone who doesn't consider herself a regular coleslaw eater, I seem to be peculiarly compelled towards this Germerican salad. Generally, I find a way in for myself by leaving out the onion, and throwing in the odd chopped scallion instead, as earlier recipes of mine will testify. So you have my blessing to leave it out here, but consider this: I am a complete wuss about raw onion and yet I love this coleslaw. Flecks of scallion look very seasonal alongside the overwhelming rubied redness of the rest of the slaw, so either way, it's a go-er.

❄ Finely shred the red cabbage; it should be very fine, so if you're patient and dextrous use a knife, otherwise use the slicing disc of a processor.

❄ Peel and slice the red onion into fine half-moons.

❄ Peel and cut the beets into matchsticks or julienne. You might want to wear vinyl disposable gloves to do this.

❄ Finely slice the fennel, then combine the cabbage, onion, beets and fennel in a big bowl.

❄ Mix the chutney, mayonnaise, garam masala and buttermilk in a bowl. Dress the coleslaw with it, and check the seasoning, adding salt – or whatever you want – to taste.

Serves at least 20 as part of a spread

1 head red cabbage (approx. 2 1/4 lbs)
1 red onion
2 large uncooked red beets (approx 1/2 lb)
1 fennel bulb

FOR THE DRESSING:
1/4 cup mango chutney (preferably Sharwood's)
1/4 cup mayonnaise, preferably organic
1 teaspoon garam masala (see note below)
1/4 cup buttermilk
salt to taste

Look for garam masala in the spice section of the supermarket.

MAKE AHEAD TIP:
The day before, mix together the dressing ingredients, cover and store in the refrigerator. On the day, about 3 hours before serving, mix together the shredded cabbage, sliced onion, beets and finely sliced fennel in a sealable bag. Store in the refrigerator. Toss the salad together about 30 minutes before serving.

CHOC CHIP CHILI

Serves 12

10 (or 5 linked pairs) chorizo sausages (not the salami sort), approx. 1 1/4 lbs

3 1/4 lb boneless beef shank, cut into 3/4 inch cubes

3 onions (about 1 lb), peeled

3 cloves garlic, peeled

1 fresh long red chile, seeded

1/4 cup vegetable oil

seeds from 3 cardamom pods

2 teaspoons ground cumin

1 teaspoon ground coriander

1 teaspoon ground cinnamon

1 teaspoon dried red pepper flakes

1/4 cup tomato paste

1/4 cup tomato ketchup

4 x 15 oz cans red kidney beans, drained

3 x 14 oz cans diced tomatoes

1/4 cup bittersweet chocolate chips

1 cup water (swished out in one of the diced tomato cans)

If you're not buying your meat from a butcher, you can use regular stew meat from the supermarket, but you'll need to cube it smaller and it is unlikely to get quite as tender as shin. I often buy shank.

MAKE AHEAD TIP:
Cook the chili in the oven for 2 1/2 hours only. Cool, cover and store in the refrigerator for up to 2 days. When ready to use, tip the chili into a pan and bring slowly to the boil on the stove top, stirring occasionally. Cover tightly and return to the oven for 1 hour until piping hot.

FREEZE AHEAD TIP:
Cook the chili for 2 1/2 hours only. Cool and freeze. Thaw overnight in the refrigerator, then reheat as above.

I've always made chili with ground meat and added a dash of cocoa to bolster. This time, I wanted to play a little, to achieve something more along the lines of a dark, spicy-sauced cassoulet: that's to say, together with the beans, I use beef, cut into fairly small chunks, and fiery Spanish sausages. In place of the cocoa there is a sprinkling of dark, dark chocolate chips, which adds real depth and a velvety savoriness. This chili is not for light eaters, but something spicy and substantial that is just what you need to soak up seasonal excess.

The Fully Loaded Potato Skins, overleaf, obviously beg to accompany this, but a splodge of the brightly hued Christmas Coleslaw on p.37 goes very well alongside, too. Under normal conditions, I'd also dollop out an unchiled guacamole with this, but I worry about having avocados sitting around going grungy, so only make this if you know it won't be hanging around: simply mash 3 ripe avocados with 3 finely chopped scallions and add the juice of a lime or two and some salt to taste, stir in 3 tablespoons of chopped fresh cilantro, spoon into two or three bowls, and sprinkle a little extra cilantro over.

❋ Preheat the oven to 300°F.

❋ Finely chop, or process the onion, garlic and chile.

❋ Heat the oil in a large ovenproof pan (with a lid) or cast-iron or enameled Dutch oven and fry the onion, garlic and chile until soft, on low for about 10 minutes, then add the cardamom seeds, cumin, coriander, cinnamon and red pepper flakes.

❋ Stir the oniony spiced mixture together and then add the chorizo, sliced into 1/4-in. coins, letting them ooze their paprika-orange oil.

❋ Drop in the cubes of beef, turning them in the pan with the chorizo and onion mix, to brown the meat.

❋ Stir in the tomato paste, ketchup, drained kidney beans and diced tomatoes. Add the water and bring the chili to a boil.

❋ Once it's started bubbling, sprinkle the chocolate chips over the chili and give it a good stir. Put on the lid and transfer to the oven.

❋ Cook at this low heat for 3 hours. Once cooked it is best left overnight to improve the flavor.

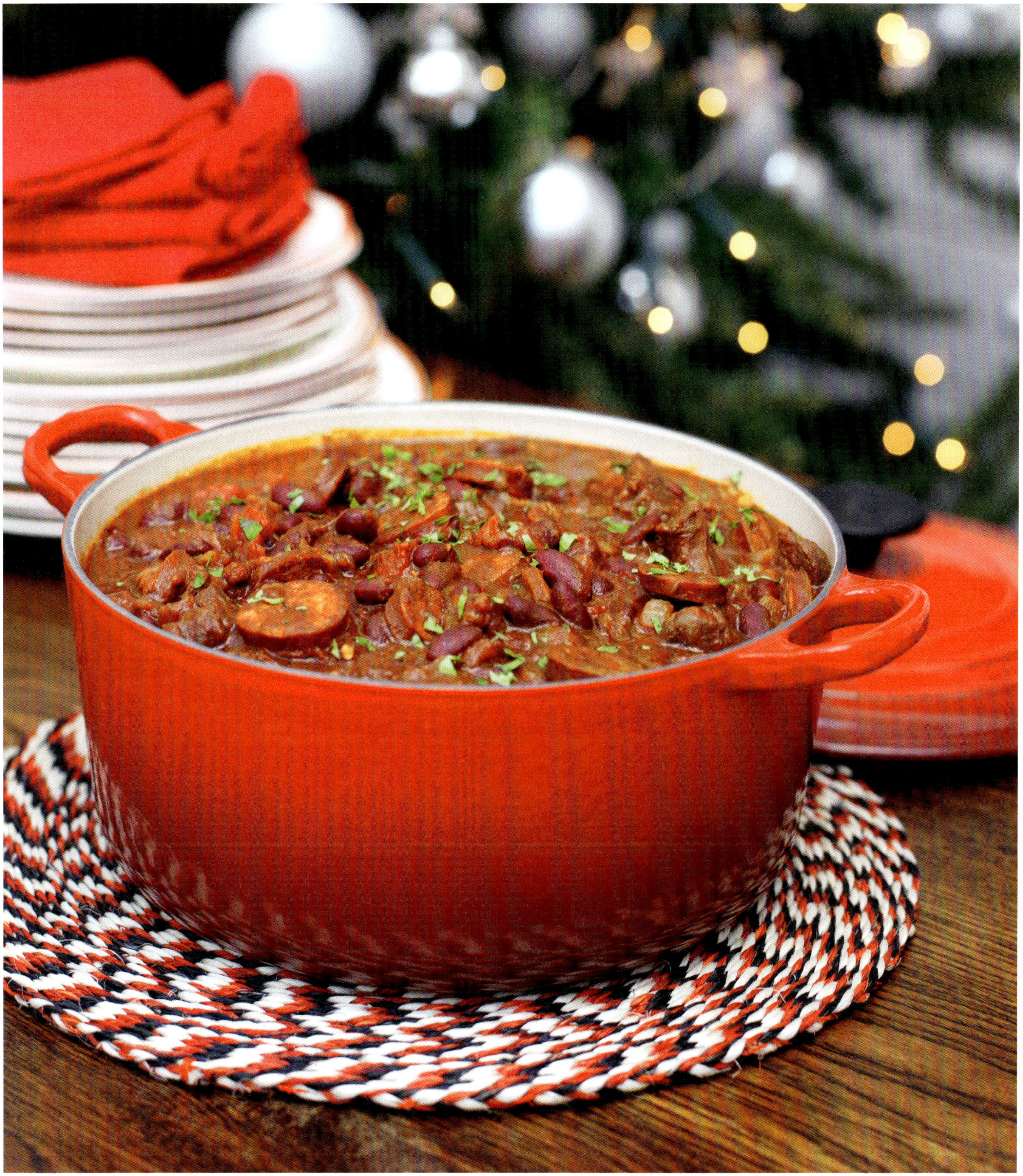

FULLY LOADED POTATO SKINS

Makes 20 stuffed potato skins

10 baking potatoes (such as Russet)
2 cups grated sharp cheddar cheese
1 cup sour cream
4 scallions
1 teaspoon kosher salt or 1/2 teaspoon table salt (or to taste)
good grinding of black pepper
1 tablespoon Lea & Perrins Worcestershire sauce
10 slices bacon
oil for frying

MAKE AHEAD TIP:
Fill the potato skins, as directed, and sprinkle with the cheese and crispy bacon (or add the crispy bacon after cooking if preferred). Cover loosely and keep in the refrigerator for up to 2 days. Cook as directed.

FREEZE AHEAD TIP:
Fill the potato skins as above, wrap in plastic wrap and freeze for up to 1 week. To cook, lay the frozen potato skins on a baking sheet and cover loosely with aluminum foil. Bake in the oven for 35–40 minutes, removing the foil after the first 15 minutes.

The first time I did these – having longed to write my own recipe for Fully Loaded Skins – I didn't bother with the bacon. I was eating them alongside meat, so it didn't seem necessary. But then I figured, without bacon they're only *partially* loaded, and that wouldn't do at all. So here I've gone, as you can see, the whole hog. However, in the seasonal spirit, you might want to serve them without the bacon, or with the crisp bacon bits in a separate bowl for sprinkling, since it seems unnecessarily antagonistic to make potatoes that your veggie friends can't eat at a party.

❋ The day (or up to 2 days) before you load them, preheat your oven to 400°F, and bake the potatoes (pricking them first) for about 1 1/2 hours, or until the skins are crisp and the insides fluffy.

❋ As soon as you can bear to tackle the hot potatoes, cut them in half lengthways and scoop the insides into a bowl.

❋ Put the husk-like skins of the potatoes on a tray and, when cool, cover until you are ready to fill them. Let the potato pulp cool in the bowl, and then cover until needed.

❋ When you are ready to fill the potatoes, preheat your oven to 400°F. Add 1 3/4 cups of the cheese to the cold potato pulp along with the sour cream.

❋ Finely chop the scallions and add to the potato pulp, with the salt, pepper and Worcestershire sauce.

❋ Spoon the potato filling into the potato skins, and lay each half on a sheet pan so they fit snugly together. Sprinkle over the remaining cheese, giving each potato skin a light covering, and cook for 20–30 minutes until golden.

❋ Fry the bacon slices in oil (or broil them) until crispy, then crumble them and sprinkle half a slice's worth over each potato skin to make them fully loaded.

THE MORE THE MERRIER 41

THE BOOZY BRITISH TRIFLE

Enough for 20 portions easily

FOR THE CUSTARD:
4 cups heavy cream
8 egg yolks (I use the whites to make the Prodigious Pavlova on p.45, but you could freeze the whites in an airtight freezer bag for up to 6 months)
2 whole eggs
1/4 cup superfine sugar
1 teaspoon vanilla extract

FOR THE BASE:
2 plain pound cakes (12 oz each)
1 x 12 oz jar strawberry or blackberry preserve
2 cups cream sherry or sweet sherry
2 x 12 oz bags frozen mixed berries, thawed
zest of 1 orange
2 tablespoons superfine sugar (not needed if using *fresh* fruits)

FOR THE TOPPING:
2 cups heavy cream
1/3 cup shelled pistachios
1 tablespoon crystallized rose petals (or crystallized violet petals)

Crystallized rose petals or violet petals are easy to find at specialist cake decoration stores or online (see Suppliers p.267).

MAKE AHEAD TIP:
Make the trifle (without the whipped cream) up to 2 days ahead. Keep, covered, in the refrigerator. When ready to serve, finish with the whipped cream, pistachios and crystallized rose (or violet) petals, as directed.

I think this really says it all. I have written so many recipes for trifle, I scarcely dare reiterate my love for it, but this, perhaps the most traditional of my offerings, shows the sensational, time-honored pud at its glorious, many-layered best: the jam-slashed and sherry-sodden sponge, the sharp fruity layer of flavor-oozing berries, the eggy custard and the whipped cream. On top, my favorite color combination: the Victorian pink of crystallized rose petals with the tender green of chopped pistachios. Perfection.

❊ To make the custard, heat the cream in a large, wide, heavy-based pan and while it's heating, whisk the egg yolks, whole eggs and superfine sugar in a bowl.

❊ When the cream's at boiling point – though *don't actually let it boil* – take it off the heat and pour it over the eggs and sugar, whisking as you go.

❊ Wash out the pan (boring but it does have to be done), then pour the uncooked custard back into it and return to the heat.

❊ Cook over a medium heat (people will tell you it should be low heat but that is just too tedious for words), stirring all the time, until it has thickened. *It must never boil!*

❊ After 10–15 minutes, it should be thick enough, so straightaway pour it into a cold, clean bowl, add the vanilla extract, and whisk a bit to help bring the temperature down.

❊ Cover the very top of the custard, as well as the bowl, with plastic wrap and leave to cool, while you start assembling your trifle.

❊ Cut each pound cake into 16 slices and make into sandwiches with the preserve. Squidge these into the base of your trifle bowl. A trifle bowl should, I feel, be glass so you can see the layers from the outside. The proportions vary and, since the point of a trifle is the layers, the dimensions of your bowl will determine how these build up and the amount of cake etc. you will need.

❊ Pour the sherry over the cake sandwiches and let it soak in.

❊ Now tumble in the thawed berries, with a little of their liquid. (It might seem unseasonal to use "summer" fruits, but I love their tartness against the sweetness of the custard that will drape over them.) Then grate the zest of the orange

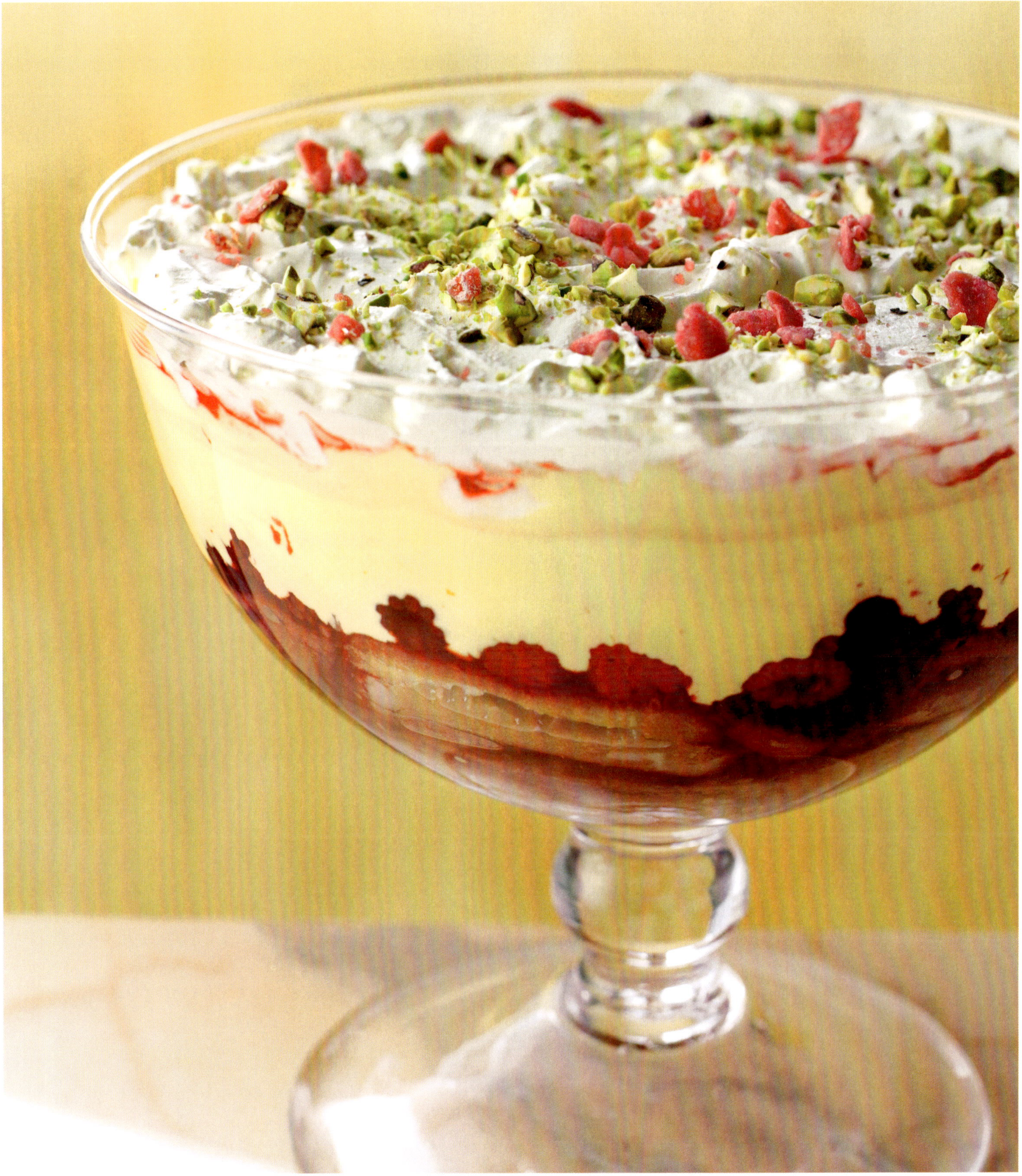

over the fruit and sprinkle with the superfine sugar; if you're not using frozen fruit (which tends to be sour), don't bother with the sugar.

❋ When the custard's cool, remove the plastic wrap. Pour and scrape the custard on top of the berries. It will be soft-set: thickened but far from solid. Cover the bowl (not the custard this time) with some fresh plastic wrap and refrigerate for at least half a day or up to 2 days – it's this standing time that makes the difference.

❋ When you are ready to serve, take the trifle out of the refrigerator to stand for about 1 hour. Whisk the cream until softly whipped. You don't want it to merge with the custard, but nor do you want it stiffly peaking.

❋ Remove the plastic wrap from the trifle bowl and spread the whipped cream on top of the custard with a rubber spatula.

❋ Finely chop the pistachios, sprinkle over the top of the trifle and adorn with a few, beautiful crystallized rose petals (or crystallized violet petals, if you prefer).

PRODIGIOUS PAVLOVA

This is indeed prodigious: a billowing, regally magnificent mega-meringue, marshmallow within, crisp and almost candied at its sugary edge, dolloped with whipped cream, lychees and passion fruit and drizzled with a vividly red, vibrantly sharp raspberry sauce.

If, like me, you live in the northern hemisphere, this being the deep midwinter, I presume the raspberries will be frozen; and since these berries tend to be sharper, I don't spritz fresh lemon juice into them as I blitz them into a sauce. If you're using fresh raspberries, add a squeeze of lemon as you blend.

I do think the raspberry sauce (coulis to those who remember the 1980s) makes a difference: I love the note of Christmas that the lucent redness brings, and the way, when you cut into it, you get a streak of winter raspberry ripple.

❄ Preheat the oven to 350°F. Line a cookie sheet with parchment paper and draw a rough 10-inch diameter circle on it; I pencil around a cake pan that size.

❄ Whisk the egg whites until satiny peaks form, then whisk in the sugar, a tablespoonful at a time, until the meringue is stiff and shiny.

❄ Sprinkle the cornstarch, vinegar and vanilla extract over the egg white, and fold in lightly with a metal spoon. Mound the meringue on to the parchment paper within the circle and, using a spatula, flatten the top and smooth the sides.

❄ Put in the oven and immediately reduce the heat to 250°F. Bake for an hour. Then turn off the oven and leave to cool completely. Once it's cool, take the meringue disc out – and you can keep it in an airtight container for a couple of days or freeze for a month.

❄ When you are ready to assemble the pavlova, invert the cooled meringue disc onto a large plate or a stand you can serve it on, and peel off the parchment paper.

❄ Whip the cream until thickened but still soft, and pile onto the meringue – on the squidgy part that was stuck to the parchment paper – spreading it to the edges in a swirly fashion.

❄ Cut the passion fruit in half, and scoop out the seeds, and any pulp and juice, into a bowl. Peel the fresh lychees (if using) over the bowl to catch any juice, then remove the stones, tear the lychees into pieces and let them drop into the passion fruit. Tear the drained, canned lychees (if using) likewise, and drop them in, too.

Makes 14 generous slices

FOR THE BASE:
8 egg whites (reserved, perhaps, from The Boozy British Trifle custard on p.42)
2½ cups superfine sugar
4 teaspoons cornstarch
2 teaspoons white wine vinegar
½ teaspoon vanilla extract

FOR THE TOPPING:
2⅔ cups heavy cream
10 passion fruit (see below)
10 fresh or canned lychees, drained if canned
3½ cups (12 oz) raspberries (frozen are fine)
3 tablespoons confectioners' sugar

Look for passion fruit in speciality markets and Asian and Latino grocers. When they are ripe they will look quite wrinkly so don't be put off. (See also Suppliers p.267)

MAKE AHEAD TIP:
Make the meringue disc and store in a deep, airtight container for up to 2 days. About 3–4 hours before serving, top with whipped cream and keep in the refrigerator. Just before serving, add the fruits and raspberry sauce.

FREEZE AHEAD TIP:
Make and freeze the meringue disc for up to 1 month. Thaw in a cool room and finish as recipe.

THE MORE THE MERRIER

46 THE MORE THE MERRIER

✻ Leave the passion fruit and lychees sitting in their bowl for a moment, while you liquidize the raspberries with the confectioners' sugar in a blender.

✻ Dollop the cream-topped pavlova with the passion fruit and lychees, and their juices, then zigzag some red, red, red raspberry sauce over the top, putting the rest in a small jug for people to add to their slices as they eat.

48 THE MORE THE MERRIER

SEASONAL SUPPORT
SOUPS, SALADS, SAUCES AND SERVE-LATER SIDES

THERE IS AN ABSENCE in this book, an absence that is at the heart of this very chapter – and that is a roast chicken. To some extent, its exclusion makes sense. After all, this is the turkey's time; a chicken, puny by comparison, doesn't seem to deserve much of a place in a Christmas book. But, for me, there is no kitchen, no life, without it: no way a roast chicken is not always central. It is the simplest feast: the oven cooks it without interference from you. You just need to be there to put it in the oven, and to take it out. And it's not just lack of time or laziness that makes it crucial: a roast chicken is the taste of home.

Still, there's nothing wrong with laziness or lack of time as motives for cooking particular sorts of food. So long as greed is rewarded at the same time, I am happy. This really is what the recipes in this chapter are all about. Not every meal, even at Christmas, can be a full-on, time-consuming procession of courses. Sometimes I need to know that all I have to do is bung a chicken in the oven and, with one of these salads or soups beforehand or, indeed, the same salad or one of the dishes alongside, a proper dinner can be served. You don't need to make the soup or vegetable dishes in advance, but I find it helpful to do so. For me, cooking in advance is the way of tackling Christmas, and all the meals it involves, express-style. There's too much to do to manage everything at the last minute (though the salads are the work of moments), so what makes life simpler is to stagger tasks, to get food cooked earlier, only to be idly reheated at the last minute.

The salads, too, whether brought out as a first course or side dish to bulk out a dinner, or to add tang and flourish to a tableful of leftovers, are the nearest, neatest thing to a stress-busting, seasonal shortcut.

Maybe it goes without saying – a quick glance at the ingredients list and all is made clear – but my approach at Christmas is "scatter with pomegranate seeds." Their jewelled beauty gives instant Christmas oomph. And I'm unembarrassed about buying the seeds, already popped out into containers, from the supermarket.

So, the roast chicken I mentioned may exist, or may be just the notional main part of the meal you're planning, without a lot of time to fuss over it; the recipes that follow are what make this meal, and others like it, possible.

SOUPS

CHESTNUT SOUP WITH BACON CRUMBLES

Enough to fill 10 soup bowls or 20 cups or small (8 oz) mugs

1 onion
1 leek
3 carrots
2 stalks celery
3 tablespoons garlic oil
2½ cups red lentils
3 quarts vegetable broth (or chicken broth if preferred)
3½ cups (1 lb) vacuum-packed or jarred peeled chestnuts
½ cup dry Amontillado sherry
salt and pepper

FOR SERVING:
small bunch of parsley (optional)
1 teaspoon garlic oil
10 slices bacon

MAKE AHEAD TIP:
Make the soup and liquidize in a blender. Cool, cover and keep in the refrigerator for up to 3 days. Reheat with the sherry, adding more broth if needed. Check the seasoning before serving. Fry the bacon, cool and crumble into a sealable bag. Keep in the refrigerator for up to 3 days.

FREEZE AHEAD TIP:
Make the soup as above and freeze in an airtight container for up to 2 months. Thaw overnight in the refrigerator and reheat as above.

This is not a million miles away from the chestnut soup in my first book, *How to Eat*, but the fact that I can't leave it behind tells you not only how good it is, but how important familiarity, tradition and continuity are, especially at this time of year.

I confess, I'd planned a celery root and chestnut soup to go here: I've cooked it; I've loved it; I'd written the recipe. But as I sit writing, I find it's my older, more basic soup that writes itself into the page. Taste it and you'll see why: a meal in itself with a hunk of warm bread, or a make-ahead starter to bring some cold cuts to party-life, this soup manages to be comforting, elegant and simple all at the same time.

Much as I love the golden intensity of chicken broth (and I'll take mine from a carton; it doesn't always have to be homemade), I do think when you're catering for groups of people it's wise to make up meat-free soups with vegetable broth, so you can keep the vegetarians happy. Thus the bacon crumbles are, I suggest, better served apart, for those carnivores who might like to sprinkle them over their sweet, grainy soup.

❈ Either by hand, or using a food processor, finely chop the onion, leek, carrots and celery.

❈ Heat the oil in a large, heavy-based pan, and add the chopped vegetables, cooking for about 10 minutes on a medium to low heat, until softened a little.

❈ Add the lentils, and turn them in the vegetable mush.

❈ Add the broth and bring to the boil, then, with the heat down a little, let simmer for about 40 minutes, or until the lentils are soft.

❈ Add the chestnuts and liquidize the soup in a blender in batches, adding more water if it's too thick. However, if you're going to serve this at a later time, I wouldn't bother to add water now, as the soup will inevitably thicken as it stands.

❈ When you want to eat the soup, heat it in the pan along with the sherry, adding more liquid if needed, and season with salt and pepper to taste.

❊ While the soup's getting warm and ready, finely chop the parsley (you will need about 3 tablespoonfuls), and heat the garlic oil in a large frying pan for the bacon.

❊ Fry the bacon until it is crisp and scorched and remove to some paper towels. Crumble the bacon into a bowl or a couple of bowls and put them on the table.

❊ As you serve the hot soup, sprinkle with parsley if wished.

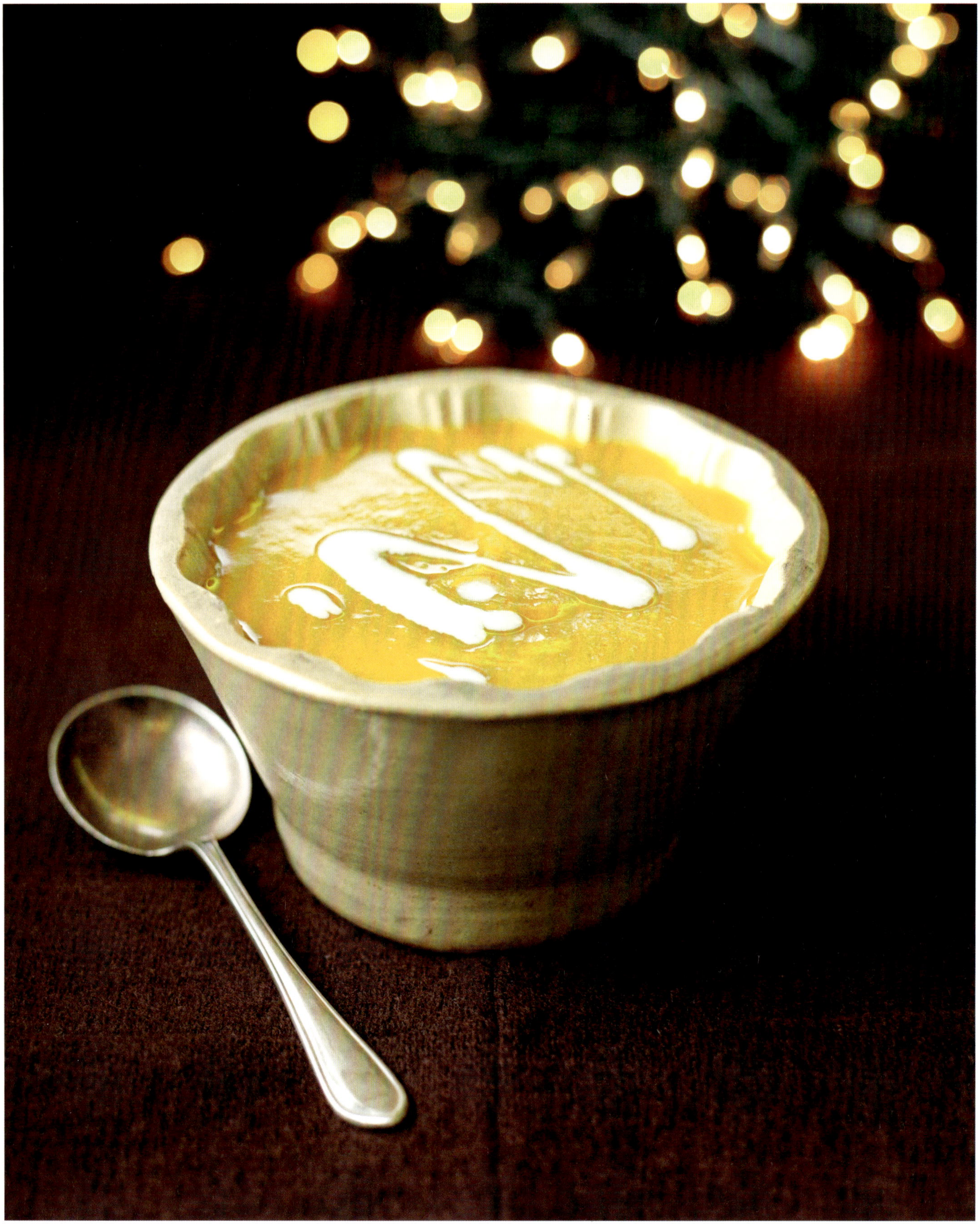

ROAST SQUASH AND SWEET POTATO SOUP WITH BUTTERMILK–BLUE CHEESE SWIRL

It may seem a bit fiddly to have a soup prepared in two parts: one in the oven; one in the pan. But I do this not only because I think it intensifies the flavor dramatically, but because it actually makes my life easier.

The thing is this: when you roast a butternut squash, you can go ahead and liquidize it without ever having to peel it (I found this out when I made the Butternut Orzotto on p.134) and when I'm thigh-deep in cooking season, this is a real boon. Plus, I love the slightly flecked look that the spice-sized specks of skin give the soup, as well as the hint of texture.

The robust sweetness of this soup is countered by the buttermilk and blue cheese drizzling-mix that I swirl over the soup as I serve it and, indeed, I think it's the two together that really make it.

❄ Preheat the oven to 400°F. Put the chopped onion, chopped butternut and sweet potato (again, don't worry that neither of these last two are peeled) onto a cookie sheet.

❄ Drizzle the oil over them and sprinkle with the cinnamon and nutmeg, then roast in the oven for about 1–1$^{1}/_{4}$ hours, by which time all should be tender. Remove from the oven.

❄ While the vegetables are still warm or at room temperature, liquidize them in a blender in 2 batches, adding 2 cups of vegetable broth to each batch.

❄ Pour the blended vegetables into a saucepan. Swish another 2 cups of vegetable broth in the blender to get out all the remnants of the soup, and pour into the pan. You have now added 1$^{1}/_{2}$ quarts of liquid to the vegetables.

❄ On reheating to serve, add the marsala, and taste for seasoning. You may need to add up to another 2 cups of water if the soup's too thick for your liking.

❄ As the soup warms up, liquidize the blue cheese and buttermilk in a clean blender and spoon into a jug or bowl.

❄ On serving, drizzle some of this mixture over each bowl. Leave the jug on the table for your guests to have more if they wish.

Serves 8–10 as a starter, 6 as a main course

1 onion, peeled and roughly chopped
1 butternut squash (unpeeled), halved, seeded and sliced into 1$^{1}/_{2}$ x 1-inch chunks
2 large (1 lb) sweet potatoes or yams (unpeeled), cut into 1-inch rings
$^{1}/_{4}$ cup olive oil
teaspoon ground cinnamon
$^{1}/_{2}$ teaspoon ground nutmeg
1$^{1}/_{2}$ quarts vegetable broth
$^{1}/_{2}$ cup marsala wine
salt and pepper

FOR SERVING:
1 cup crumbled blue cheese
1 cup buttermilk

If you have any buttermilk–blue cheese mixture left over, put it into a clean glass jar with a fierce squirt of lime juice, and seal. It will keep for a day in the refrigerator and serve as a good salad dressing with or without an avocado blended into it.

MAKE AHEAD TIP:
Make the soup and liquidize in a blender. Cool, cover and keep in the refrigerator for up to 3 days. Reheat with the marsala, adding more water if needed. Check the seasoning before serving.

FREEZE AHEAD TIP:
Make the soup as above and freeze in an airtight container for up to 2 months. Thaw overnight in the refrigerator and reheat as above.

54 SEASONAL SUPPORT

TORTILLA SOUP

When I went to Dallas, I became somewhat obsessed with ferreting out this Southwestern speciality and, although I was nominally there to work (under the auspices of Janet McLeod who had, fantastically, been Elvis's publicist), my overwhelming concern was this soup. However, my version is not attempting to ape the various ones I tried on my travels; I don't want to enter into the debate as to what is authentic or not. For one, I lack the credentials. I'm probably about as far from a southern belle as you could get, though I love the twang, adore the manners and could eat tortilla soup until the cows come home.

If you don't know what this is, the name is probably misleading. The tortilla refers to the soft corn tortillas which are cut into shreds and fried to be tossed into a spiced chicken broth, along with some shredded cheese, diced avocado and chopped cilantro. Naturally – and it has a particular bearing, given the season – this can be made with turkey in place of chicken.

The chicken broth plays such a part here, it's worth making sure you use a good one. That doesn't have to mean homemade, though it's not difficult to make. Either follow the method on p.265 or cover the fresh carcass and leavings from a roast chicken with $4^1/_2$ quarts of water and boil with onion, leek, carrot, bay and salt for about 3 hours. With a turkey carcass you could make double this, easily.

❄ Heat the broth in a large pan, and add the celery salt, cumin, bay leaves, garlic, chiles and scallions.

❄ Let the soup boil gently for about 10 minutes, then take off the heat and add the shredded chicken.

❄ While the soup's bubbling, put about a third of the vegetable and chile oils into a frying pan to heat. Take a pair of soft corn tortillas, roll them up like a cigar and, with scissors, snip into approx. $1/4$-inch strips. Do likewise, in pairs, with the remaining 6 tortillas.

❄ Fry about a third of the tortilla strips in the hot oil and, as they scorch, remove to some waiting paper towels. Add and heat another third of the oil and continue like this, with the rest of the tortilla strips and oil. The home-fried tortilla chips may seem disappointingly soft in the pan, but they seem to crisp up as they cool slightly on the paper towels and, later, serving plate.

❄ Ladle the hot soup into bowls, and arrange the hot tortilla strips, the cheese, avocado, cilantro and lime wedges (for spritzing) in separate dishes on the table to add to the glory of the occasion and to the soup.

Serves 6 as a main course

$3^1/_2$ quarts chicken broth
2 teaspoons celery salt
2 teaspoons ground cumin
3 bay leaves, preferably Turkish
1 small clove garlic, peeled and minced
2 fresh red chiles, seeded and chopped
4 scallions, finely sliced
3 cups cooked shredded chicken (or turkey)

FOR SERVING:
2–3 tablespoons vegetable oil
1 teaspoon chile oil
8 soft corn tortillas
2 cups grated cheddar cheese
1 avocado, peeled and diced
3 tablespoons chopped fresh cilantro
3 limes, cut into quarters

MAKE AHEAD TIP:
Make the soup then cool, cover and keep in the refrigerator for up to 1 day. Bring slowly to the boil to reheat then simmer very gently until piping hot. Avoid too much stirring or the chicken will become stringy.

THREE SEASONAL SALADS

CHRISTMAS SALAD

Serves 6

2 heads red endive or treviso
1 large head radicchio
2 red bell peppers (optional)
seeds from 1 pomegranate, or 1/2 cup pomegranate seeds from a container

FOR THE DRESSING:
1 teaspoon Dijon mustard
1/2 teaspoon honey
juice of 1 clementine
1 teaspoon lime juice
pinch of salt
3 tablespoons extra virgin olive oil

It is predominantly the color – for all that I have another red salad on p.58 – that makes me think of this as a Christmas salad. But then, the starring role played by *the* Christmas fruit – the pomegranate – would surely be justification enough. This is the salad I bring out time and time again at Christmastime, either to bring a little joy and color to a quickly gathered together tableful of leftovers, as a side dish when the food really needs no more than a light accompaniment, or even as an appetizer, so people have something to pick at as I do a little last minute this-or-that.

At this time of year, given my pomegranate-predilection, my refrigerator is full of those cartons of all-done-for-you seeds, and the amount here represents half what I'd expect to find in a carton. If you're going for the whole fruit, use the seeds from a whole pomegranate.

If the salad is an appetizer, I tend to throw in the red bell peppers; as a simple side dish it is elegant perfection without.

❈ Tear the endive or treviso and radicchio into pieces into a salad bowl.

❈ If you are using the red bell peppers, seed them and cut into 3/4 -inch strips, and add to the salad.

❈ Sprinkle some of the pomegranate seeds over, then whisk together the dressing ingredients to pour over the salad.

❈ Toss everything together, then do a final sprinkling of pomegranate seeds over the top before serving.

MAKE AHEAD TIP:
Whisk together all the dressing ingredients, pour into a clean jar or an airtight container and refrigerate for up to 3 days.

OPPOSITE:
Char-grilled Peppers with Pomegranate (back left);
Christmas Salad (back right); Red Salad (front)

56 SEASONAL SUPPORT

SEASONAL SUPPORT **57**

RED SALAD

Serves 8

2 x 15 oz cans red kidney beans
1 red onion, peeled and finely chopped
4 teaspoons good-quality red wine vinegar
1/2 lb cherry or grape tomatoes
2 tablespoons extra virgin olive oil
a few tablespoons finely chopped parsley (optional)

This is a fantastic fallback not least because it's a speedy, low-effort way to turn something as basic as cold meat or baked potato into a substantial supper. Indeed, you could fork a little best-quality drained, canned tuna straight in and be done. However, even as someone as far from the vegetarian end of the spectrum as could be, I am more than happy to have this, quite simply, as is.

❊ Drain and rinse the kidney beans in a colander to get rid of the dark sludge from the cans, then rinse again and put into a serving bowl or dish.

❊ Put the chopped onion into a small bowl and pour over the vinegar. Leave to macerate for at least 15 minutes and up to 2 hours.

❊ Halve the tomatoes and put them into the serving bowl.

❊ Now tip in the macerated onions and toss through the beans and tomatoes. Drizzle over the oil and toss again, sprinkling with some parsley if you want; I like the way its greenness brings out the red.

MAKE AHEAD TIP:
Make the salad, without adding the tomatoes, up to 1 day ahead. Cover and keep cool. Add the tomatoes and parsley, if using, about 1 hour before serving.

CHAR-GRILLED PEPPERS WITH POMEGRANATE

Serves 8

6 bell peppers (ideally a mix of red, orange and yellow, but never, ever, ever green; all red is fine though)
seeds from 2 pomegranates, or 1 cup pomegranate seeds from a container
2 tablespoons fresh pomegranate juice
2 teaspoons lime or lemon juice
1/4 cup extra virgin olive oil
1 tablespoon garlic oil
1/2 teaspoon kosher salt or 1/4 teaspoon table salt
3 tablespoons drained capers

It was only a matter of time before I came back to the pomegranate. I am relaxed as to how you combine the bell peppers with the pomegranate. I often make this with frozen bags of char-grilled peppers, which I tip out, unthawed, onto a cookie sheet and roast in a hot oven for about 20 minutes. These I often eat warm, with some olive oil and lemon juice (or freshly squeezed pomegranate juice mixed with lime) tossed through, along with a handful of pomegranate seeds. For my cold version I simply use char-grilled peppers from a jar or deli, in place of the roasted bagged ones.

Opposite is the method you'll need if you're char-grilling the peppers yourself. It isn't difficult, just fiddly. Sometimes, I like an excuse to busy myself undemandingly in the kitchen. At other times, I unashamedly take the shortcuts above.

This salad is also good if you leave the bell peppers raw, just seeded and cut into 1/4-inch-wide strips, all juicy and crunchy, as are the pomegranate seeds, only the peppers are markedly sweeter.

58 SEASONAL SUPPORT

If I know all parties will be agreeable, I make a dressing by blending or whisking 2 anchovy fillets with a tablespoonful of red wine vinegar and three of olive oil. Otherwise, the dressing below is perfect.

To turn this into a first course, simply add some crumbled feta or sharp goat's cheese. And whether I'm using raw, bagged, jarred or home-charred peppers, I like to go for a mix of red, orange and yellow, to create an edible flame on the plate.

❋ Preheat the oven to 450°F.

❋ Cut the peppers in half, remove the stem and seeds, and sit them cut-side down on a sheet pan or a couple of pans. Roast in the hot oven until they blister; about 15 minutes should do it.

❋ Take out of the oven, and quickly tip the blackened peppers into a big bowl. Cover the bowl tightly with plastic wrap and leave the peppers to cool enough to handle.

❋ Use your hands to peel off strips of charred skin (don't worry if some is left on) and, as you go, put torn strips of peppers into a serving dish.

❋ When you've done all of them, add most of the pomegranate seeds to the peppers and toss well.

❋ Whisk together the pomegranate and lime juices (or lemon juice, if using), the olive oil, garlic oil and salt. I often just put everything into an old glass jar with a lid, and shake. Pour the dressing over the salad and toss gently but well.

❋ Add the crocodile-green capers, the perfect salty counterpart to the juicy sweet red peppers, and toss again, taste for seasoning, then add a final scattering of rubied seeds.

MAKE AHEAD TIP:
Make the salad, without the capers, up to 1 day ahead. Cover and keep cool. When ready to serve, add the capers and toss again. Check the seasoning, then scatter with extra pomegranate seeds.

SERVE-LATER SIDES

RED CABBAGE WITH POMEGRANATE JUICE

Serves 10

2 tablespoons vegetable oil
1 red onion, peeled and halved
scant 1 tablespoon kosher salt or 1 teaspoon table salt
2 red apples
1 head red cabbage
3 tablespoons packed soft dark brown sugar
2 teaspoons ground allspice
3 cups pomegranate juice

I couldn't have Christmas without red cabbage, and I never veer far from the way my mother cooked it – that's to say, I give it a long, slow stewing with something sharp, something sweet. This recipe takes in my unabating pomegranate pash but, instead of using the seeds, I go for the juice that comes in bottles. Make sure you go for the unadulterated, unsweetened variety; that much is crucial.

I love this with ham (hot or cold), or with turkey or roast pork, but I think it might be at its unsurpassed best (it's a close-run thing) with the Roast Goose on p.149. The important thing to bear in mind is that, as with all stews, this improves as it stands, so not only does it help you to make it in advance, it positively helps the red cabbage and, thus, your dinner, too.

Although as a regular side dish, this is fine for 10, it stretches easily to half that again as part of a Christmas dinner; when there are so many components, people tend to take relatively small helpings – and I'm talking about my family here, which is really saying something.

❋ Heat the oil in a large, heavy-based saucepan (with a lid) or a cast-iron or enameled Dutch oven. Finely slice each halved onion into thin half-moons and add to the pan along with the salt. Fry for about 5 minutes until the onion begins to soften but doesn't burn; the salt will help to prevent it from burning.

❋ While this is going on, quarter the apples (no need to peel), cut away the cores and chop them roughly, and add them to the softening onions and cook, stirring occasionally, for another 5 minutes.

❋ Finely shred the cabbage and add it to the onion–apple mixture in the pan, stirring slowly and patiently to mix. Add the brown sugar and allspice and stir, then pour the pomegranate juice into the pan.

❋ Let the mixture come to a bubble, then give another stir, turn down the heat, put on a lid and cook very gently at the lowest possible heat for 2–3 hours, stirring occasionally. It really won't get overcooked. Taste for seasoning only when you're ready to reheat, as the flavors won't have mellowed and come together properly until then.

❋ To reheat, put the pan back on the stove over a medium to low heat, stirring occasionally, for 15–20 minutes.

MAKE AHEAD TIP:
Make the red cabbage up to 3 days ahead. Transfer to a non-metallic dish or bowl then cool, cover and keep in the refrigerator. Put the cabbage back in the pan, and reheat as directed. Check the seasoning before serving.

FREEZE AHEAD TIP:
Make the red cabbage as above and leave to cool. Spoon into an airtight container and freeze for up to 2 months. Thaw overnight in a cool room and reheat as above.

BOSTON BAKED BEANS

This continues the seasonally warming vegetable theme – here, a pale pulse, after the deep-red cabbage with pomegranate juice – that combines the savory and the sweet, and although this is less obviously Christmassy than the others, tell me that after you've had a vat wafting its spiced way through the kitchen as you cook. The scent is heady and welcoming as the beans seem to mull in the bacon, mustard, spice and sugar.

These might not be baked beans as a Bostonian (or Messrs Heinz or Campbell for that matter) would cook them, but they work for me – and for anyone I've ever, proudly, fed them to. I warn you now: they are addictive. Must be the salt and sugar, which also – alas – explains why they taste so good.

It may be an obvious pairing, but this begs to be eaten with sausages.

Serves 8

2½ cups dried navy beans
2 tablespoons garlic oil
¼ lb thick-sliced smoked bacon, chopped somewhere between finely and roughly
1 onion, peeled and chopped
¼ cup grainy mustard
2 tablespoons tomato paste
½ cup packed soft dark brown sugar
1 quart water, plus ¼ cup
1 tablespoon cider vinegar
2 teaspoons kosher salt or 1 teaspoon table salt, or to taste

❄ The night (or day) before you want to make this recipe (which could be 2 days before you plan to serve it), soak the beans in plenty of water for 24 hours.

❄ Once the beans are soaked, drain and rinse them and put aside. Preheat the oven to 300°F and heat the oil in a large, cast-iron Dutch oven or an ovenproof pan with a lid.

❄ Fry the chopped bacon briskly in the hot oil and, after about 5 minutes, turn down the heat and add the chopped onion. Cook alongside the bacon for about another 10 minutes.

❄ Add the mustard, tomato paste and sugar and 2 cups of the water, stirring everything together well.

❄ Stir in the rinsed beans, and then add a further 2 cups of water. Bring to a boil and let it bubble for 10 minutes.

❄ Put a lid on the Dutch oven or pan and transfer to the oven for 2–2½ hours or until tender.

❄ Remove from the oven and add the remaining ¼ cup water along with the vinegar and, after tasting carefully (don't burn your mouth), the salt if wished.

MAKE AHEAD TIP:
Cook the beans for 2 hours, then cool and spoon into an airtight container. Keep in the refrigerator for up to 2 days. To reheat, return to the pan and stir in the extra ¼ cup water along with the vinegar and salt. Cover with the lid and bring slowly to the boil, stirring occasionally. Simmer for 10–15 minutes or until piping hot.

FREEZE AHEAD TIP:
Cook and cool the beans as above. Freeze for up to 3 months. Thaw overnight in the refrigerator, then reheat as above.

SEASONAL SUPPORT

SEASONAL SUPPORT

PISELLI CON PANNA E PANCETTA
(Peas with Pancetta in Cream All'Italiana)

Even though we constantly read how Italians use olive oil and never butter or cream, of course this is not the case – or certainly not in northern Italy. Funnily enough, however, it is a southern Italian, a Calabrese by the name of Lisa Grillo, who brought this combination into my life. And as grateful as I am to her for so very much, this must be chief of the blessings she has brought me over the years.

Yes, it's rich, yes it's got lots of cream, *bla, bla, bla*, as the Italians say, without an "h," but it is Christmas for goodness' sake.

This is good with absolutely everything – plain chicken or fish, or heaped over pasta or rice or *anything*.

❅ Heat the garlic oil in a large, heavy-based pan (with a lid) or a cast-iron Dutch oven and tumble in the *cubetti di pancetta* or bacon cubes (however you like to think of them) and let them cook for about 5 minutes.

❅ Add the scallions, stir well, and cook for a further 3 minutes.

❅ Add the butter and thyme to the pan or Dutch oven, stir well, then tip in the frozen peas. Cook for a few minutes, stirring, until the frost begins to leave the peas and they start to look a brighter green.

❅ Add the water, give another stir, then stir in the cream. Bring to a bubble, put the lid on and let it cook for 15 minutes.

❅ Take the pan off the heat, and remove the lid while you stir in the shaved Parmesan flakes, then put it back on to let the peas cool in their flavorsome cream. The peas will dull down, losing their bright green color as they cool and sit. This is as it should be, and don't worry about it; they may look less vibrant but they taste more vivid.

❅ To reheat, put the pan over a low to medium heat and keep it covered – opening it only to stir occasionally – for 5–10 minutes.

Serves 8

1 tablespoon garlic oil
1 1/2 cups (7 oz) cubed pancetta or slab bacon
6 scallions, sliced
1 tablespoon butter
1 teaspoon dried thyme
8 cups (2 lbs) frozen petits pois or baby peas
3/4 cup boiling water, from a kettle
1 cup heavy cream
heaping 1/2 cup shaved Parmesan cheese

MAKE AHEAD TIP:
Complete the recipe but without the Parmesan cheese. Allow to cool, cover and keep in the refrigerator for up to 1 day. To reheat, put the pan over a low to medium heat and stir in the Parmesan. Cover and reheat gently, stirring occasionally, for about 5–10 minutes.

POTATO, PARSNIP AND PORCINI GRATIN

Serves 8

1/3 cup dried porcini, or cepes
2/3 cup boiling water, from a kettle
1/2 stick (8 tablespoons) butter
1 tablespoon garlic oil
2 cups whole milk
2 cups heavy cream
3 star anise
1 teaspoon kosher salt or 1/2 teaspoon table salt
good grinding of pepper
2 lbs (approx. 6) potatoes such as Yukon Gold
2 lbs (approx. 8) parsnips

Cooking potatoes for large numbers of people is not always easy. This gratin makes it so, not least because I don't peel the potatoes (or the parsnips for that matter). Obviously, you don't need to make it ahead, but knowing you can is a help. There is a fabulously musky scent to this gratin, which comes in part from the star anise, in part from the porcini, and also from the culinary alchemy of all the ingredients together. And the thing is, for something so sweetly comforting, it is – I cannot explain why – somehow grand and exquisite, too.

❈ Soak the porcini in the boiling water for about 20–30 minutes.

❈ Preheat the oven to 450°F. Heat the butter and garlic oil in a large pan.

❈ Drain the porcini, reserving the liquid, then finely chop the mushrooms and add them to the pan to cook for a couple of minutes.

❈ Add the mushroom liquid, milk, cream, star anise and salt and pepper.

❈ Without peeling the potatoes or parsnips, slice them into 1/4-inch-round slices and add to the pan.

❈ Bring the pan to a bubbling simmer and then gently cook, partially covered, for 20 minutes, or until the potatoes and parsnips are tender but not mushy.

❈ Decant into a gratin-type, ovenproof pan (mine is a round shallow cast-iron braiser, about 5-quart capacity).

❈ Bake in the oven for about 40 minutes (it will need longer if you have cooked it ahead and left it to cool before putting in the oven) or until the top is colored in places and the gratin looks bubbly underneath.

MAKE AHEAD TIP:
Decant the vegetables into the gratin pan and leave to cool. Cover tightly with plastic wrap and keep in the refrigerator for up to 1 day. To cook, leave the pan at room temperature for about 40 minutes. Cook in the oven as directed.

FREEZE AHEAD TIP:
Cool and cover the vegetables as above, then freeze for up to 1 week. To use, thaw overnight in the refrigerator, and cook as above.

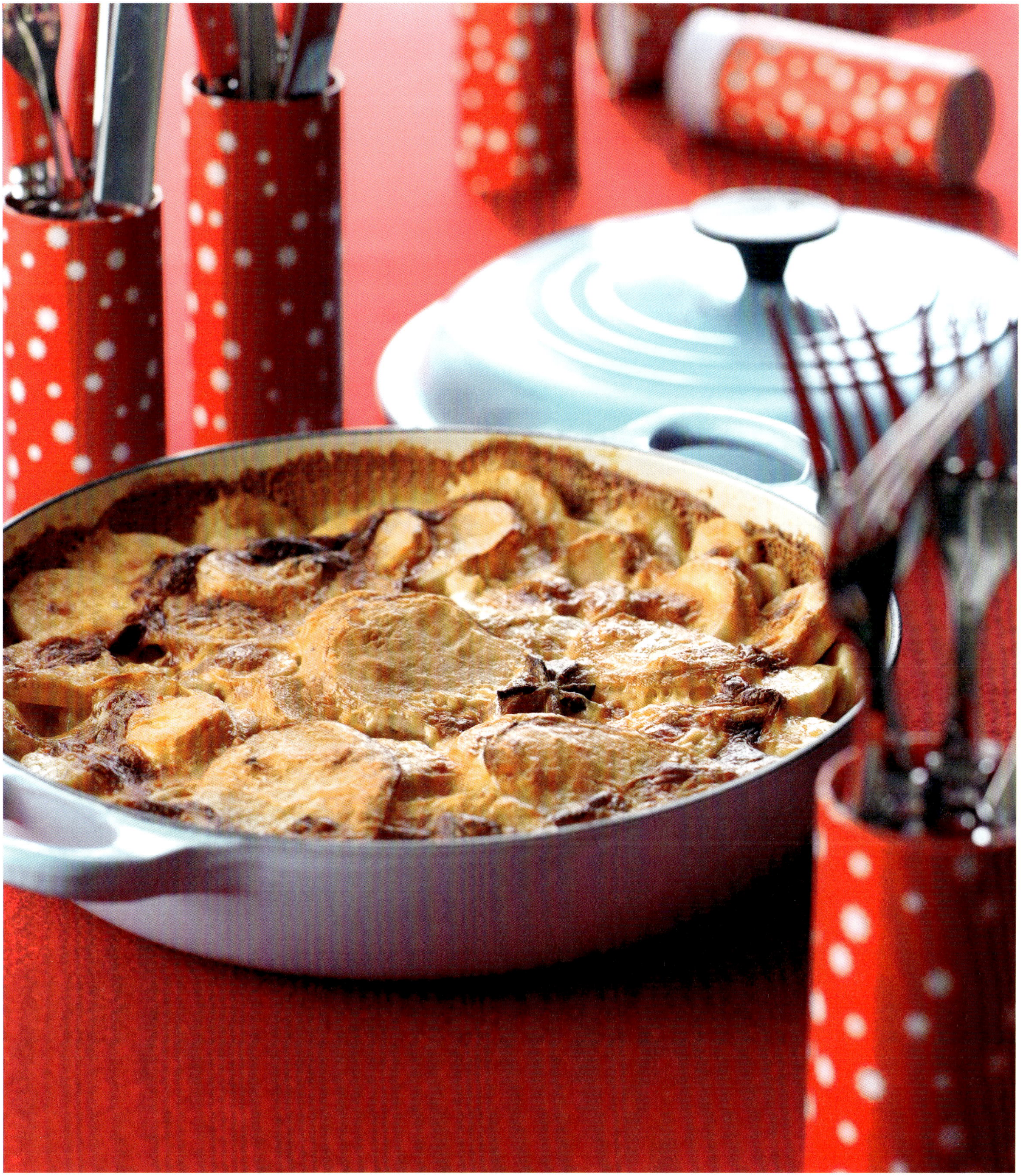

THREE STIR-TOGETHER SAUCES

This trio of sauces is just what you need to be able to prink something into dinner-party fare. And sometimes, it's not so much partifying as adding a crucial touch that makes everything feel complete. There is something about the contrast of components in each whisked-up sauce that offers complexity to the taste while being simple to make: the sweetness of the red beets plays against the heat of the horseradish; the pepperiness of the mustard counters the fruity sweetness of the jelly; and the sharpness, again of the mustard, undercuts the richness of the mayonnaise.

WHOLE-GRAIN HONEY MUSTARD MAYONNAISE

Makes enough to serve as a condiment for 8 people

1 cup good-quality, store-bought mayonnaise, preferably organic
¼ cup whole-grain mustard
1 teaspoon runny honey
squeeze of lemon
salt to taste

I love the combination of mustard and mayonnaise, my earliest savor of which was years ago, frightening how many, dolloped alongside some hot skinny French fries in Amsterdam. The one here is very different, and different again from the smooth, but equally delicious Dijonnaise I've run into since. This is sweet and nubbly and gorgeous with cold chicken, cold turkey, ham, hot baked potato or in any sandwich.

❈ Put the mayonnaise into a bowl and dollop in the mustard, whisking well to combine.

❈ Add the honey and a spritz of lemon and whisk again, tasting for balance and seasoning.

It may be helpful to think in terms of ratios rather than amounts: in volume (not weight), you have a quarter mustard here to mayo; add honey and lemon juice (and indeed salt) to taste.

MAKE AHEAD TIP:
Cover and keep in the refrigerator for up to 1 week.

OPPOSITE:
Whole-grain Honey Mustard Mayonnaise (left); Red Currant and Whole-grain Mustard Sauce (right)

66 SEASONAL SUPPORT

RED CURRANT AND WHOLE-GRAIN MUSTARD SAUCE

This has a distinctly Scandinavian taste, and is the perfect accompaniment to baked ham, eaten hot or cold. It can also make a quick glaze for sausages or, indeed, the ham before you've baked it.

❉ There is really nothing to this: you simply put the ingredients together and whisk till they're combined. If you've kept either of them in the refrigerator and they're too hard to mix, just whisk them in a saucepan over a low heat until they do what they're told.

Makes enough to serve as a condiment for 8 people; it's easy to augment, as you're using equal amounts of each

$1/2$ cup whole-grain mustard

$1/2$ cup red currant jelly

MAKE AHEAD TIP:
Cover and keep in a cool place for up to 3 days or longer if in the refrigerator.

RED BEET AND HORSERADISH SAUCE

Makes enough to serve as a condiment for 8 eaters

1 cup hot horseradish sauce
2 tablespoons crème fraîche or sour cream
1 small, uncooked red beet

This, in effect, is the Jewish *chrayn*, which makes an unorthodox outing in a Christmas book. I include it here because it enlivens cold turkey and other leftovers, and is particularly wonderful with roast goose or, it must be said, pork.

Because I'm usually pressed for time, I grate the beet into hot horseradish sauce from a jar (to which I've added the crème fraîche) but if you have time, you can grate 3 tablespoons of horseradish (use a Microplane grater, as for the beet) and the small beet into a scant cup of crème fraîche and add half a teaspoon of Dijon mustard, and salt to taste, stirring well to combine.

❋ Whisk or stir together the hot horseradish sauce with the crème fraîche in a wide bowl (this makes it easier when you grate in the beet).

❋ Put on disposable gloves (if you know what's good for you) and peel the beet before pressing it through a fine Microplane grater held over the horseradish bowl. Rap the grater when you've all but finished (don't grate so far that you risk mixing your own blood with the beet's) to knock in all the red gunge.

❋ Stir or whisk to combine and decant to a serving bowl or a jar.

MAKE AHEAD TIP:
Cover and keep in the refrigerator for 1 day.

SEASONAL SUPPORT

COME ON OVER...
STRESS-FREE SUPPERS

I DON'T THINK I CAN REMEMBER when I last gave a dinner party. This isn't an admission of regret or guilty confession, but a thankful statement of fact. Friends over for supper is a different matter, though. Around Christmas, I love to pile people in and I don't mind if it's every evening; in fact, that's what I want to happen. From mid-December onwards, sometimes even earlier, I want the house to be filled with people sitting around a table, talking and eating.

But this is very much about supper and not dinner. For one thing, I invite people over unfashionably early. I get things ready, but not fussily organized. I plonk cutlery, red napkins in snowflake rings and the shiny multi-colored tea light holders I bought at one of the children's school Christmas fairs on the bare wood table, along with a pile of plates, add drinks and wait for people to come, sit around and help themselves. I don't go in for serving drinks in one room, with everyone having to get up and shuffle into another to eat. I like to keep the scene of the crime contained. I think it feels cozier, but it makes life easier, too. Besides, I don't like having to act as some sort of MC or white-knuckled party organizer, desperately trying to herd people through the evening. That's not relaxing for anyone.

And, although I'm very happy to have company while I'm pottering stoveside, the food I make for my season of suppers requires so little last-minute attention, I'm never in hostess-meltdown. Most of the menus I suggest here can be prepared largely in advance, or else practically cook themselves. I don't factor in a first course, because I just have never found them necessary. You don't have to agree with me, and the soups and salads in Seasonal Support (from p.50) can help you bump up a two-course supper into a tripartite dinner with gratifying ease. I certainly do, however, put something – most usually one of the Crostini or the Seasonally Spiced Nuts from The More The Merrier (see pp.15–17 and 21) – on the table for people to graze on over drinks as they arrive.

I also feel that, around Christmas, you have to have bowlfuls of lychees and clementines to bring out either with dessert or even instead. And, please, the season surely demands a bowl of nuts with a nutcracker nestling in them, as well.

All I want, at this time of year, is to be able to have the people I love round a table with me and the food that follows makes me know I can do this, and enjoy it.

A LUSCIOUS DINNER FOR 6–8

LAMB AND DATE TAGINE
RED ONION AND POMEGRANATE RELISH
GLEAMING MAPLE CHEESECAKE

The symbolic aspect of feast foods has always been an important part of the ritual of celebration; sweet ingredients are there not just to please the palate, but also to bring corresponding harmony to the home. *La douceur du foyer*, that ironic Baudelairean yearning for home, sweet home, and the pleasures of the hearth, is never more keenly felt (or often, indeed, as futilely) as it is at this time of year. I know that good food does not automatically create a good mood, but friends and family gathered around a treat-laden table can make the difference, to both cook and eater. And this indulgent, aromatic menu is the perfect way to begin our season of spirit-lifting suppers.

If the dessert sounds rich after the sweet substantiality of the main course, well – what can I tell you? – it is Christmas, after all. But, while I make no claims for the dietary restraint of this menu – *as if* – it is actually the case that the cheesecake has, in each more-ish mouthful, just the tang and the melting lightness that you want after the tagine. The maple syrup that cascades lightly on top and sometimes down the sides is sweet enough to hold its own after the swelling fruitiness of the dates, but not so sweet that it creates overload.

An easy, no-cook alternative for getting this balance of sweet first, tang after, is to provide, instead of dessert, a snowy log or two of tender goat's cheese, and perhaps some honey to drizzle over it.

And I'm sure you know my views by now on the enduring desirability of loading the table with seasonal fruits, so both you, and those you're feeding, can play it any way you or they want, to finish dinner.

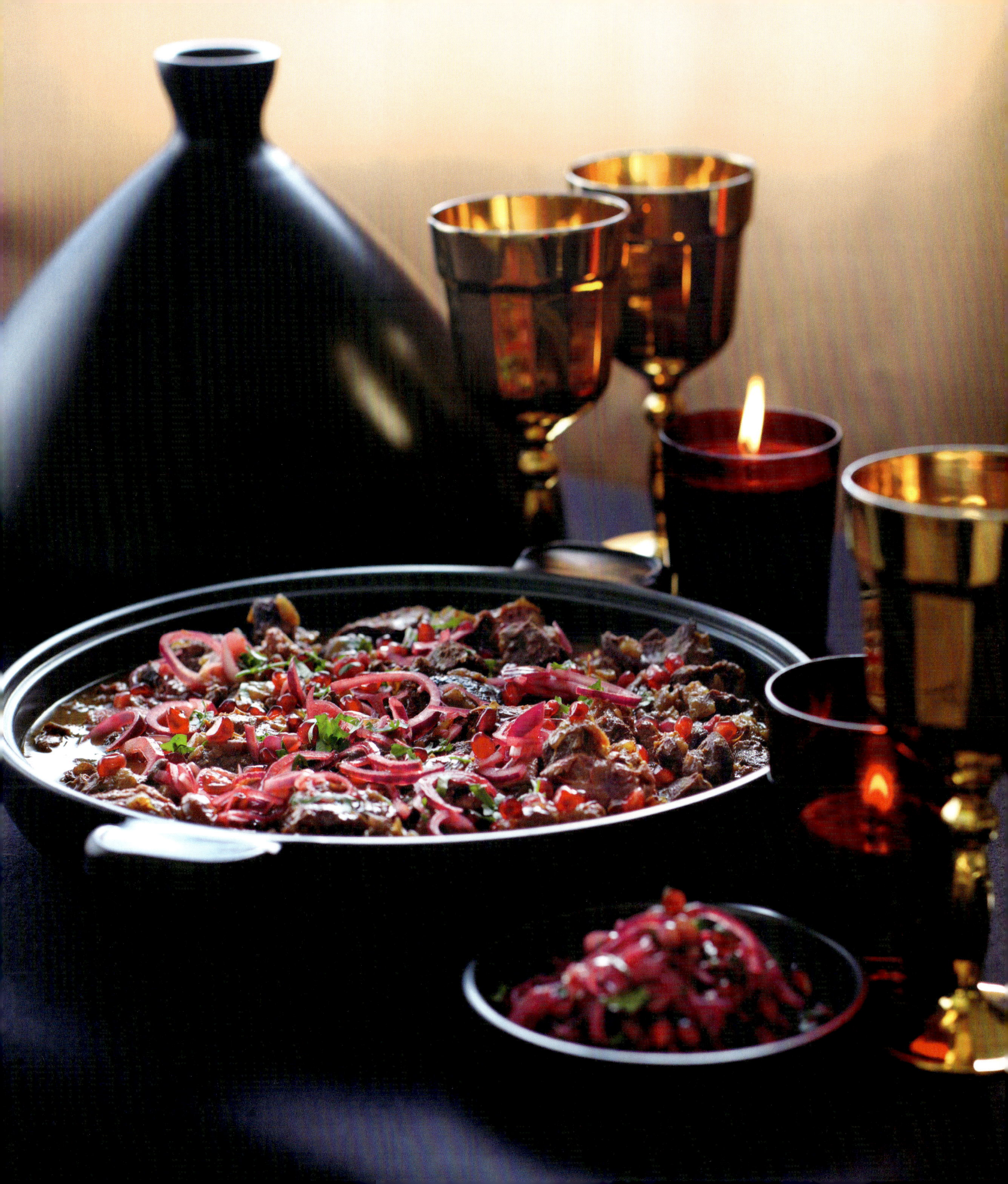

LAMB AND DATE TAGINE

3–4 tablespoons goose fat (or olive oil)
2 onions, peeled and chopped
1 teaspoon ground cinnamon
1 teaspoon ground turmeric
1 teaspoon ground ginger
1 teaspoon ground cumin
1 teaspoon ground allspice
2¼ lbs cubed leg of lamb
2 cups (½ lb) soft dried pitted dates, or pitted Medjool dates
1 cup pure pomegranate juice, from a bottle
1 cup water
2 teaspoons kosher salt or 1 teaspoon table salt, or to taste

If you're not using a funnel-lidded tagine, but a regular, preferably shallow, braiser, then you do have the option of cooking this for 2 hours in a 300°F oven.

MAKE AHEAD TIP:
Make the tagine, then transfer to a non-metallic bowl to cool. Cover, and store in the refrigerator for up to 3 days. When ready to serve, return the tagine to the pan and add ⅓ cup water. Bring slowly to the boil, stirring occasionally, and let it bubble very gently for 2–3 minutes. Reduce the heat to a bare minimum and simmer the tagine, still stirring, for 15–20 minutes or until piping hot. Be prepared to add a little more water to thin it out as it reheats.

FREEZE AHEAD TIP:
Make the tagine as directed and freeze in an airtight container for up to 1 month. Thaw overnight in the refrigerator and reheat as above.

I admit, I often call a stew a tagine because it sounds more appealing, but this can more authentically claim rights to the title: it is, after all, Moroccan in substance and inspiration and I have indeed cooked it in the tagine – that Moroccan funnel-lidded pan – which gives the stew its name.

You don't need to have a tagine to cook it, so don't worry. What the traditionally shaped tagine – with its shallow base and conical lid – does is to allow a lot of steam to circulate so that a relatively small amount of liquid gives a lot of flavor and intensity to the dish. But, conversely, I find using a pan into which all the ingredients fit snugly, with a tight-fitting lid, does the trick just as well. As to size, what you need here is a tagine base, or wide, shallow, lidded pan or casserole, with a 3-quart capacity.

I have chosen goose fat as a cooking medium here only because I always have some in the house over Christmas, but do use regular olive (not extra virgin) oil if you prefer.

The dates make this tagine rich and sweet, which is just how it should be; the fragrant, almost-sourness of the pomegranate helps to punctuate this. The spices permeate the atmosphere with warmth and festive spirit. If you wish to, you could serve some plain couscous alongside – prepare 3 cups as for the Festive Couscous on p.97, but leave out the golden raisins and the post-soaking adornment.

❊ Warm the goose fat (or oil) in your cooking vessel of choice and scrape in the onions from the chopping board, letting them cook gently over a low heat for 10 minutes or until softened, stirring occasionally.

❊ Add the ground cinnamon, turmeric, ginger, cumin and allspice, and turn well in the onions.

❊ Turn up the heat and add the meat, turning it patiently in the pan so that it sears equally; this is why a wide, shallow pan is better than a narrow, deep one.

❊ Drop in the dates, pour in the pomegranate juice and water, then add the salt and bring to a bubble. Put the lid on, turn down the heat to an absolute minimum; it's important that this cooks ultra-gently for 2 hours. Or choose the oven option (see left) if appropriate.

❊ I prefer to cook this a day or two in advance and reheat; on serving, top with some of the Red Onion and Pomegranate Relish (see opposite), transferring the rest to a small bowl.

COME ON OVER...

RED ONION AND POMEGRANATE RELISH

I don't normally like raw onion much, but the pomegranate and lime juices take any acrid sting away. I could eat this by itself, frankly. It gives a fruity, sharp edge to the gratifying richness of the tagine – and is worth bearing in mind whenever you need to add glorious seasonal adornment to a meal fast; it is as delicious with some cold turkey as heaped onto a hot, fluffy-fleshed baked potato.

1 red onion
1/4 cup lime juice
juice and 1/4 cup seeds from 1 large pomegranate, or 1/4 cup pure pomegranate juice from a bottle and 1/4 cup pomegranate seeds from a container
2 tablespoons chopped fresh cilantro
salt to taste

❋ Peel and cut the onion in half, then slice into very thin half-moons.

❋ Put the onion slices into a bowl with the lime juice and pomegranate juice, and let them steep for half an hour.

❋ Drain the steeped onion into a little bowl, discarding the too-oniony juice, and add the pomegranate seeds.

❋ Toss with the chopped cilantro and season with a little salt.

❋ Strew a little relish on top of the tagine and put the rest in a small bowl for people to add to their own portions.

COME ON OVER... 73

GLEAMING MAPLE CHEESECAKE

FOR THE BASE:
1 1/3 cups graham cracker crumbs
3/4 cup pecan halves
3/4 stick (6 tablespoons) butter

FOR THE FILLING:
3 x 8 oz bars cream cheese, at room temperature
1/4 cup sugar
2 teaspoons cornstarch
1/2 cup maple syrup, plus more for drizzling
4 eggs
1/2 teaspoon cider vinegar or lemon juice

I've broached the sweetness issue earlier, but know that this dessert makes converts of even those who claim never to want something sweet: it's a cheesecake (baked in a bain-marie, which is the smartest route to the lightest, most delicate set) sitting on a base made of graham crackers, crushed pecans and a dash of maple syrup, the cheese layer itself smokily sweetened with the syrup. This cheesecake is best made well in advance, so you can sit back at dinner and enjoy the feast.

The one thing I need to be strict about is that the cream cheese be taken out of the refrigerator a good 2 hours before you start. I know you'll obey me when I tell you to bake the cheesecake in a pan of water (don't worry, it's perfectly straightforward) but I suspect that the stipulation for room-temperature cream cheese may not be as dutifully observed. But it must be: you will never get the requisite voluptuously smooth texture if the cream cheese starts off cold.

❋ Preheat the oven to 350°F.

❋ Put the cracker crumbs in a food processor, then add the pecan halves and blitz again to a crumb mixture. Add the butter and process everything together until it clumps up, and then press into the bottom of an 8-inch springform pan to make a smooth base. Sit the pan in the refrigerator to chill while you get on with the topping.

❋ Put the cream cheese into the cleaned processor bowl with the sugar, cornstarch and maple syrup.

❋ Turn the motor on and, with the processor running, break the eggs down the feed tube, processing until you have a smooth mixture. Add the vinegar or lemon juice, and pulse to mix.

❋ Take the springform pan out of the refrigerator, and line the outside with a layer of special ovenproof plastic wrap, bringing it up around the top outer edge of the pan; this is to make a waterproof layer for when the cheesecake is cooked in a water bath. Do the same again, cover the plastic wrap, with a double layer of aluminum foil, making sure that this, too, is brought right up to the top edge of the pan.

❋ Sit the foil-wrapped springform in a roasting pan, then pour in the smooth filling. Fill the roasting pan with freshly boiled water, to come about halfway up the wrapped springform.

If you can't get ovenproof plastic wrap, just use the double layer of aluminum foil.

COME ON OVER... **75**

❉ Bake the cheesecake in the oven for about 1¼ hours, though start checking it after an hour; it should be set on top but still have a hint of a wobble in the middle.

❉ Take the whole shebang-marie out of the oven and carefully lift the cheesecake out of its water bath. Peel away the foil layers and let it cool in its pan on a rack. Once cooled, refrigerate the cheesecake for at least 4 hours, or ideally overnight.

❉ The following day, or up to 2 days later, let it come to room temperature before springing it out of the pan.

❉ Sit it on a serving plate and pour some maple syrup over the top of the whole cake, drizzling a little more over each slice as you serve the cheesecake.

MAKE AHEAD TIP:
Make the cheesecake and leave to cool as directed. When cool, cover the pan with plastic wrap, making sure the wrap doesn't touch the top of the cheesecake, or pop a plate on top. Keep in the refrigerator for up to 2 days. Add maple syrup only on serving.

FREEZE AHEAD TIP:
Only cheesecakes made with full-fat, softened cream cheese will freeze. Leave the cheesecake in the pan to cool, cover with plastic wrap, as above, and freeze for up to 3 months. Thaw overnight in the refrigerator. Add maple syrup only on serving.

GROWN UP NURSERY SUPPER FOR 6

I have never much liked formal entertaining. I love coziness: I want people to feel welcomed, not impressed and I want to feel happily surrounded by my friends rather than wind myself up into a frenzy of hissing, self-loathing panic because I've got people coming for dinner.

And this time of year, above all, should be about relaxed expansiveness, about succor as well as celebration. This menu says it all: the supper you want to eat to make you feel that all will be well.

The fish gratin is the lazy person's answer to a fish pie. I *love* fish pie, but mashing a sinkful of potatoes is no one's idea of a low-effort enterprise; of course, it's not hard, but it takes time when time itself is at a premium. Topping the fish with finely sliced, unpeeled baking potatoes is the easy answer. And as for the fish itself, rather than cook and flake it and then make a sauce, I simply make an extra-thick white sauce (my version is too basic, really, to be called a béchamel), turn it green with a garden of freshly chopped parsley and leave it for up to 3 days before snipping in some smoked and unsmoked fish, giving it a stir-up, topping with the sliced potatoes and whacking it in the oven. You don't have to make the sauce in advance, but I find it makes my life easier. If you're not making it in advance, slice the potatoes before you put the fish into the warm sauce so that the minute the raw fish is in the sauce you can top with the potatoes and put the gratin straight in the oven.

This is best eaten with a big bowl of buttery peas, fresh from the freezer. I love to add a few handfuls of snow peas to the pea-cooking water for the last minute of cooking time, before draining and dousing them in butter and a fresh grinding of white pepper.

The dessert must be made up in advance; though, again, this is a boon not a burden for me.

PARSLEYED FISH GRATIN

PROSECCO AND POMEGRANATE GELATIN

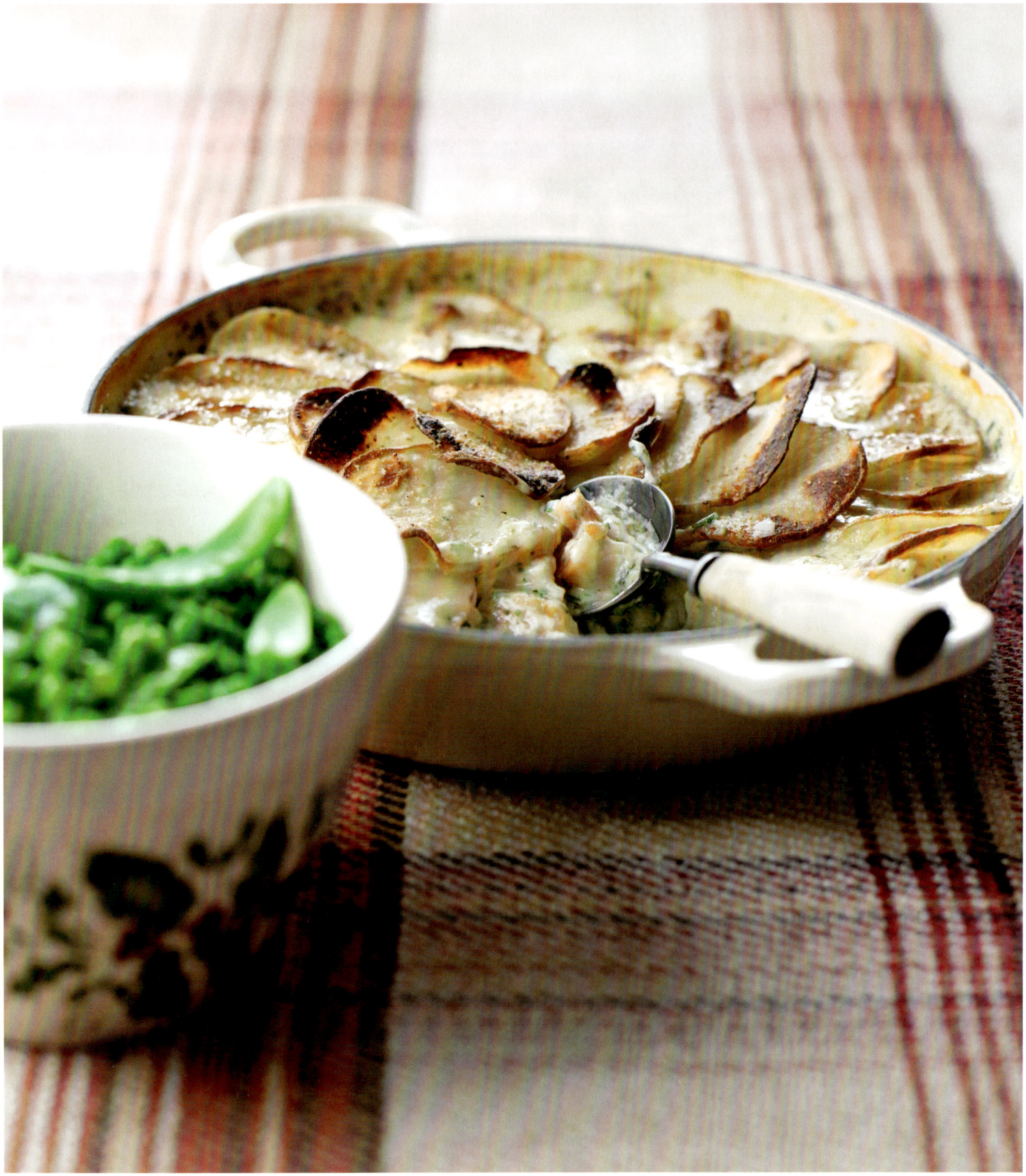

PARSLEYED FISH GRATIN

❋ Make a white sauce by first melting the butter in a large saucepan and then adding the flour, stirring together for a minute or so. Then, off the heat, whisk in the vermouth (or wine), mace (or nutmeg), salt and mustard.

❋ Next, whisk in the milk, and put the pan back on the heat, continuing to whisk the sauce as it thickens. Once the sauce appears to be getting thicker, which will be a matter of 3 or so minutes, keep cooking it for a further 3 minutes until very thick.

❋ Take it off the heat and stir in the chives and parsley. Then decant into your gratin-type dish (mine is a round shallow braiser about 5-quart capacity).

❋ Once cool, you can leave this dish covered, in the refrigerator overnight or for up to 3 days.

❋ When ready to cook, preheat your oven to 400°F and slide a cookie sheet in as you do so. Take your gratin dish out of the refrigerator and uncover it.

❋ Slice the unpeeled potatoes as thinly as you possibly can.

❋ Scissor or cut both types of fish into large bite-sized pieces (approx. 2 inches x 1 1/2 inches), and mix into the parsley sauce, along with the shrimp.

❋ Layer the potatoes in concentric circles over the fish in parsley sauce, overlapping halfway across each potato slice as you go around the dish.

❋ Melt the garlic oil and butter in a small pan, then paint the circles of potato with this mixture, using a silicone pastry brush (or just dribble it over), to slick the top of the gratin.

❋ Grind some fresh white pepper over the top and place in the oven to cook for 50–60 minutes; the top should be golden and the underneath of the gratin bubbling.

FOR THE SAUCE:
3 tablespoons butter
1/3 cup all-purpose flour
1 tablespoon dry white vermouth or dry white wine
1/4 teaspoon ground mace or nutmeg
1/2 teaspoon kosher salt or 1/4 teaspoon table salt
1/4 teaspoon Dijon mustard
1 1/2 cups whole milk
1 1/2 tablespoons finely chopped chives (or 1 scallion, finely chopped)
1 cup finely chopped parsley

FOR THE FISH MIX AND POTATO TOPPING:
2 medium-sized (14 oz total) white potatoes (such as Yukon Gold), unpeeled
3/4 lb skinless salmon
3/4 lb skinless cod, or similar white fish
3/4 lb shelled large raw shrimp (31-40 count), defrosted if frozen

FOR THE GLAZE:
1 teaspoon garlic oil
2 tablespoons butter
good grinding of white pepper

MAKE AHEAD TIP:
Make the parsley sauce up to 3 days ahead. Decant into gratin dish and cover directly with plastic wrap or the lid to prevent a skin forming. Cool and keep in the refrigerator.

FREEZE AHEAD TIP:
For fresh, not previously frozen fish and shrimp, make the parsley sauce, and leave to cool in its dish. When cool, stir in the fish, then cover and freeze for up to 1 month. Thaw overnight in the refrigerator, then, when ready to cook, finish with the potatoes and cook as directed.

PROSECCO AND POMEGRANATE GELATIN

1 x 750ml bottle Prosecco or other white wine
1 cup water
1 1/2 cups superfine sugar
1 cup water
4 teaspoons unflavored powdered gelatin
1/2 teaspoon vanilla extract
1 tablespoon Cointreau, Grand Marnier or Triple sec, plus more to serve
seeds from 1 pomegranate, or 1/2 cup pomegranate seeds from a container
flavorless oil for greasing
heavy cream to serve (optional)

I love wine and liqueur gelatins, and I think I've had a version – sauternes and lemon balm, gin and tonic, slut red raspberries in chardonnay gelatin, blackberries and Muscat – in pretty well all of my books. They are delicate, luscious and incredibly easy to make.

There's no absolute need to use Prosecco: any good white wine would do. What's important is simply to make this: the pale glint of the jelly against the red jewels of pomegranate makes it as beautiful to look at as to eat.

❋ Lightly grease a 1-quart gelatin mold with flavorless oil and sit it on a small tray so it's easy to convey it to the refrigerator later.

❋ Pour the Prosecco into a saucepan, add the sugar and stir to help it dissolve (but do not stir once the pan is on the heat). At the same time, put the water into a large jug or bowl and sprinkle over the gelatin, letting it soak for 5 minutes.

❋ Put the pan on the heat, bring to the boil and let it boil for a minute.

❋ Add the vanilla and keep the pan bubbling gently for another minute, before taking it off the heat.

❋ Carefully ladle about 1 cup of the wine–sugar mixture into the jug and stir well until the gelatin has dissolved completely.

❋ Pour the jugful of liquid back into the pan (which must be still off the heat), whisk again, and tip it all back into the jug, before pouring it into the prepared gelatin mold. (This may sound a kerfuffle, but it ensures the gelatin is thoroughly dispersed.)

❋ Put the filled-to-the-brim mold, still on its tray, into the refrigerator and leave to set overnight. It has a gentle set, which is what makes it so delectable.

❋ Just before you are ready to serve, fill a sink or plastic washing-up bowl with warm water to come about halfway up the mold, and sit the as-yet-unturned mold in the warm water for half a minute.

❋ Take the mold out of the sink, wipe the water off the outside and place your serving plate on top. Then, with one hand on the plate and the other on the mold, tip them both over and lift off the mold to reveal the gelatin. It will look smaller than it did in the mold; that's expected.

The amount of gelatin powder is deliberately low; packets will instruct you to use more, but a voluptuously soft set is desirable. This does mean, however, that the gelatin needs an overnight set in the refrigerator and cannot be unmolded in advance.

MAKE AHEAD TIP:
Make the gelatin up to 3 days ahead. If it's possible to cover the mold with a tight seal of plastic wrap without it touching the gelatin, then do so. Otherwise, leave uncovered and put in the refrigerator, but make sure you have nothing heavily flavored with garlic in the refrigerator at the same time!

❉ Dribble the Cointreau (or your choice of alcohol) over the gelatin (putting the bottle on the table so people can anoint with more as they eat) and scatter with pomegranate seeds, a few on top, but most around the side. It spoils the jewel-like clarity of the gelatin, but this is out of this world with a little heavy cream poured over each portion. Put a small jugful on the table as encouragement.

If you want to dispense with the worry of unmolding, simply divide the warm gelatin mixture between six stemmed glasses of under 1-cup capacity each and set in the refrigerator.

MEANWHILE, BACK AT THE RANCH...

BOURBON-GLAZED RIBS
SPOON BREAD
SPINACH AND BACON SALAD
GIRDLEBUSTER PIE

...A FINGER-LICKIN' SUPPER FOR 8–10

This is the perfect relaxed holiday supper, though there's no reason it couldn't be a button-bursting lunch when you're not at work, either. It's big and friendly and gives an atmosphere of homestead warmth. You may feel mightily full when you get up from the table, but you will feel happy.

BOURBON-GLAZED RIBS

24 St. Louis–style pork spareribs
1/2 cup packed dark brown sugar
3/4 cup bourbon
2 tablespoons soy sauce
2 tablespoons prepared yellow mustard
2 tablespoons tomato ketchup

I can't think of any way of cooking ribs I dislike, but this bourbon and brown sugar marinade-cum-glaze does double-duty, tenderizing the meat before it cooks and slicking it with a chestnut-shiny, delicious-beyond-words glaze after, and is frankly more inviting – the rich scent in the air as it cooks, the sweet stickiness as you eat – than is decent. I salivate both in memory and in hope.

❋ Put the ribs into a resealable plastic bag and add the other ingredients to form a marinade. Place in the refrigerator, putting the bag into a bowl to avoid drips or spillages, and leave overnight.

❋ The next day, remove the ribs from the refrigerator, and preheat the oven to 425°F.

❋ Pick the ribs out of the marinade and put them into a shallow roasting pan (lined with aluminum foil for easier cleanup), then pour the marinade into a saucepan.

❋ Cook the ribs for 1 hour, turning them over halfway through cooking.

❋ When the ribs are cooked, bring the marinade to a boil and cook for about 7 minutes, or until it is thick and glossy. Plate up the ribs, then pour the bourbon sauce over them.

MAKE AHEAD TIP:
Chill the ribs in the marinade for up to 3 days.

FREEZE AHEAD TIP:
Freeze the ribs in the marinade for up to 1 month. Thaw overnight in the refrigerator, and cook as directed.

COME ON OVER... **83**

SPOON BREAD

3/4 stick (6 tablespoons) soft butter, plus more for greasing
3 cups drained canned corn
4 scallions, roughly chopped
1 1/4 cups grated sharp cheddar cheese
4 eggs
2 cups yellow cornmeal
2 teaspoons baking powder
4 cups whole milk

This is something of a cross between cornbread and creamed sweet corn – a kind of Southwestern polenta. It is perfect with ribs as here, but I love it, too, with some sizzled bacon (in which case no need to add bacon to the salad) or to jazz up a refrigeratorful of cold cuts.

I mostly use the kernels drained from their cans, but do use frozen corn if you prefer; if you haven't got time to let it thaw, put it in a sieve and pour boiling water over it for a quick defrost.

I like to bake this in a round, shallowish copper roasting pan (11 x 2 inches deep with a capacity of 2 1/4 quarts), or an 11-inch cast-iron skillet, so be prepared to adjust cooking times if your ovenproof pan has different dimensions.

❋ Preheat the oven to 425°F. Grease your ovenproof pan or skillet, melt the 3/4 stick butter in a saucepan over a low heat and leave to cool.

❋ Put the corn, scallions and cheddar into a food processor with the eggs.

❋ Process to chop the vegetables and cheese, then add the cornmeal and baking powder.

❋ Process again until the mixture becomes paste-like, then, with the motor running, add the milk and melted butter.

❋ Pour into the greased pan or skillet and bake for 1 hour until just set.

❋ Remove the spoon bread from the oven and let it stand for 10 minutes – it will continue cooking as it stands – before taking to the table.

SPINACH AND BACON SALAD

I love those Eighties salads, tossed with bacon-cubes and a warm dressing that makes the leaves begin to wilt. "Begin" is the operative word: though spinach, even young, relatively tender-leaved spinach, stands up to the warm drizzle well, as does the endive. I like to go for the rusty-red blades, but if all you can find is the regular pale jade endive, it won't make any difference: they taste the same; my preference, here, is aesthetic.

And even though this is a spinach salad, some other bag (or two) of salad leaves would do just as well. Similarly, if you haven't got any pancetta, just snip up some slices of bacon.

8-10 cups (8 oz) baby spinach, or similar salad
4 small heads red endive or treviso
1 teaspoon garlic oil
1/2 cup (3 oz) cubed pancetta
3/4 cup pecan pieces
2 1/2 tablespoons cider vinegar or white wine vinegar
2 tablespoons maple syrup

❋ Arrange the spinach in a large salad bowl. Add the endive, separated into leaves and then torn into bite-sized pieces, and toss together.

❋ Warm the garlic oil in a frying pan over a medium heat, and drop in the pancetta cubes, cooking until they are crisp and bronzed.

❋ Add the pecans, and mix well with the pancetta in the fatty pan.

❋ Take off the heat, and stir in the vinegar – be prepared for a lot of sizzle.

❋ Now stir in the maple syrup, quickly pour over the salad and toss swiftly, serving immediately.

86 COME ON OVER...

GIRDLEBUSTER PIE

I confess: it was the title that lured me. Tell me you don't feel the same. I came across this in a recipe by Elinor Klivans, whom I often turn to for chocolatey solace, in her *The Essential Chocolate Chip Cookbook*, which includes the wonderful phrase "let the chocolate chips fall where they will."

Although her recipes always work to the letter, my recipe is not hers. I am inspired by the graham cracker and chocolate base and coffee ice cream filling (though if you're feeding children, I'd suggest vanilla) but I like a butterscotchy topping, which sets the minute it hits the ice cream. Sometimes bits of ice cream bubble up to the surface, making the top gloriously Florentined.

And the joy of the girdlebuster (as it is known for short at home) is that, should there be any left, you can put it back into its dish and just stash in the freezer again for midnight feasts. Admittedly, this is not huge, but a small slice is all that's needed. Do not let it "ripen" out of the freezer before slicing because it all gets too sticky and drippy and messy.

❊ Process the graham crackers with the butter and chocolate pieces or chips until it forms a damp but still crumb-like clump.

❊ Press into a 9-inch pie plate or flan dish. Form a lip of cracker crumbs a little higher than the plate or dish if you can. This process takes patience as you need ideally to form a smooth even layer. Sorry.

❊ Freeze this crumb-lined layer for about an hour so it gets really hard. In the meantime, let your ice cream soften, just enough to be scooped, in the refrigerator.

❊ Spread the ice cream into the hard-crumb-lined dish to form a layer. Then cover in plastic wrap and replace in the freezer.

❊ Put the syrup, sugar, salt (if using) and butter into a saucepan and let it melt over a low to medium heat, before turning it up and boiling for 5 minutes, then turn off the heat and add the bourbon, letting it hiss in the pan.

❊ Add the cream and stir to mix into a sauce, then leave to cool. And once the sauce is cool, but not set cold, pour it over the pie to cover the ice cream layer and then put it back in the freezer. Once frozen, cover with plastic wrap again.

❊ When ready to serve, remove from the freezer, take the whole pie out of its dish and cut into slices. Should you have any pie left over, slip it quickly back into the dish and return, covered with plastic wrap, to the freezer.

FOR THE BASE:
1 x 14 oz box graham crackers
3/4 stick (6 tablespoons) soft butter
1/4 cup bittersweet chocolate, chopped or chips
1/4 cup milk chocolate, chopped or chips

FOR THE ICE CREAM FILLING:
1 quart coffee ice cream

FOR THE TOPPING:
1 cup golden syrup, such as Lyle's
1/2 cup packed soft light brown sugar
3/4 stick (6 tablespoons) butter
pinch of table salt (optional)
2 tablespoons bourbon
1/2 cup heavy cream

FREEZE AHEAD TIP:
Make and freeze the pie in its dish, as directed, but cover with plastic wrap *and* a double layer of foil. Freeze for up to 6 months.

EASY ELEGANT DINNER FOR 8

EFFORTLESS HOME-CURED PORK
APPLE AND ONION GRAVY
TIRAMISU LAYER CAKE

I actually did this dinner for my brother Dominic's birthday last year, but I think of it as a Christmastime menu simply because his birthday is 17th December and so he helps usher in the family festivities. My seasonal celebrations, anyway, are regulated by the family diary: my daughter's birthday is the 15th and so no tree, no mention of Christmas, no festive distractions of any kind are allowed to intrude until after that date. To tell the truth, it is a very convenient curtailment.

When I say that the curing of the pork is effortless, I am not making any false promises. I suppose it is not quite accurate to call it "curing," since that implies preserving: what I am really doing is "brining" (as with my Spiced and Superjuicy Turkey on p.115). But I avoid that word because it hardly tempts, whereas the effect it produces, which is rather to tenderize and imbue with flavor, is more of an obvious inducement. All it involves is putting the pork in a pan or bowl, covering it with water, apple juice, spices and a few other bits and pieces and your work is done, save for bunging it in the oven later.

With this, I make an apple and onion gravy, which is really halfway between a gravy and a sauce; it's thick but just pourable. All this, the light-toned pork and the equally pale apply, oniony gravy that anoints it, is not supercharged aesthetically and I would go for a vegetable to add depth of color as well as taste. My choice is the Red Cabbage on p.60, though I love it with the bacony, creamy peas (*Piselli con Panna e Pancetta*) on p.63 as well. But it's an either or; don't do both. And you can either bake fluffy potatoes in their jackets alongside, and put some chive-flecked sour cream on the table to dollop in them, or steam some small, sweet and tight-fleshed baby potatoes.

I created the Tiramisu Layer Cake especially for my brother, since there is nothing he likes more than coffee, chocolate and creaminess all in one over-indulgent package, but I also recommend here the Christmas-Spiced Chocolate Cake on p.183, a seasonal favorite I came up with to celebrate another seasonal birthday – on the 21st December – for the voice coach and pocket venus, Joan Washington.

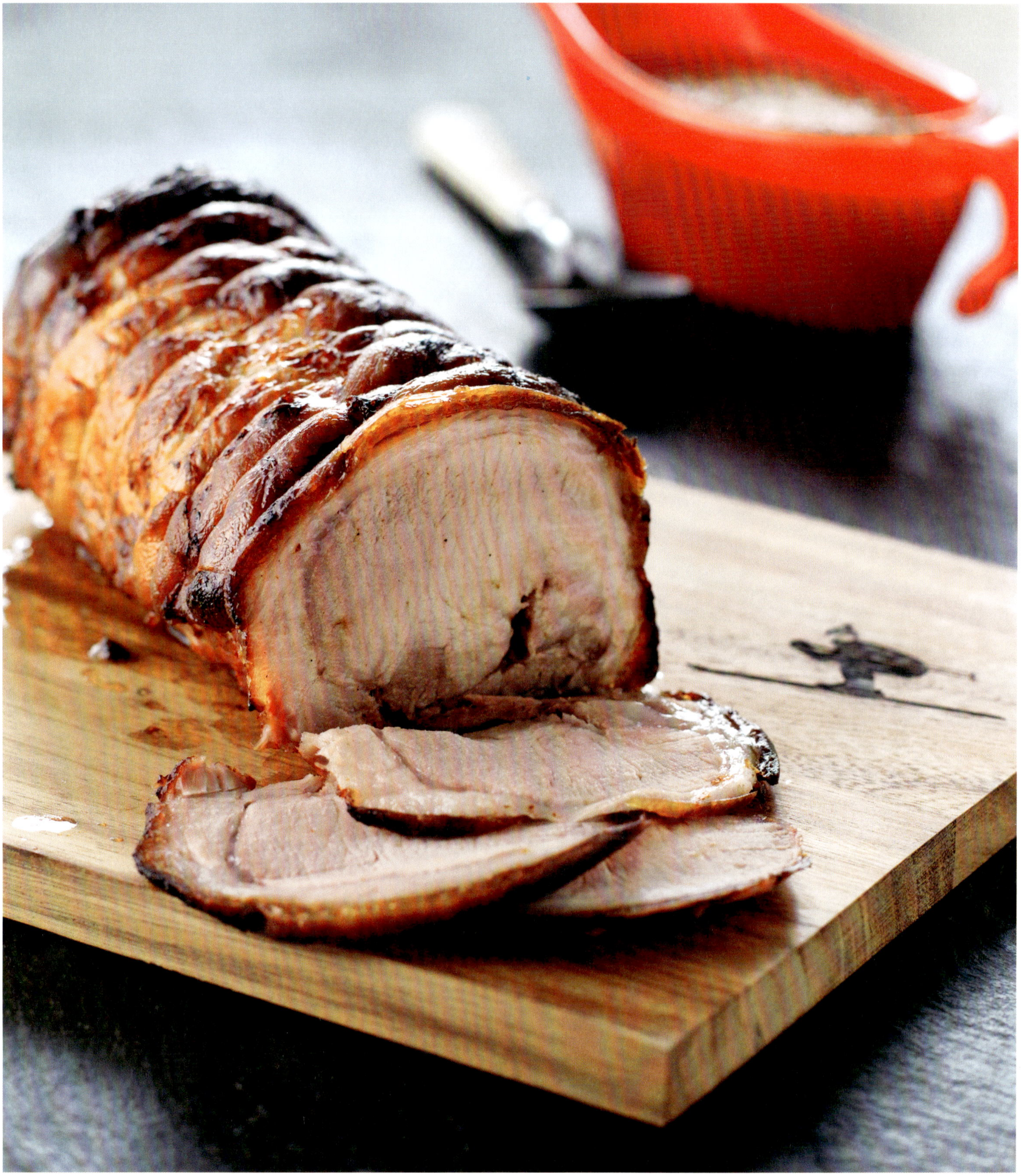

EFFORTLESS HOME-CURED PORK

3 1/2 lbs boneless center cut pork loin
4 cups apple juice, preferably pressed
4 cups water
1/2 cup kosher salt or 1/4 cup table salt
1 cup cider vinegar
4 small onions, peeled and quartered (or 2 large onions, cut into eighths)
stalks from large bunch of parsley (optional)
cloves from 1 head garlic, bruised but not peeled
1/3 cup maple syrup
1 teaspoon cardamom seeds
1 teaspoon caraway seeds
4 teaspoons garlic oil

These days pork is reared to be so lean that it is barely digestible when you just plain roast it. Of course, you can stuff and roll it, as I do when going all-out in my Rolled Stuffed Loin of Pork on p.158, but that is work – work that rewards, but work just the same. This is altogether easier. Indeed, it is impossible to think of any kind of preparation that would involve less effort; not only does it make the pork juicily delicious, but it also makes it easier to carve thinly, which means it goes a lot further, too.

Because of the magic-soaking treatment, a supermarket pork loin is just fine, though go for organic or proper farm-sourced for choice. And it comes all ready for you – fat removed, boned, rolled and tied. This size loin certainly looks small, but once carved ultra-thinly – as the cure helps you do – there's plenty to go round.

❋ Put the skinned, boned and rolled pork loin in a pan or stockpot with a lid.

❋ Add the remaining ingredients except the garlic oil, put the lid on the pan or stockpot and place in the refrigerator or in a cold place for at least a night and a day and up to 2 days.

❋ Half an hour before the pork needs to go into the oven, preheat the oven to 400°F, then take the pork out of its brine and sit it on a rack in the sink to let the liquid drain off and the meat get less cold.

❋ Transfer the pork to a roasting pan, pour the garlic oil over it and roast for 1 1/2 hours, before removing to a carving dish. An instant-read thermometer, inserted, should read 160°F when the pork is cooked through.

❋ Carve the pork thinly – the joy of the quasi-cure is that it makes it easy even for a bad carver like me to do this, and you can be sure of feeding 8 people. Serve with the apple and onion gravy, opposite.

MAKE AHEAD TIP:
Keep the pork in its "curing" mixture for up to 2 days. Leave it in a cold place or in the refrigerator if you have room.

APPLE AND ONION GRAVY

Although I'd pretty well go along with the Wildean aphorism that one should try anything once except incest and morris dancing, I am in certain matters, most of them culinary, rather a novelty-eschewing traditionalist. If I'm having pork, I want to have applesauce with it. My grandmother always mixed her applesauce with horseradish, a radical departure I, too, am happy to make. I can also accommodate the corresponding tart fruitiness of cranberry sauce, but not with this apple-brined pork roast; it wouldn't be right.

And while I wouldn't want to upset anyone who just wants plain old regular applesauce alongside, I happen to feel better myself when I make this apple and onion gravy. Not that it's quite a gravy in the traditional sense, but it's runnier than the customary sauce: you pour it from a jug, maybe with a little cutlery-coaxing; it's a grauce.

Somewhat untraditionally, I use eating apples here: Gala would be my first choice, although Braeburn or Granny Smith should be fine, too. And because I think bacon fat is such a wonderful cooking medium, I always pour off the fat from the pan when I've been cooking bacon, to keep in a little cup in the refrigerator for exactly these occasions, and advise you to do likewise (fish fried in bacon fat is fantastic), but otherwise use butter. The onions, which are mushed up with the apples then fried, give depth and savoriness, and the maple syrup – yes, maple syrup again, and I don't have shares in any Vermont orchard I promise – brings its resiny sweetness to play along with the peppy heat, just a hint though, of the ginger.

2 onions, peeled and quartered
2 apples, peeled, cored and quartered
2 tablespoons bacon fat (or butter)
1 teaspoon garlic oil
1 tablespoon maple syrup
2 teaspoons cornstarch
1/4 teaspoon ground ginger
2 cups chicken broth
4 teaspoons soy sauce

❄ Put the onions and apples into a food processor and process to mush.

❄ Put the bacon fat (or butter) and the garlic oil into a pan and cook the processed onions and apples over a very gentle heat for about 30 minutes, stirring every now and again.

❄ Add the maple syrup and cook for another 15 minutes.

❄ Stir in the cornstarch and ground ginger, then turn up the heat as you, still stirring, pour in the broth.

❄ Continue stirring as you bring the gravy to a boil and season with the soy sauce. Cook until the gravy has thickened slightly, almost into a sauce, and there is no floury taste; this is probably no longer than 3 minutes.

MAKE AHEAD TIP:
Make the gravy, then transfer to a non-metallic bowl, cover with plastic wrap and keep in the refrigerator for up to 2 days. You may need to add some more broth or water on reheating.

FREEZE AHEAD TIP:
Make the gravy, pour into an airtight container and freeze for up to 1 week. Thaw overnight in the refrigerator, then pour into a pan and gently reheat, with a little extra liquid if needed, until piping hot.

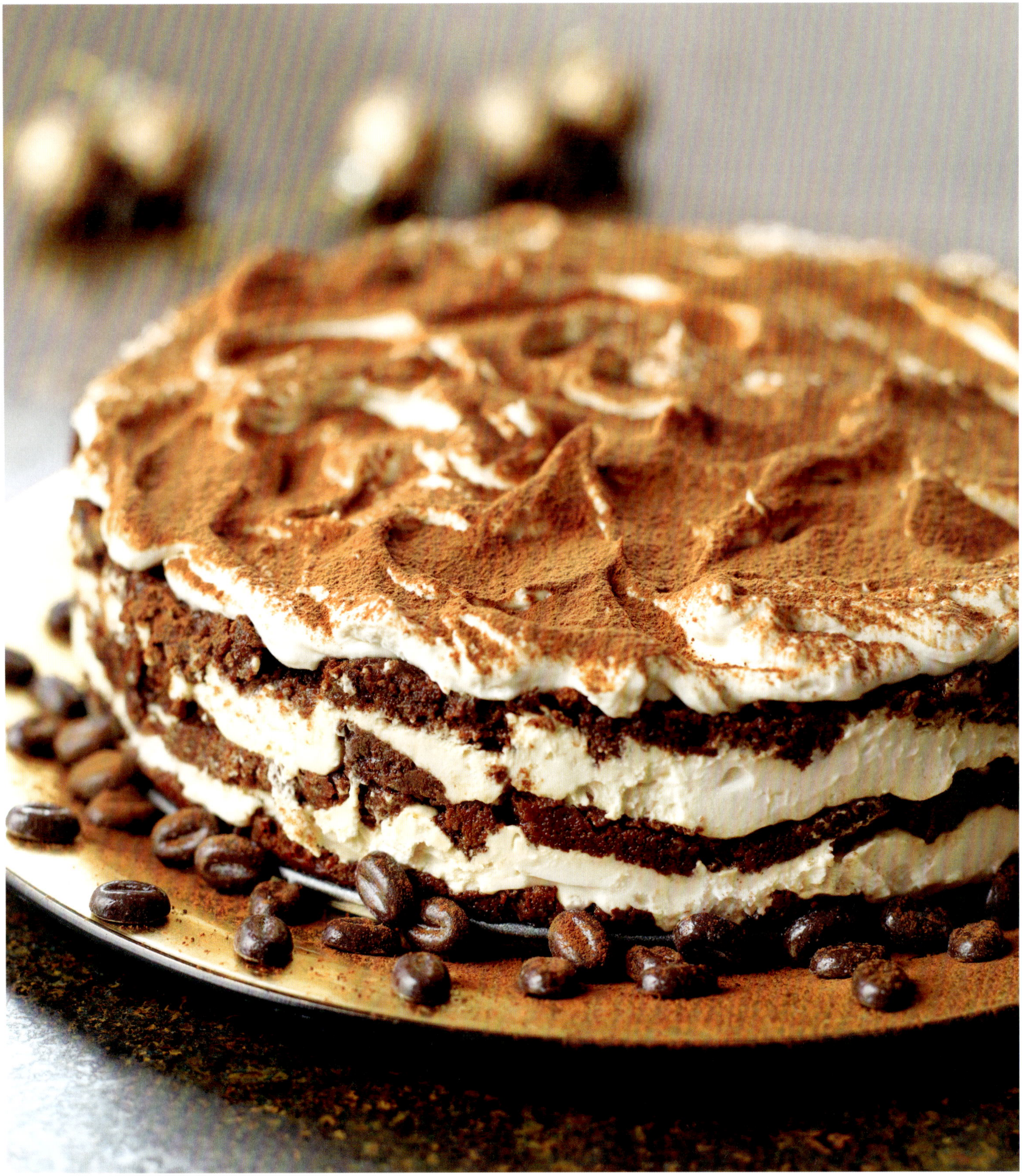

TIRAMISU LAYER CAKE

There is no shortage of tiramisu recipes in the world, many of them emanating from me. I started off with a certain hauteur, stemming from the certainty that tiramisu was the Black Forest gâteau of the Nineties; you can see how long ago the prejudice and the countering compulsion started. But now I know that when things work, they work, and that I'm happier adding to, rather than chipping away at, the canon.

This recipe reads harder than it cooks. Or rather, doesn't cook. It's an assembly job more than anything, and it doesn't take very long or require much in the way of skill or patience: it's just that the number of layers make the recipe on the page seem more complicated than it is.

I don't deny its vulgarity: the original, hardly the apotheosis of chic, relies on *savoiardi* (ladyfingers), dunked in coffee and liqueur, before being built up with eggy, marsala-laced mascarpone and topped with a dusting of cocoa; I cut to the chase, by using chocolate muffins and dousing it only in coffee liqueur, before layering up into a big fat cake which cuts easily into greedy wedges.

I wish I were the sort of person who could make enough but no more, but that's never going to be the case: when I made this for my brother's birthday, he came back round for a couple of slices the next day. And that's the way I like it.

❋ Wrap the outside of a 9-inch springform pan with some plastic wrap or aluminum foil to avoid leaks from the base.

❋ Slice the chocolate muffins thinly with a serrated knife, and pour the 1¼ cups (or more if needed) of Tia Maria into a shallow dish, ready for soaking the muffin slices as you need them.

❋ Before you start to layer the cake, whisk the eggs and sugar, and then beat in the mascarpone and heavy cream; I use an electric whisk for this, but there is no need to if you're feeling muscley. Then add, gradually, the ½ cup Tia Maria to make a creamy spreadable layer for the cake.

❋ Using approx. 2 muffins per layer, dunk the slices in Tia Maria before lining the pan with them. Squidge them down, pressing confidently as you go; each layer should not be too thick, but juicily compact and solid. If the muffin slices are tricky to dunk then press them into the pan and spoon over ½ cup Tia Maria.

❋ Spread a third of the cream mixture over the soaked muffin slices.

❋ Repeat with another layer of soaked chocolate muffin slices, and then cream again.

---

6 jumbo-size chocolate muffins (3 lbs total weight)
1¼ cups Tia Maria
1–2 teaspoons unsweetened cocoa powder for dusting
chocolate-covered coffee beans (optional)

FOR THE FILLING:
2 eggs
⅓ cup superfine sugar
2 cups (1 lb) mascarpone cheese
1 cup heavy cream
½ cup Tia Maria

MAKE AHEAD TIP:
Make the tiramisu, cover with plastic wrap, and store in the refrigerator for up to 4 days. Unmold and finish as directed.

FREEZE AHEAD TIP:
Unmold the tiramisu, finish with the remaining cream then open freeze. When solid, cover securely with a double layer of plastic wrap and return to the freezer for up to 3 months. To use, unwrap the tiramisu, place on a serving dish and thaw overnight in the refrigerator. Dust with cocoa and serve.

❋ Finish with a layer of chocolate muffin slices – not as soaked as the first 2 layers – reserving the last third of the cream mixture for later in a covered bowl.

❋ Press the layer down to make it as smooth as possible, then cover it with plastic wrap and put the cake in the refrigerator overnight, or for up to 4 days.

❋ When you are ready to serve, take the cake out of the refrigerator, unmold, sit it on a plate or cake stand, then spread with the final third of cream mixture, before dusting with cocoa and serving. The cake is too deliciously damp to lift it off the pan's base, but I shouldn't let that worry you; if you want, though, you can scatter some chocolate-covered coffee beans around the cake, once it's sitting on its serving plate, to deflect critical gaze away from the visible edge of metal.

SEDUCTIVELY SIMPLE SUPPER FOR 6

PARTY CORNISH HENS
SPICED ROAST SQUASH
FESTIVE COUSCOUS
CHESTNUT CHOCOLATE POTS

The French call Cornish hens *poussins*, so the shorthand for this, chez moi, is pouss-pouss with couscous, and there is a reason for that: this is one of the most reliable fallback suppers that can be stuck in the oven and left to cook itself, with only a bit of stoveside fiddling, in order to provide a party-mood, feel-good festive supper even when you're chock-a-block with after-school activities, office parties, or sackfuls of wrapping; this is my seasonal get-together without tears.

I love the silky richness of the Chestnut Chocolate Pots afterwards, but if you don't have the sort of timetable that accommodates advance preparation, simply pile up some Quickly Scaled Mont Blancs in glasses at the last minute. These were my mother's seasonal specialty, and need no further full-on explanation from me, since I have banged on about them before (in *Nigella Express*, for instance) but, just in case, here's what you need to do: get out 6 smallish glasses, with a capacity of about $1/2$ cup each, and in them drop a layer of chopped bittersweet chocolate (you'll need a 4-ounce bar or $1/2$ cup chips altogether); on top of the rubbly shards of chocolate, dollop some sweetened chestnut cream from a can or jar (a 1-pound can is more than generous); then whip 2 cups heavy cream until thick but still soft, fold in 2 meringue cookies from a box and spoon this on top of the chocolate and chestnut layers; then crumble another 2 meringue cookies in a snowy layer on top. Couldn't be easier – but then nor could the silky Chestnut Chocolate Pots on p.98. The choice is undemandingly yours.

PARTY CORNISH HENS

6 Cornish hens
1/4 cup chile oil or olive oil
1 tablespoon kosher salt or
   1 1/2 teaspoons table salt
pinch of sugar
1/4 teaspoon ground cinnamon
1/2 teaspoon paprika
1 lemon, preferably unwaxed
1 head garlic

These small birds make a big feast, and with ease. For me, one reason why this produces such a relaxing supper is that there's no work once you're at the table, either. It's not only that I am a bad carver (though I am), but elaborate serving-up makes me feel flustered. This must obviously be avoided – but without sacrificing the sense of occasion.

The Cornish hens need no more than the couscous to eat alongside, but I often like to make (since I have room in the oven and the flavors are so right) a tray of Spiced Roast Squash at the same time. In fact, this is a regular festive fallback of mine, as it provides a luscious accompaniment, without much work. You need a whole butternut squash – about $2^{1}/4$ pounds in weight – and don't bother to peel but seed it and cut into, roughly, $1^{1}/2$-inch cubes. Arrange these on a low-lipped sheet pan (I use a jelly roll pan) and pour a couple of tablespoons of regular olive oil over, sprinkle with 1 teaspoon each of ground mace and paprika and smoosh everything around to mix, before baking on the rack below the Cornish hens for about the same amount of time. If you're cooking the squash on its own, you may find 50 minutes at 450°F is enough. Either way, I love the squash served with a generous sprinkling of kosher salt and a judicious spritz of lime juice; both bring out the earthy sweetness of the squash.

And incidentally, if you have any butternut or couscous left over, add the one to the other to make a very more-ish salad. A final note: the Cornish hen carcasses, after, make a great stock or soup.

❋ Preheat the oven to 425°F. Sit the Cornish hens snugly in a roasting pan, and pour the oil slowly over, making sure you get good, equal coverage.

❋ Mix together the salt, sugar, cinnamon and paprika in a small bowl, and sprinkle this spice mixture over the Cornish hens.

❋ Cut the lemon into quarters, then cut each quarter into 4 so you have 16 small pieces, and tuck these pieces along with the garlic separated into cloves, but unpeeled, around and in between the baby birds.

❋ Cook the Cornish hens for $1–1^{1}/4$ hours, until the juices from the thickest part of the leg run clear, then let them rest for about 10 minutes in their pan out of the oven before serving.

MAKE AHEAD TIP:
Put the Cornish hens in the roasting pan with the oil, salt, sugar and spices. Cover with a roof of plastic wrap and leave in the refrigerator overnight. The next day, add the lemons and roast as directed.

96 COME ON OVER...

FESTIVE COUSCOUS

The correct way of cooking couscous is to cover it with cold water for about 20 minutes, and then place the dampened couscous in the top part of a couscoussier or a steamer to steam it. The best way to tell when it's ready is to put a thin slab of butter on top: when the butter starts melting, the couscous is done.

However, even though the following method is, strictly speaking, incorrect, it is the way I most often do it, and feel it is only fair to encourage you down this shameful, lazy path, too. If you want, do replace the golden raisins with dried cherries or dried cranberries or even, should you live near a Middle-Eastern store, some dried barberries.

3 cups quick-cook couscous
1/2 cup golden raisins
1/4 teaspoon ground cinnamon
1/2 teaspoon paprika
1/2 teaspoon ground cumin
1/2 teaspoon ground coriander
2 teaspoons kosher salt or 1 teaspoon table salt
3 1/3 cups freshly boiled water, from a kettle
seeds from 1 pomegranate, or 1/2 cup seeds from a container
handful fresh cilantro leaves, chopped

❊ Just before the Cornish hens come out of the oven, put the couscous into a heat-proof bowl or a pan with a tight-fitting lid, add the golden raisins, spices and salt, and give everything a stir.

❊ Pour the freshly boiled water over and cover with plastic wrap or the lid; let it sit for 10–15 minutes, by which time it should have absorbed the water.

❊ Fluff the couscous through with a fork to separate the grains, then carefully pour in some of the juices that have collected in the roasting pan of Cornish hens.

❊ Fork through again and check the seasoning before transferring to a serving dish.

❊ Drop half the pomegranate seeds over the mounded couscous, mixing them in gently with a fork.

❊ Scatter the remaining pomegranate seeds over, sprinkle with some chopped cilantro and serve.

❊ Serve each person not only a Cornish hen and some couscous but some oven-charred lemon pieces and garlic cloves as well – and some Spiced Squash if you've chosen to add it (see opposite).

CHESTNUT CHOCOLATE POTS

heaping 3/4 cup best-quality bittersweet chocolate, chopped or chips

1/2 cup heavy cream, plus more to serve if wished

1/2 cup whole milk

1 egg

3/4 cup (9 oz can) sweetened Chestnut cream (see Suppliers p.267)

2 tablespoons dark rum

I'm almost embarrassed by how easy these are. It's true that you do need a food processor, though you could just chop well and whisk using a lot of elbow grease. Or you could make the machinery-eschewing Quickly Scaled Mont Blancs (see p.94) if that suits better.

As an experiment, I also tried the chestnut chocolate pots as chestnut chocolate mousses: the mousses were more work and not as good; this – lazy – way provides a much more meltingly luscious texture. Good to know . . .

Any remaining of the chestnut cream can either be brought out to make these for another day, or can be profitably put to use to make the Hot Chocolate-Chestnut Sauce, unspeakably good swathed over ice cream, and see p.169.

❋ Crush the chocolate to smithereens in the food processor.

❋ In a saucepan, heat the cream and milk until just about boiling and, with the motor off, pour into the processor through the funnel over the chocolate.

❋ Let it stand for 30 seconds. Process for 30 seconds, then crack the egg down the funnel and process for 45 seconds more.

❋ Add the chestnut cream and rum through the funnel, and process until everything is incorporated.

❋ Remove the blade and, using a rubber spatula and a spoon, fill 6 x 4-ounce (1/2 cup) glasses or pots.

❋ If wished, put a jug of unwhipped heavy cream on the table and let people pour it over their pots as they eat.

MAKE AHEAD TIP:
Make the pots up to 2 days before, cover with plastic wrap and store in the refrigerator.

FREEZE AHEAD TIP:
Spoon the mixture into freezable, ceramic serving dishes, cover and freeze for up to 1 week. Thaw overnight in the refrigerator.

COME ON OVER... **99**

MY CHRISTMAS EVE SUPPER FOR 10–12

GINGER-GLAZED HAM
MACARONI AND CHEESE
SPRUCED-UP VANILLA CAKE (P.198)
MIXED BERRY COMPOTE

The tradition in Continental Europe is to have fish on Christmas Eve. That's never felt right for me. I rather plan ahead and make the supper before Christmas Day something I can call into service afterwards. My mother routinely baked a ham to go with the turkey on Christmas Day but, given all the vegetables and bits and pieces that need to be seen to, I think that is making life hard on yourself. This, then, is my way of ensuring there is cold ham to eat alongside cold turkey for the rest of the week.

It also provides the perfect cross-generational supper. When my children were younger, I didn't do dinner on Christmas Eve, preferring instead to have a big late lunch – sausages and mash and a rhubarb crumble – and to pack the children off early to bed where, excitedly, they didn't sleep. Now, I invite friends and their families over for an early supper, knowing that ham and mac and cheese will keep everyone happy.

The Spruced-Up Vanilla Cake, with its snowy fir-tree peaks, is a must for my Christmas Eve table, though you'll find the recipe for this impressively festive yet simply made cake in the baking chapter (see p.198) where it, strictly speaking, belongs. But, with the Mixed Berry Compote that follows here, it makes the perfect dessert to give everyone a feeling that Christmas has come. Furthermore, should you not want to bother with the Christmas Morning Muffins the next day (see p.214), know that this cake, toasted, makes for the most fabulous breakfast, with or without the compote drizzled over. With a scoop of vanilla ice cream, the toasted cake doubles as an exquisite dessert; think unfried French toast, a creation of extreme vanilla-and-eggy scrumptiousness.

GINGER-GLAZED HAM

I make no excuses for the fact that this is far too big a ham for the planned supper. Even were I to invite a crowd, I know I could count on leftovers. But that, after all, is the point. Anyway, you can adapt it freely, depending on the number of people you want to feed at the first sitting (I did this for 11 adults and 6 children last year) and how many days you want to eke it out for afterwards. I prefer to buy an uncooked ham and cook it myself as it is delicious served hot and isn't dry when served cold later. But what *is* important, given that this is probably the most labor-intensive time of year in the kitchen, is that this dispenses with any fiddly steps. The ham is simply simmered in ginger ale and, although you need to strip off the rind to glaze it, the glaze is straightforward. My patience is pretty well exhausted by Christmas Eve and knowing that I've still got the stockings to fill and the next day to get through, I don't go in for clove-by-clove studding on the ham: instead I let the golden cubes within the ginger preserve (or jam) give a crisscross effect as they rise to the surface. It works glowingly well.

It won't give that same crowning effect, but if you cannot get hold of ginger preserve, you could use ordinary orange marmalade and add a teaspoon of ground dried ginger or, indeed, grated fresh, as you heat it up.

1 x 12-13 lb bone-in uncooked ham (see Suppliers p.267)
6 quarts ginger ale
1 cup chunky ginger preserve or orange marmalade (see Suppliers p.267)
2 tablespoons hot English mustard
1/2 cup packed dark brown sugar
1/2 teaspoon ground cloves

MAKE AHEAD TIP:
About 6 hours before serving, cook the ham for 3 hours only, take the pan off the heat, remove the rind and return the ham to the hot liquid. Set aside in a cool place for about 3 hours. One hour before serving, preheat the oven to 425°F. Put the ham in a shallow, aluminum foil–lined roasting pan, cover with a tent of foil and place in the oven for 20 minutes. Then glaze and return to the oven for 20–30 minutes or until golden and burnished.

FREEZE AHEAD TIP:
Any leftover ham can be thinly sliced, wrapped in a double layer of foil, or put into a sealable bag, and kept in the freezer for up to 1 month.

❊ Soak the ham in cold water for 48 hours (or 24 hours if you like a saltier ham), changing the water every 8 hours.

❊ Place the ham in a large pan on the stove top and pour the dry ginger ale over it, topping up with water so the ham is just about covered with liquid.

❊ Bring to the boil, then lower the heat to keep the ham bubbling gently for 3 1/2–4 hours.

❊ Towards the end of cooking, preheat the oven to 425°F, and start on the glaze.

❊ Put the chunky ginger preserve (or marmalade) into a small bowl, and spoon in the hot English mustard. Add the soft, dark brown sugar, sprinkle in the ground cloves and stir to mix.

❊ After the ham has had its 3 1/2–4 hours (and check that it's ready by inserting an instant-read thermometer – it should read 160°F), gently lift it out of the pan – no mean feat – and place in an aluminum foil–lined roasting pan. Carefully cut away the skin, leaving a thin layer of fat. There is no need to score the surface, simply slap on the glaze and place in the hot oven for 20 minutes.

❊ Transfer to a carving board where it can be admired before being carved as thinly as possible; I try to get someone else to do this.

MACARONI AND CHEESE DELUXE

1 1/2 sticks (12 tablespoons) soft butter, plus more for greasing
1 cup all-purpose flour
2 teaspoons Dijon mustard
2 cups evaporated milk, (1 1/2 x 12 oz cans)
1 1/2 quarts reduced-fat milk
2 x 1 lb boxes macaroni (elbows)
Cheese:
2 3/4 cups grated Emmental cheese
3 cups grated cheddar cheese
1 1/2 cups shredded Parmesan cheese
salt

I'll come clean, I am making a vatful here, but I can't stop myself. At any time of the year, I take the view that welcome is conveyed by plenty and am, frankly, never knowingly undercatered. However, at Christmas, there isn't a pan that isn't overflowing, a dish that isn't full to the brim, a table that isn't groaning. I'm not apologizing, and nor do I suggest you minimize quantities (though you could probably halve the amounts here if you have a different temperament). I admit I had more than enough for the children and 11 adults, packing up half the leftovers for my sister to take home, and half to heat up for tea when I couldn't be bothered to cook later on in the week.

If the notion of evaporated milk appals you, use light cream in its stead (or replace both the evaporated and reduced fat milk with 2 quarts of whole milk), but it's the former that gives that very necessary almost-packaged taste which makes the mac and cheese so sweetly comforting and gorgeous against the pink saltiness of the ham.

You could add a simply dressed crisp green salad to the supper table, but nothing more is worth considering.

❋ Preheat the oven to 425°F, lightly grease a roasting pan (approx. 14 x 10 x 2½ inches deep) with butter, and start heating a large panful of water on the stove to cook the pasta.

❋ Put another pan with a lid, though not quite as big, to heat on the stove for the cheese sauce; melt the butter over a medium to low heat, add the flour, stirring until you have formed a paste – roux – in the pan. Cook, still stirring, for 5 minutes over a low heat.

❋ Add the Dijon mustard to the pan, stir well, then take off the heat.

❋ Pour the evaporated and the fresh milk into a jug and slowly whisk this into the roux. Be patient or you will get lumps.

❋ When you have whisked in all the liquid, put the pan back on the heat and cook, stirring with a wooden spoon, for about 10–15 minutes, or until all the flouriness has gone.

❋ When the sauce is ready, add the cheeses (reserving a small handful). Stir until the cheese has melted, season to taste and take off the heat, with a lid on so no skin forms.

❋ Meanwhile, when the water in the first pan has come to the boil, salt it extravagantly and cook the macaroni for a couple of minutes less than directed on the box, and drain.

❋ Tip the drained pasta into your prepared roasting pan, and scrape the cheese sauce on top. With a couple of spatulas or your already dirty wooden spoon and a spatula (why add to the washing up?), mix the two together until the pasta is coated with the sauce.

❋ Sprinkle over the reserved cheeses and transfer to the oven and cook for 15–20 minutes, or until the top has scorched slightly and the underneath is bubbling. This is best left to stand for another 20 minutes or so out of the oven before serving.

MAKE AHEAD TIP:
Make up the mac and cheese, pour into the prepared roasting pan, cool, cover with plastic wrap and keep in the refrigerator for up to 3 days. When ready to use, preheat the oven to 400°F. Remove the macaroni from the refrigerator while the oven is heating and cover with aluminum foil. Place the pan in the oven for 20 minutes, then uncover, sprinkle over the reserved cheese and reheat for a further 20–30 minutes until piping hot and golden (the time will depend on the depth and thickness of your pan). To check, push a metal skewer or table knife into the center of the pan; if the macaroni is hot enough, the tip of the skewer or table knife will be piping hot.

FREEZE AHEAD TIP:
Make the macaroni, cool, cover and freeze for up to 3 months. Thaw overnight in the refrigerator and reheat as above.

SPRUCED-UP VANILLA CAKE WITH MIXED BERRY COMPOTE

(see p.198 for cake recipe)

8 cups (2¼ x 12 oz bags) frozen mixed berries

1 x 12 oz jar best-quality strawberry preserve

One of my oldest friends – school, university and now children the same age – Tracey had a grandmother who, over-rouged and frizzy-haired, was known cruelly by us when we were young as Elizabeth I. She was, though, a fantastic old-fashioned cook and at the end of the summer used to make a pie with berries from her garden. This is my deep midwinter version, made with frozen berries and a pot of good strawberry preserve (Wilkin & Sons Little Scarlet is the favorite, but any good strawberry or raspberry preserve will do). It could scarcely be easier and can cook, and cool, while the cake bakes and cools. I love it, too, with Greek yogurt, or you can fold it into whipped heavy cream to make a heavenly fool.

You can also serve the Spruced-Up Vanilla Cake, in all its glory, with the Antioxidant Fruit Salad on p.254 or with an accompanying bowl of crème fraîche or whipped cream sprinkled with pomegranate seeds.

❋ Put the berries into a saucepan with a lid with the preserve and stir together.

❋ Put the lid on the pan, and over a low to medium heat cook for 10 minutes, removing the lid only briefly now and then to give a stir.

❋ Then, take the lid off altogether, and turn up the heat so that the pan bubbles away for about 4 minutes.

❋ Tip into a wide-mouthed measuring jug and allow to cool, before transferring to a prettier jug or two for the table, to be poured at will over the yellow, eggy, thick slices of Spruced-Up Vanilla Cake (see p.198).

MAKE AHEAD TIP:
Make the compote, spoon into a heat-proof bowl and leave to cool. Then cover and chill for up to 3 days. To reheat, place over a pan of gently simmering water (you may need to add a splash of water or a squeeze of orange juice) until liquid again. Pour into a jug and allow to cool before serving.

FREEZE AHEAD TIP:
Make the compote and freeze for up to 1 week. Thaw overnight in the refrigerator and reheat as above.

THE MAIN EVENT

THIS IS IT. The title of the chapter says it all, and if this unsparing statement of fact adds to the pressure, I have to admit, there is no point denying it. This is not just lunch: it is the focus of our expectations. It is also a huge undertaking. So, to feel a twinge of anxiety is not a sign of weakness or impending failure. It's reasonable. No one, absolutely no one, can just breeze through Christmas Day. I love the whole thing, so I'm not complaining, but I think it is best to accept that it's going to be a stretch.

The work itself, however – all the preparation and organization needed to pull everything together – is actually not so terrible. Like most things in life, when you actually do what you dread, you find that the fear is dispelled. But then, most things are better to do than to think about. Having to make the best lunch of the year feels daunting: peeling potatoes and trimming Brussels sprouts, writing out a list of what must be done, and ticking it off as you go, is hugely satisfying. You don't have to operate quite like this, but I find it helps, and so have included here a tight timetable that demands, but delivers. This doesn't need to be followed to the letter, but I suggest that if you want to go off piste, you chart your own proposed trajectory. You need some means of containing and controlling your workload. I have concentrated on two days, Christmas Eve and Christmas Day, simply because that's my favored M.O. You may find it easier to start the preparations a few days earlier, and sometimes – if you're at work on Christmas Eve, for example – you will have no choice. But if you look at the Make Ahead suggestions printed alongside each recipe, you can check how many days you can work ahead and finesse the timings to suit your schedule. Should you be someone who finds long-term, advance preparation and freezer-filling the best way to diminish panic and prep-proliferation, then look at the Freeze Ahead tips beside each recipe, and plan a strategy that works for you.

That – the nuts and bolts of the lunch as a purely practical undertaking – is the easiest part. But the stress-factor, incipient panic, the general hysteria that can color this day – this is where the danger lies. I think we all have to make a conscious effort to keep this under control; and by under control, I don't mean keep it to yourself, but rather ensure you don't risk getting worked up into a state of explosive, put-upon martyrdom. No lunch is worth that. What is the use of fabulous food and blip-free efficiency if everyone is cowed into misery by the stress you give off? My mother's hysteria is an enduring lesson to me. By Christmas Eve, every year, she'd be in tears, and her tension leaked throughout the house. Now, I want to enjoy Christmas.

To some extent, this means working out a way of making this feast your own. Friends of mine who get the nerviest are those who have mothers (or mothers-in-law) coming over and, haunted by the perfect Christmas these dames have apparently delivered effortlessly, they live in fear of the harsh judgment their own shameful simulacrum will surely elicit. You have a choice here: you either take charge of your Christmas and enjoy (as I do) the slightly less structured event you decide to let unfold; or you recognize that disapproval of your slap-dash efforts bestows such a sense of superiority in those finding fault that you are in fact doing them a favor. Think how threatened they'd feel if you'd upstaged them.

But that brings us to a difficult area. What makes Christmas lunch so important is also what makes it so fraught; reader, I have one word to say to you, and it is *family*. I love to have as many of mine around me as I can, but I have learned they need to be leavened. Why not invite some friends, and not necessarily old friends, though it's lovely to have them round the table, too? What you need is the stabilizing effect of the stranger factor: someone with whom your family doesn't feel quite at home enough to behave badly. And I include myself here, too. We can all regress quite alarmingly with family, and we need to be inhibited out of this behavior.

As I said, I want the lunch to have a certain relaxed informality, and if that seems at odds with the brisk, clipboard-and-pen style of my detailed preparations, well, it's because only the military precision of the planning enables me to relax for the lunch.

And, for the meal itself, I want – as will become clear – the food to be plentiful but I want, too, the feel of a feast not a banquet. I have, in recent years, let my lunch become more of a help-yourself than a silver service affair. That's to say (not least because I make so much food there's too much of it to go on our table and still leave room for us) I put all the food on another table, and let everyone pile up their own plates as they go. Sometimes, I hover, adding spoonfuls or helping people if I feel the need, but, generally, I'm happy to carve or get someone else to, and make sure they all know exactly what everything is. Then we can all take ourselves to the main table to eat, returning for a refill at will. It's not an elegant solution, but it feels cozy.

My other, more recent, accommodation was suggested by my sister. I was worried that I wouldn't fit everyone around one table, and I didn't want a sprawled out affair but something warm and compact. So, at my sister's bidding, I put an oilcloth out on the floor underneath the Christmas tree and let the children have a Spruceside picnic lunch. They couldn't have loved it more, munching under the baubles and the lights, and everyone was happy. So much energy can be wasted trying to make sure small children stay seated, that not having this to worry about aided the mellowness of proceedings.

Informality doesn't preclude attention to detail. I want the table to look right, which, for me, means special cloths or napkins and bits and bobs of decoration, brought out once a year, with ceremony. It has to feel festive. I bring them out soon after the 15th December, and they are packed away again on Twelfth Night. I don't insist on a tablecloth – I like the warm gleam of plain wood – but I must have tea lights or candles, and proper napkins, and I'm not beyond the odd bauble or pine cone. My favorite china, seasonally stashed away, is the somewhat obsessively collected, mainly 1950s Crown Devon Stockholm (and see my proud display, left), but I can go a number of pleasurable ways.

So aside from this basic, number one Christmas Table, I love, too, the elemental Christmas Red – you can see from the pictures, on pp.48 and 131, how glorious it looks when tablecloth, napkins, crockery are all aglow with hollyberry brightness. But, although the season allows for vibrant display, it doesn't depend on it. There is a part of me that longs, throughout Christmas, to evoke the wood cladding and rustic cozy calm of some alpine hut and this is the part that brought the table setting on pp.110 and 166 into being. It's hard to choose between my two other favorite tables, different as they are. One I think of as "I'm dreaming of a white Christmas" mode (p.109); the other, my designer and art director, Caz Hildebrand, nicknames Barbie Goes to Bollywood (right and p.viii). There is a brightness, airy calm and serenity about the white-on-white approach; and yet the other, with its preposterous pinkness and odd clashing touch of brazen orange, manages a spirit-lifting glamour despite its (or my) best efforts. But these are just my ways of playing with the Christmas table, and you, no doubt, will have yours. Of course, no one wants a new set of china each year, but it's surprising how different you can make a setting look just by playing about with a cloth, some napkins and a tea light or two.

I try to be as permissive about the content of the lunch itself, and I am, I am, but I make no secret of the fact that *my* Christmas lunch is the one that opens this chapter: the lunch presided over by the turkey with all the traditional trimmings; the lunch I ate as a child, and the one I eat so much more joyfully now, and which, with occasional variations, I've written about before. But I am, I'd hope, a zealot rather than a bully and happy to include ideas for those of you who want something different for a change, or who cannot embrace or even meekly go along with my exuberant championing of the Christmas turkey. A Christmas goose is the most obvious alternative, and a fabulous one (especially with pear and cranberry stuffing), but once I've ventured beyond the traditional, I am ready to take a broadly inclusive approach. So that means a vast and gorgeous rib of beef with a seasonal port and Stilton gravy; or a slightly Italianate, rolled, stuffed loin of pork, both of which bring their own splendor and specialness to the occasion. A glazed ham (p.32), if you wanted to bring this into the equation, and were not already following my Christmas Eve supper plans (see p.100), would also do the trick. Within all these suggestions are provisions for vegetarians, but I'm happy, too, to include a full-on, meatless Christmas Feast, in the form of a beautiful, whole, stuffed pumpkin. Some of you may have teenage children and their tyrannical fads to accommodate, others may simply prefer, if in mixed carnivore and veggie company, to have just one meal for all, and this is one that everyone can relish.

And, although each of the menus makes any Christmas lunch feel like the Main Event it is, these are meals that can also lend themselves to any big-deal dinner throughout the season.

THE MAIN EVENT 107

MY TRADITIONAL CHRISTMAS LUNCH

CHRISTMAS LUNCH MENU FOR 10–16

SPICED AND SUPERJUICY TURKEY WITH ALLSPICE GRAVY
REDDER THAN RED CRANBERRY SAUCE
MY MOTHER'S BREAD SAUCE
GINGERBREAD STUFFING, PANETTONE AND ITALIAN SAUSAGE STUFFING OR CHESTNUT STUFFING
BACON-WRAPPED CHIPOLATAS
PERFECT ROAST POTATOES
MAPLE-ROAST PARSNIPS
BRUSSELS SPROUTS WITH CHESTNUTS
BUTTERNUT ORZOTTO
RED CABBAGE WITH POMEGRANATE JUICE (p.60)

ULTIMATE CHRISTMAS PUDDING WITH EGGNOG CREAM
CHOCOLATE PUDDING FOR CHRISTMAS PUDDING HATERS WITH CHOCOLATE SAUCE

SATSUMAS OR CLEMENTINES
LYCHEES
FRESH MIXED NUTS IN THEIR SHELLS

When I read the menu that follows, I feel exhausted, hungry, flabbergasted and proud. How could I have cooked so much? How could we all have eaten so much? But how I want to eat it now. I am warmed by recollection and anticipation.

For this is what I made last year, which is – give or take – what I make every year and will be making every year that – *d.v.* – follows. It used to be worse, I used to make two stuffings; now, I concede that one suffices. But then, in my two-stuffing days, I went without bacon-wrapped chipolatas, so a balance has been maintained.

In fairness, I should say that the menu is inflated, as two of the people (out of a total of nine adults and five children) round my table were vegetarians and I wanted to make sure they could feast as richly as the rest of us. In previous years, I had only intermittently added the red cabbage and never the butternut orzotto, but both made sense and neither was any trouble since I prepared them in relative quiet the day before and simply reheated them as I cooked the rest. I had to do something for non-meat eaters as I knew I couldn't forgo the goose fat on my roast potatoes (although I had decided to take pancetta out of the sprouts). I did *think* about the goose fat, and consulted my sister who was, after all, bringing the vegetarians. I gave her three options: cook the potatoes in vegetable oil; cook them in goose fat and don't tell the vegetarians; cook them in goose fat, tell them and deprive them. She felt strongly that we'd already given up the pancetta, so enough was enough – they would have the orzotto, plus we hadn't forced them to become vegetarians. At this time of year, one can get frenzied and beyond reason – so I was grateful for her coolly brutal logic.

I have printed a timetable for guidance, my own Christmas Lunch Countdown, but obviously there are variables. I hope, at least, it helps you to structure your own timetable. That much is crucial: if you don't run the cooking like a military campaign, you won't get lunch on the table in time. Having said that, I should admit one thing: I invited everyone for 2 pm, with a thought that we would eat at 2.30 pm, and got started in the kitchen at 10 am, having not been released from rapacious present-opening by my children before then. By the time everyone arrived, I was unmade-up, shiny-faced with the exertions and still in my dressing gown. So I'm not pretending that any of this can be done with a mere snap of the fingers or wiggle of the nose. But the pleasures that are to be had from the slow build-up as you prepare a feast, as well as from quickly eating it, are not to be underestimated. For me, this lunch is the lynchpin of the year.

The menu opposite, in the quantities I cook, is what I'd do for 10, and it would certainly stretch to 16. This may sound odd, but caterers routinely downsize portions the greater the number of guests. The one thing you needn't worry about is not having enough: there are so many elements to a proper Christmas feast, you'd be surprised just how little people take of each. And simply, the fewer the guests, the more leftovers you'll have. That, too, is part of the rich, full point of the exercise.

THE MAIN EVENT 109

AT-A-GLANCE CHRISTMAS LUNCH COUNTDOWN

There is no reason why you couldn't do some of what follows in advance, but this is how I tackle it.

CHRISTMAS EVE (at the latest)

- First thing, take the turkey out of the refrigerator. (Take the giblets out as soon as you get the bird home and stash them separately in the refrigerator, throwing away the liver, I'm afraid to say.) Put all the giblets into a saucepan with a lid along with the other ingredients to make the broth for your Allspice Gravy (see p.118), then put it all on the heat and get on with preparing the turkey while the broth comes to a boil.
- Get out a very large pan with a lid – a pan that will fit the turkey roomily – or a clean bucket or plastic trash can and add all the ingredients you need for brining the Spiced and Superjuicy Turkey (p.114). Stir well and lower the turkey into the brine, adding more water if needed. Cover with the lid and put it somewhere cold. This now just sits, infusing, until Christmas morning.
- Meanwhile, once the giblet-water has started boiling, cover with the lid, turn down the heat to very low and leave for 2 hours.
- You could use this time to get on with everything else, so in whatever order you like – or you can man several pans at once, which is more efficient so long as it doesn't stress you out:
  – Redder Than Red Cranberry Sauce (p.119); or make this further ahead.
  – your chosen stuffing (pp.122–26), but don't add the eggs yet.
- The above are non-negotiable, I feel. You may want to add (or not) the following, and if so, start on these today:
  – Bacon-Wrapped Chipolatas (p.127): wrap them ready for cooking.
  – Red Cabbage (p.60); or this can be made further ahead.
  – Butternut Orzotto (p.134), but only up to the point before the mascarpone is added.
- When the above are either done or under control:
  – Take the giblet-water, after its simmering time, off the heat, remove the lid and leave to get cold.
  – Check you've got all the plates, cutlery and napkins you need for tomorrow and that there's champagne, white wine, fizzy water (or any combination you want to serve) in the refrigerator, or in a small clean plastic trash can stuffed with ice, to save refrigerator space.
  – Count the Christmas crackers and, if this applies, put them beyond any child's reach.
  – Slice a good-quality white loaf, cut crusts off and leave on a rack to stale for the Bread Sauce tomorrow (p.121).

110 THE MAIN EVENT

CHRISTMAS DAY

This is a brutal schedule, but better to go into battle properly prepared than enter the fray buoyed up with optimistic ignorance. You can draw up your own timetable, and it's often wise to, as the act of scribbling things down on paper helps you to get a good measure of what's involved, more than just reading can. I still scrawl down my own schedule. Plus, of course, you may have a different weight turkey, want to eat later or introduce any number of your own traditions and elements or have to fiddle and edit to accommodate your particular kitchen set-up.

The following, unsparing, schedule is based on a 2.30pm lunch, cooked with the benefit of a double oven. I know not all of you will have two ovens, and this is all perfectly possible, if harder, with one oven. In many ways it's more of a conjuring trick than a culinary exercise. Once cooked, the turkey can sit for an hour, or longer, out of the oven so long as it is not in a draught; and as it comes out, the oven can be turned up for the potatoes. A hot oven for the spuds is the only crucial factor – or that and the gravy. As I've said before, so long as the turkey is cooked, the potatoes are crisp and the gravy piping hot, everything else can be warmish, whatever the health and safety officers say.

No doubt, you would give yourself a less frenetic timetable were you to schedule lunch for later, say 4pm, but old habits die hard, so that's too late for me. I hear my mother's voice in my ear talking disdainfully about "Spanish hours". Besides, if you have a later lunch, you run into the difficulties of having hungry people hanging around the kitchen wanting to be fed beforehand. But the choice is yours. Good luck!

10.00am
- Peel and cut potatoes, then leave in cold water, as directed (p.128).
- Take bacon-wrapped chipolatas out of the refrigerator.

10.30am
- Take turkey out of brine, sit it on a rack in the sink (or over a pan) and leave to drip, drain and come to room temperature.
- Preheat first oven to 400°F.
- Trim brussels sprouts and leave in a colander.
- Take prepared stuffing out of the refrigerator.

10.40am
- Put chipolatas in oven.
- Infuse milk for Bread Sauce (p.121).
- Measure out ingredients for Chocolate Sponge Pudding (p.140) and set aside.

11.00am
- Put prepared potatoes (p.128) in pan on heat to parboil.

11.10am
- Take chipolatas out of oven and leave wrapped in aluminum foil.

11.20am
- Melt basting liquid for turkey (p.114).

11.30am	• Baste turkey with half the liquid, and put in first oven. • Potatoes should be at parboiling stage, or will be within the next 10 minutes, so keep an eye on them, then drain, dredge (p.128) and leave in pan.
12 noon	• Baste turkey with remaining liquid. • Put large pan of water with steamer attachment (for puddings) on to heat. • Now sit down calmly with a glass of wine, or cup of tea, and look over everything else that needs to be done so you are not panicked by the quick-fire work later. • Lay the table.
12.45pm	• Put Christmas Pudding (made a few weeks earlier, p.137) in bottom part of pan-with-steamer attachment to steam (for 3 hours).
12.50pm	• Prepare Maple-Roast Parsnips (p.130), and leave in a pan, preferably an aluminum foil throwaway one. • Put sprout water on and let it to come to the boil. You can leave it with its lid on, with the heat switched off once it boils.
1.00pm	• Preheat second oven (if available) to 500°F, putting in a roasting pan with goose fat to heat up at the same time (this will be for the potatoes).
1.30pm	• Put potatoes in hot fat in second oven.
1.45pm	• Add prepared bread to infused milk and finish off Bread Sauce (p.121). • Put parsnips in oven on rack below potatoes. • Check sprout water, bring back up to boil, then cook and drain sprouts. • Finish off stuffing, by adding eggs etc. (pp.122–26), put in dish and pop in oven below turkey. • Baste turkey at the same time.
2.00pm	• Turn potatoes over. • Check turkey; it should be done. Take out of oven and leave tented with foil. • Pop aluminum foil–parcel of chipolatas in oven to reheat. • Process ingredients for Chocolate Sponge Pudding (p.140), put in basin, and put basin in steamer above Christmas pud to steam.
2.10pm	• Put Red Cabbage (p.60) on to reheat. • Put Butternut Orzotto (p.134) on to reheat. • Warm chestnuts in butter, add drained sprouts and toss in pan (p.132), leaving with lid on and heat off till lunch. • Fork through Cranberry Sauce (p.119).
2.20pm	• Finish Allspice Gravy (p.118). • Take parsnips out and plate up. • Check seasoning and heat of bread sauce. • Take stuffing out of oven.
2.30pm	• Bring everything to the table, leaving potatoes and hot gravy till last. • **LUNCH**
3.30pm	• Have a quick nip out to the kitchen, whip up Eggnog Cream (p.140) and melt ingredients for Chocolate Sauce (p.140).

THE MAIN EVENT 113

114 THE MAIN EVENT

SPICED AND SUPERJUICY ROAST TURKEY WITH ALLSPICE GRAVY

I know I have done an awful lot of jumping up and down and shouting about my way of making sure your turkey is going to be surefire-succulent, but I don't think I can rest until I have converted every last person. This is feasible: you have only to try this method to be utterly convinced. It's not egomania that motivates me here: indeed, I take no credit for an age-old tenderizing technique; brining is a discovery not an invention. My evangelical zeal is more a combination of altruism, control-freakery (if I'm honest) and enthusiastic faith. But then, these factors are probably behind all kinds of evangelism – and cookery books.

But I don't wish to be lacking in compassion for those who don't choose this path. I can offer another way of making sure a turkey doesn't end up stringy and dry, namely my Sausage Meat–Bosomed Turkey (see photo p.110). It is simple, consisting of a minor, but amply satisfying, procedure. You take your turkey and, using your fingers, wiggle some space between the skin and breast of the bird, being careful not to tear the skin. (Mind you, turkey skin is so tough, you'd probably need talons to rupture it.) Into this space you've made, squeeze good sausage meat, or the contents of your favorite butcher's sausages (2 pounds of either should be enough for a 12-pound turkey), pushing, pressing and coaxing so that it covers the whole breast. Then from on top of the skin, mold it a little with your hand so that the breast is voluptuously but smoothly bulging. Secure the flaps of skin over the cavity with a metal skewer so that the sausage meat doesn't escape during cooking. The skin really crisps up as this turkey roasts, and the sausage meat, which drips down into the breast as it cooks, keeps the meat from drying out. To ensure the turkey doesn't brown too rapidly, cover it loosely with a sheet of buttered aluminum foil until halfway through the cooking time. You could then dispense with the chipolatas (or stuffing if you can live without it), so this is a good way of cutting down on dishes to prepare, without making huge sacrifices.

But still, my Christmas turkey is the brined one. For not only does it tenderize and add subtle spiciness, but it makes carving the turkey incredibly much easier.

And I mean to say: how hard is it to fill a pan or large plastic trash can or bucket with water and spices and lower a turkey into it? At this time of year, it's fine just to leave it in a cold place. I sit mine by an open window in the kitchen. It means everyone freezes, but who am I going to put first – my turkey or my family? Out in the garden if you're lucky enough to have one would also be fine, though the pan must be securely covered: if I've got a bucket or bin out in the open, I cover it twice with foil and then put my son's skateboard on top to prevent foxy foraging.

As I've said before, though you might find it hard to believe sight unseen, a raw turkey covered in brine – with its oranges, cinnamon sticks, and scattering

Serves 10–16 as part of the Christmas feast, or 8–10 if not

approx. 6 quarts water
1 large orange or 2 smaller, quartered
1 cup kosher salt or ½ cup table salt
3 tablespoons black peppercorns
1 bouquet garni
1 cinnamon stick
1 tablespoon caraway seeds
4 whole cloves
2 tablespoons allspice berries
4 star anise
2 tablespoons white mustard seeds
1 cup sugar
2 unpeeled onions, quartered
1 x 2-3 inch piece unpeeled ginger, cut into 6 slices
¼ cup maple syrup
¼ cup honey
stalks from medium bunch of parsley (optional, if you have some parsley hanging around)
12 lb turkey

FOR THE BASTING GLAZE:
⅓ cup goose fat or butter
3 tablespoons maple syrup

MAKE AHEAD TIP:
Leave the turkey submerged in the brine, securely covered, in a very cold place for up to 2 days.

THE MAIN EVENT 115

of spices – looks so beautiful as it steeps that I can never help lifting the lid for quick, blissfully reassuring peeks.

I give a turkey this size, without stuffing, 2½ hours' cooking. You have read correctly: as long as it goes into the oven at room temperature, that is enough time, along with 20–40 minutes' standing time, tented in foil, once it's out of the oven. See the chart opposite for a slightly more structured guide. But remember that ovens vary enormously, so check by piercing the flesh between leg and body with a small sharp knife: when the juices run clear, the turkey's cooked. Or, if you want to be really scientific, put an instant-read meat thermometer in, and when it reads 170°F, you know it's cooked. Don't worry: the note opposite will explain everything fully.

❋ Put the water into your largest cooking pot or a bucket or plastic trash can. Squeeze the juice from the orange quarters into the water before you chuck the peels in, then add all the other ingredients, stirring to combine the salt, sugar, syrup and honey.

❋ Remove any string or trussing from the turkey, shake it free, remove the giblets, if not already done, and put them in the refrigerator (or straightaway set about making the broth for the gravy), then add the bird to the liquid, topping up with more water if it is not completely submerged. Keep covered in a cold place, even outside overnight or for up to a day or two before you cook it, remembering to take it out of its liquid (and wipe it dry with paper towels) a good hour before it has to go into the oven. Preheat said oven to 400°F.

❋ Melt the goose fat (or butter) and maple syrup together slowly over a low heat. Paint the turkey with the glaze before roasting in the oven, and baste periodically throughout the cooking time. Roast for 2½ hours.

❋ When you think it's ready, pierce the turkey with the point of a sharp knife where the body meets the leg, and if the juices run clear, it's cooked; if still pink, cook it for longer until they run clear, or use an instant-read thermometer. Then take the turkey out of the oven, and let it sit, tented with aluminum foil, for 20–40 minutes or even longer if you like, as I do.

HOW LONG TO COOK YOUR TURKEY FOR

The cooking times here always seem shockingly short to other people, but the truth is we've all been overcooking turkeys for years, and then complaining about how dull and sawdusty they are. If your turkey starts at room temperature, and is untrussed and without stuffing, and your oven thermostat is working correctly, these cooking times hold.

I've given instructions on how to check your turkey is cooked through, opposite, but so long as you use my brining method, if you want to ignore me and give your poor old bird longer, you can rest assured that a turkey so prepared is not going to taste dry, even if it is untrustingly overcooked. I beg you, though, for the sake of succulence, to have the courage of my convictions.

A turkey is generally held to be cooked through when an instant-read thermometer, inserted into its thickest part, reaches 165°F, though some cooks recommend 170°F. However, Paul Kelly of KellyBronze Turkeys (a company which rears free-range heritage-breed turkeys in the UK) says his birds are cooked through at 150°F and this is what his turkey thermometer indicates. Any such free-range turkey also cooks faster than a very lean, more mass-produced bird, since the free-range turkeys have more marbling and this conducts the heat faster. The timings here are for free-range birds, put in the oven at room temperature rather than refrigerator-cold. If you have stuffed the bird, add the weight of the stuffing to the weight of the bird to calculate the total weight and cooking time; if you choose to stuff the cavity, do so loosely and add a further 1/2 hour.

TURKEY COOKING TIMES

Weight of bird	Cooking time
5 lb	1 1/2 hours
8 lb	1 3/4 hours
10 lb	2 hours
12 lb	2 1/2 hours
15 lb	2 3/4 hours
17 lb	3 hours
20 lb	3 1/2 hours
25 lb	4 1/2 hours

The USDA recommends that turkeys are cooked to a minimum internal temperature of 165°F.

ALLSPICE GRAVY

giblets from turkey (not including liver)
1 quart water
1 tablespoon allspice berries
1/2 teaspoon whole black peppercorns
3 bay leaves, preferably Turkish
1 x 2-inch stick cinnamon
1 stalk celery, halved
2 carrots, peeled and halved
1 unpeeled onion, halved
1 tablespoon kosher salt or
  1/2 tablespoon table salt
juice of 1 clementine (approx. 1/4 cup), plus pulp from fruit
2 tablespoons all-purpose flour
2 tablespoons honey

Generally speaking, the best gravies are made by deglazing a roast's cooking juices in the roasting pan, but, with a brined bird, the liquid it gives off is just too salty; you can't use more than 2–3 tablespoonfuls. You could, of course, simply drain off the excess, but given the stress of Christmas Day, making the gravy in a saucepan is a better route: you avoid the smoking you can get from a roasting pan on the stovetop; and you can make it all ahead – the stovetop will be quite busy enough as it is.

❋ Put all the ingredients, except the flour and honey, into a saucepan and bring to a boil. Cover with a lid and simmer gently for 2 hours.

❋ Strain the gravy broth through a strainer (or just pour, holding back the bits) into a large measuring jug: this should give you approx. 1 quart. All this can be done well ahead (and see tips).

❋ On the Day itself, whisk the flour in a saucepan with 2 tablespoons of the salty juices from the turkey roasting pan, then put the saucepan on the heat and slowly whisk in the rest of the broth and the honey.

❋ Let the gravy bubble away, stirring every now and again with a wooden spoon, until it thickens a little and the floury taste disappears.

❋ If you are preparing the gravy broth ahead, make sure when you add the flour and juices and reheat that it gets piping hot; preferably fill the gravy jug with hot water for 10 minutes before draining, drying and filling it with hot, invitingly aromatic allspice gravy.

You can use the unused juice and pulp of one of the clementines/satsumas from the Gingerbread Stuffing on p.124, if making.

MAKE AHEAD TIP:
Simmer the gravy broth for 2 hours, and stir in the honey. Cool, cover and keep in the refrigerator for up to 2 days. Finish the gravy with flour and turkey juices as directed.

FREEZE AHEAD TIP:
Make the broth as directed, cool and freeze for up to 1 week. Thaw overnight in the refrigerator, and finish as above.

REDDER THAN RED CRANBERRY SAUCE

When I was a child, I don't think fresh cranberries were ever seen in England. For me, cranberry sauce came out of a jar – and my mother was the sort of person who made her own mayonnaise. Actually, I have nothing against store-bought cranberry sauce (and recommend it in various recipes), but I personally don't quite see the point: it is ridiculously easy to make, and tastes so much better homemade that it feels like the wrong thing to cut out of your cooking schedule.

Having a kitsch weakness for déclassé liqueurs, I love the cherry brandy element (not the sophisticated see-through kirsch, but the rich, red, sweet and viscous maiden-aunt's tipple), though Cointreau, Grand Marnier, Triple Sec or ruby port would be just dandy, too. But you can simply substitute some freshly squeezed orange juice (blood orange juice out of a carton would keep you tonally correct) and be prepared to up the sugar slightly – probably by an extra 1/2 cup, but don't add it all at once – as the sweet liqueurs counter the fierce sharpness of the cranberries. If you're squeezing an orange for juice, go that extra inch and zest it first over the cranberries in the pan.

Serves 10–16 as part of the Christmas feast, or 8–10 if not

1 x 12 oz bag pack fresh cranberries
1 cup sugar
3 tablespoons cherry brandy
1/3 cup water

❄ Put everything into a pan and let it bubble away until the berries start to pop, stirring every now and again with a wooden spoon. This will take about 10 minutes.

❄ The one thing you should bear in mind, though, is that the pectin-rich nature of the fruit means it solidifies enormously on cooling, so although it will be cooked when the berries have burst, it will still look runnier than you think cranberry sauce should.

❄ At this stage, give the sauce a final, vicious, whipping stir to help crush the berries into the liquid, and taste – making sure not to burn your mouth – to check whether it needs more sugar; if you find it too sweet, which is unlikely, just spritz in some lemon juice. Transfer to a bowl to cool.

❄ If you cook this sauce way in advance, it will jellify a lot so thrash it through with a fork before serving.

MAKE AHEAD TIP:
Make the sauce up to 1 week ahead. Cover and keep in the refrigerator. Stir well before serving.

FREEZE AHEAD TIP:
Make and freeze for up to 1 month. Thaw overnight at room temperature. Stir well before serving.

120 THE MAIN EVENT

MY MOTHER'S BREAD SAUCE

I couldn't have Christmas lunch without bread sauce: just the smell of the milk, infusing on the hob, giving off that familiar scent of onion, mace, bay and clove, lets me know it is Christmas. The idea of a bread sauce remains intensely baffling, possibly even disgusting, to any person who hasn't been brought up with British traditions, but I have, so far, been able to convert Italians, Austrians and even (admittedly with some condescension on their part) a French contingent. I regard bread sauce as not only my legacy from my mother, but every Briton's sacred and stodgy inheritance. I shouldn't have to say it but, given the kind of bread our nation willingly consumes (and my children lead the way here, eschewing all proper loaves), let me warn you now: do not even consider making this with the plastic, sliced stuff.

Proper recipes tell you to use breadcrumbs and it isn't simply laziness that makes me cut out that step, though I suspect it played some part in my mother's decision. I don't mean that rudely: she was a wonderful cook, and much of that came from her impatience; stripping away unnecessary processes is an important part of real cooking, and no one should feel guilty about that.

The real truth is that bread sauce made with torn-up cubes and strips of bread has a much better texture than the almost gruel-like, uniformly smooth sauce made with semolina-sized crumbs.

❄ The day before you make this, slice the bread thickly, cut off the crusts (not with too much dedication, as a few bits of brown crust won't matter) and lay the slices on a rack to stale. And as you don't need the 2 end crusts for the sauce, I'd eat these while they're nice and fresh. I'm afraid I often end up eating the strips of discarded crusts from the slices, too (with a thick layer of butter and a thin one of Marmite).

❄ If you've forgotten to stale the bread, or don't have time, you can speed the process by putting the slices in a very low oven until they feel dry to the touch (though not toasted) – but just don't forget they're there.

❄ On Christmas Day (see p.111), though you could make this before, prepare the sauce, which is scarcely hard work. Put the milk into a pan. Peel and quarter the onion, stud each quarter with a clove, and drop them, as you do so, into the pan of milk. Add the bay leaves, peppercorns and the blades of mace (or sprinkle the ground mace over) along with the salt and bring to an almost boil, but *do not let it boil*.

❄ Remove from the heat, cover the pan and let it foggily infuse.

Serves 10–16 as part of the Christmas feast, or 8–10 if not

1 x 1³⁄₄ lb good-quality white loaf, sliced thickly and left to stale overnight (see step 1 below)

1 quart whole milk

1 onion

4 whole cloves

2 bay leaves, preferably Turkish

1 teaspoon whole white peppercorns

2 teaspoons kosher salt or 1 teaspoon table salt

2 blades mace (or heaped ¹⁄₄ teaspoon ground mace)

2 tablespoons butter

2 tablespoons heavy cream (optional)

fresh nutmeg

MAKE AHEAD TIP:
Make the sauce up to 2 days ahead. Remove the clove-studded onion pieces. Melt the butter and spoon over the sauce to prevent a skin forming. Cover with plastic wrap and keep in the refrigerator. To reheat, return the sauce and butter layer to the saucepan, and stir over a gentle heat for 3–4 minutes until everything has blended together. Adjust the seasoning to taste.

FREEZE AHEAD TIP:
Make the bread sauce (without adding the butter) up to 1 month ahead. Cool and freeze. To reheat, thaw overnight in the refrigerator and return to the saucepan. Stir over a gentle heat for 2–3 minutes then beat in the butter, and season as above.

OPPOSITE:
My Mother's Bread Sauce (top);
Redder Than Red Cranberry Sauce (bottom)

THE MAIN EVENT

❉ Tear the slices of bread into rough cubes over a bowl, so you catch all the crumbs, too.

❉ When you're not far off serving up, put the pan back on a very low heat, add the bread cubes and cook for about 15 minutes, by which time the sauce should be thick and warm and evocatively fragrant. I have to say I don't bother with removing any of the bits – the onions, the peppercorns and so on – but you can strain the milk before adding the bread if you want to.

❉ Just before serving, stir in the butter and, if you happen to have a carton open, the cream (otherwise, splosh in a little more milk) and some more salt if you think it needs it. Grate over quite a bit of nutmeg, adding more once you've decanted it into a warmed bowl or gravy boat.

CHESTNUT STUFFING

This is my modest reworking of the stuffing, as made by my butcher Lidgate's of Holland Park, which the constant reader will recognize. I've fiddled a little, but not in a major way – it didn't need it – and this makes enough to fill a turkey or dish of approx. 10 x 9 x 2 inches deep, though I often use a similar-sized aluminum foil pan. Neither of these needs any more than 30 minutes' baking time, maybe 40 if the oven is very loaded. I can't make any aesthetic claims for this stuffing, but it is unreasonable to expect wodged-up chestnuts and chestnut cream to cast off their claggy brown looks and, besides, the taste dispels any worries about its appearance.

    This is not a huge amount of stuffing, but I find a large spoonful per person is all that's needed, though if you want to make more – say the size of the Gingerbread Stuffing on p.124 – just double everything.

    It is the perfect amount for fitting inside the turkey's cavity, which is all well and good, but I have found that stuffing and trussing a bird on Christmas morning, while very satisfying OB/GYN work on its own account, is the one step that can tip me over the edge. And my brining method means that moisturizing from within is no longer necessary.

    As for breadcrumbs, I highly recommend you use stale real bread that you've crumbed yourself in a processor. If you need to, buy a loaf, slice it and leave it to stale overnight as for the bread sauce, above; it doesn't have to be as dry as dust, just not still squidgy. I often make breadcrumbs as I go, throughout the year – I can never throw anything away, least of all stale bread – and stash resealable bags of them in the deep freeze.

❄ Peel and roughly chop the onion and stick the pieces in the processor with the bacon and parsley. Or chop finely by hand.

❄ Melt the ¾ stick butter in a large-ish, heavy-based pan and, keeping the heat fairly low, cook the processed mixture until it softens, about 10 minutes.

❄ Remove to a bowl and, using your hands, crumble in the chestnuts so that they are broken up slightly, then mix in the breadcrumbs and chestnut cream. This isn't very hard to do by hand (a wooden spoon and brutal manner will help), but an electric freestanding mixer with the paddle attachment is the agreeably lazy option.

❄ If you are making this in advance, then let it get cold now, otherwise, beat in the eggs, season with only a little salt (remember the bacon will contain some) and a good grating of fresh nutmeg and fresh pepper.

❄ If you want to stuff the turkey with this on Christmas morning, be my guest; otherwise butter your dish or aluminum foil pan, add the stuffing, spread the extra tablespoon of butter on top, and bake, uncovered, in the oven underneath the turkey for 30–40 minutes, depending how full your oven is.

Serves 10–16 as part of the Christmas feast, or 8–10 if not

1 large or 2 small onions
¼ lb bacon
large bunch of parsley, from which you can get a good 2 handfuls of leaves
¾ stick butter (6 tablespoons), plus more for greasing dish and extra tablespoon for buttering top (if not stuffing turkey)
1 cup cooked whole chestnuts from a jar or can
5 cups breadcrumbs
1 x 1 lb can unsweetened chestnut cream (see Suppliers p.267)
2 eggs, beaten
good grating of fresh nutmeg
salt and pepper

MAKE AHEAD TIP:
Make the stuffing, leave to cool completely then beat in the eggs. Cover and keep in the refrigerator for up to 2 days.

FREEZE AHEAD TIP:
Make the stuffing, with the eggs, and freeze for up to 2 weeks. Thaw overnight in the refrigerator.

THE MAIN EVENT

GINGERBREAD STUFFING

Serves 10–16 as part of the Christmas feast, or 8–10 if not

1 lb (3 medium-sized) onions
2 eating apples, peeled and cored
3 tablespoons butter
1 tablespoon vegetable oil
1 1/2 lbs bacon
zest of 2 clementines
5 cups loosely crumbled gingerbread
2 eggs, beaten
approx. 1/2 teaspoon freshly ground pepper

Sometimes, it makes sense to use one's obsessions to advantage. I know that most people don't have trivial light-bulb moments when the notion pops into an already food-filled head to make a stuffing in which crumbled gingerbread cake replaces breadcrumbs, but that's, unfathomably, how my mind works.

You can use dark brown, dense gingerbread, or the lighter, sandier loaves. I buy spiced bread rather than make it (though those who want to could turn to p.201) and you will often find it sold, even still in loaf-shape, as ginger cake. It all works. Indeed any sweet, spiced bread would, and the Italianate version opposite is a case in point.

❋ Using a food processor or by hand, finely chop the onions and apples.

❋ Put the butter and oil in a large, wide saucepan over a medium heat and fry the chopped onions and apples until soft, about 10–15 minutes.

❋ Finely chop the bacon in the processor, or by hand, and add this to the softened onion and apple mixture. Cook everything, stirring frequently, for about 5 minutes more.

❋ Add the zest of the clementines, reserving the bald fruit (you can use some of their juice in the Allspice Gravy on p.118).

❋ Take the pan off the heat and let it cool a little before mixing in the gingerbread crumbs. You can let this get properly cold now if you want.

❋ Just before you want to cook the stuffing, add the beaten eggs and pepper, and use it to stuff the cavity of your turkey, or cook all of it (or what's left after stuffing your bird) in a buttered baking pan. I don't stuff the bird but put all of my stuffing in a very generously buttered old Le Creuset terrine, with internal dimensions of approx. 10 x 3 1/2 x 3 inches deep.

❋ Bake it in a hot oven (400°F) with your turkey for about the last 45 minutes. If the stuffing's going into a full oven – which it no doubt is – there should be no need to cover the dish. If the oven is less full, and therefore hotter and less steamy, you could cover with aluminum foil for the first 30 minutes.

❋ Let the cooked stuffing sit in its terrine for a good 10 minutes out of the oven before turning it out and slicing it. Or just spoon from the dish if that's less stressful. (I love a slice of this, cold, in a Christmas night or Boxing Day turkey sandwich.)

MAKE AHEAD TIP:
Make the stuffing, leave to cool completely then beat in the eggs and pepper. Cover and keep in the refrigerator for up to 2 days.

FREEZE AHEAD TIP:
Make the stuffing, with the eggs and pepper, and freeze for up to 2 weeks. Thaw overnight in the refrigerator.

PANETTONE AND ITALIAN SAUSAGE STUFFING

This is nothing more, really, than an Italian-inspired take on the gingerbread stuffing, opposite. The finished product is very different, however. Whereas the Olde Englishe stuffing is rich, dark and dense, this one is light, spicy and spoonable.

I go for hot Italian sausages here, since it's the contrast between the sweet, fruited bread and the fieriness of the sausage that I love; but it would work with the milder variety, too. You can't, however, substitute normal breakfast sausages: the rusk in them would add too much breadiness; that element is elegantly provided already.

If you don't like the dried fruit in panettone, then go for a tall, round loaf of pandoro or challah instead. In either case, be sure to brush off all the bits of visible sugar from the top. I just slice off the sugar-covered bits.

For broth, I simply use good store-bought carton or can. If you're starting off with hot broth, make it up first and leave it to cool a little before mixing in with the eggs.

Serves 10–16 as part of the Christmas feast, or 8–10 if not

2 onions, peeled
3 stalks celery
1/4 cup olive oil
2 lbs Italian sausages
4 eggs
2 cups chicken broth
1 lb panettone, cut into 1-inch cubes
salt to taste
large handful of chopped parsley, plus more to serve

❄ Preheat the oven to 400°F. Lay out the panettone cubes on a large baking sheet, and toast them in the oven for 10 minutes, till they are crisp and golden at the edges. Allow to cool. Obviously, this step can be done well in advance, just be sure to keep the toasted cubes in an airtight container.

❄ Chop the onions and celery finely, but don't go so far that you end up with a mush.

❄ Put 2 tablespoons of the oil into a pan and, when warm, add the celery and onion and cook gently, stirring every now and again, for 10–15 minutes until softened.

❄ Add the remaining oil to the pan, then squeeze the sausages out of their casings into the pan and squish and turn with a wooden spoon to break the pieces up as much as possible and mix with the celery and onion. Cook the sausage meat for about 10 minutes, or until the pinkness has left it, stirring regularly with your wooden spoon. You can do everything up till this stage in advance if you like.

❄ Preheat the oven to 400°F (if it isn't on already) and grease an ovenproof pan (approx. 3 x 8 inches), pretty enough to serve from, put in the toasted panettone cubes and add the sausage, celery and onion: I use my hands to blend everything together well.

❄ In the bowl that had the sausages, celery and onion (to save on washing up)

MAKE AHEAD TIP:
Make the sausage meat and celery mixture. Cool, cover and keep in the refrigerator for up to 2 days. Toast the panettone cubes and store in an airtight bag or container for up to 1 week. Finish with the eggs and broth, as directed overleaf when ready to use.

THE MAIN EVENT

whisk the eggs with the broth (adding salt if it isn't already salty, so taste the broth first) and pour this over the stuffing, leaving it to soak in for 5 minutes or so before baking, uncovered, in the oven for 45 minutes. It will be dark golden and crisp on top, eggily soft – but utterly firm – underneath.

❋ Sprinkle with chopped parsley and use a large spoon to serve.

BACON-WRAPPED CHIPOLATAS

It's embarrassing – or should be, though happily I don't believe in feeling ashamed of anything I eat – but I used to be a little sneery about bacon-wrapped cocktail sausages or chipolatas. How foolish one can be. They are now a must-have.

I make life easy for myself by cooking them early – about an hour or two in advance – and then covering with foil (in the main to stop marauders, and I include myself here as they are dangerously pickable) and reheating at the last minute in a very hot oven, such as the one the potatoes will be roasting in later.

If the bacon's not very thin, it makes sense to roll it out: you can do this most efficiently by putting lots of slices on some plastic wrap on the kitchen surface, covering with another layer of wrap, and rolling with your rolling pin. Half a slice is plenty for one little sausage.

Cooking 50 of them may seem over the top, but these get snaffled up (especially by children) faster and more greedily than you could believe. You can see these little beauties nestling around the turkey on p.114.

Serves 10–16 as part of the Christmas feast, or 8–10 if not

25 thin slices streaky bacon, or 50 very thin slices pancetta
50 skinny, breakfast sausage links or small chipolatas (see Suppliers p.267)
approx. 3 tablespoons vegetable oil

❉ Preheat the oven to 400°F; though if I'm doing this much earlier and don't need the oven at this temperature anyway, I cook them for 40–45 minutes at 350°F. Twist each sausage in the center to form 2 cocktail-size sausages and snip with scissors on the twist to separate them.

❉ Make sure your bacon is thin enough to be unbulkily pliable and if not, roll out to make thinner, then cut each slice of bacon in half vertically. Wrap each fine half-slice of bacon round each cocktail sausage; there's no need to firm with a toothpick, as I've never had any unraveling. The bacon, when thin, seems to get sticky and adheres dutifully to its sausage.

❉ Spoon the oil into a roasting pan and arrange the sausages, each with the end bit of bacon down (though they may roll), and roast for 30 minutes or so, until the bacon is crisp and the sausages cooked. The only way to be sure is to make the ultimate sacrifice and taste one.

❉ Take out of the oven and wrap the pan in aluminum foil. If you've let the sausages burn a little, however, it may be better to remove them to a large piece of aluminum foil and wrap them in it, forming a loose but tightly sealed package; otherwise the sausages will continue to fry a little in the pan.

❉ When you are almost ready to eat, reheat the sausages by posting the foil-wrapped pan, or parcel, in a hot oven for about 10 minutes. Or cook them from scratch about 45 minutes before you need them.

MAKE AHEAD TIP:
Roll the chipolatas in bacon, as directed, cover and keep in the refrigerator for up to 2 days ahead. Cook in the oven as directed.

FREEZE AHEAD TIP:
Freeze the bacon-wrapped chipolatas in sealable bags for up to 3 months. Thaw overnight in the refrigerator. Cook in the oven as directed.

THE MAIN EVENT

PERFECT ROAST POTATOES

Serves 10–16 as part of the Christmas feast, or 8–10 if not

2 cups goose fat
6 lbs potatoes, such as Yukon Gold
2 tablespoons semolina

Needs must and all that, so I have always been an open anti-perfectionist, but in truth (and I'm sorry to repeat what I've said before) it is impossible to cook roast potatoes without needing them to be perfect, which to me means sweet and soft inside and a golden-brown carapace of crunch without. And, strangely, no matter how many tricky things you may succeed at in cooking, no matter what techniques you may master, nothing gives quite the contented glow of achievement that cooking a good tray of roast potatoes does.

Unfortunately there is concomitant decline when you feel you've failed. The brutal truth is that you either get it right or you don't, and anything less than perfect is a disappointment.

There are three crucial things that I think make the difference: the first is the heat of the fat – if it's not searingly hot, you don't stand a chance, and since goose fat has a very high smoking point and tastes good, it is my annual choice here; the second is the size of your potatoes – you want them relatively small, so that the ratio of crunchy outside to fluffy interior is optimized; and, finally, I think dredging the potatoes – and this is a family practice, inherited through the maternal line – in semolina rather than flour after parboiling, then really rattling the saucepan around to make the potatoes a bit mashed on the surface so they catch more in the hot fat, is a major aid.

❋ Preheat the oven to 500°F. If you don't have a double oven, you will have to do this as soon as the turkey is out of your single oven, which, for me, is very much later than the parboiling stage.

❋ Put the fat into a large roasting pan and then into the oven to heat up, and get frighteningly hot; 20–30 minutes should do it.

❋ Peel the potatoes, and cut each one into thirds by cutting off each end at a slant so that you are left with a wedge or triangle in the middle.

❋ Put the potatoes into salted, cold water in a saucepan, and bring to a boil, letting them cook for 4 minutes.

❋ Drain the potatoes in a colander, then tip them back into the empty, dry saucepan, and sprinkle the semolina over.

❋ Shake the potatoes around to coat them well and, with the lid clamped on, give the saucepan a good shake and the potatoes a proper bashing so that their edges fuzz and blur a little: this facilitates the crunch effect later. I leave them to rest at this stage. If you don't, you'll need to have preheated the oven earlier!

MAKE AHEAD TIP:
Peel the potatoes the day before. Keep submerged, whole, in cold water in a cold place. Drain, cut and cover with fresh, salted water to parboil and then roast as directed.

THE MAIN EVENT **129**

❋ When the fat is as hot as it can be, tip the semolina-coated potatoes carefully into it (they splutter terrifically as you put them in) and roast in the oven for an hour or until they are darkly golden and crispy, turning them over halfway through cooking.

❋ If the oven's hot enough, they may well not need more than about 25 minutes a side; but it's better to let them sit in the oven (you can always pour off most of the fat) till the very last minute.

❋ When everything else is served up, transfer the potatoes to a large (warmed if possible) serving dish and bring to the table with pride in your heart.

MAPLE-ROAST PARSNIPS

Serves 10–16 as part of the Christmas feast, or 8–10 if not

2 lbs parsnips
1/2 cup vegetable oil
1/3 cup maple syrup

These used to be, until about three years ago, honey-roast parsnips, but I prefer the less intense sweetness, the smokier richness, of the maple syrup. Added to which, being runnier, the syrup makes a better, and lighter, coating for the nips. I have got a bit lazier, too: when cooking them in the very hot potato oven, I used to parboil the parsnips first and then cook them in the higher heat for 15 minutes. Now, I don't parboil, and I don't even peel. I find they are fine, and won't burn in the potato oven, so long as they are given about 10 minutes less time, plus are lower down in the oven and cut as uniformly as you can. I make sure the thick parts of the parsnip are thinly sliced and leave the thin part long and straggly. Nevertheless, do keep an eye on things and don't leave them in the oven for longer than they need.

❋ It seems foolish to say "preheat the oven," when it's frankly going to be on anyway, but if you were cooking these to go alongside, say, some cold, leftover turkey, then you need a hottish oven, say 400°F, and would need to cook them for around 35 minutes. If you're using the potato oven, 20–25 minutes should be fine.

❋ Halve the parsnips crossways, then halve or quarter each piece lengthways, so that you have a bundle of spindly, shard-like lengths. Cut any thick part into a thinner – rather than square – chunk.

❋ Put these fawn twigs of parsnip straight into a roasting pan, pour the oil over, smoosh them about and then dribble the maple syrup over them and roast until tender and stickily brown.

❋ Be careful as you taste to test: the sugar content of the parsnips, more even than the syrup, make these blisteringly hot.

MAKE AHEAD TIP:
Cut the parsnips into lengths the day before and keep in the refrigerator in a sealable bag.

CHRISTMAS SPROUTS

Serves 10–16 as part of the Christmas feast, or 8–10 if not

3 1/4 lbs Brussels sprouts
1 cup ready-cooked chestnuts from a jar or can
1 stick (8 tablespoons) butter
fresh nutmeg
kosher or table salt and freshly ground pepper to taste

This is the absolute basic, non-negotiable version of my Christmas sprouts. They need to be buttery, and they need crumbled, sweet chestnuts. I get my chestnuts in vacuum-sealed packs or jars. My mother, against all her instincts, always roasted and peeled her own chestnuts, but then again, my mother always cried on Christmas Eve.

But if this is my basic version, there are many variants on the same theme. For my Pancetta Sprouts I start off (before the chestnuts) with 1 1/2 cups pancetta cubes, fried in 2 teaspoons of vegetable oil, so that the chestnuts are softened in bacon fat (to which I add 2 tablespoons of butter) and then splosh in 1/4 cup marsala and let it bubble away to become a thick syrup before returning the drained sprouts to the pan along with 2 handfuls of chopped Italian flat-leaf parsley. For my Pecan Sprouts, I slice 4 fat or 6 thin scallions and soften them in 2 teaspoons of garlic oil before adding the butter and chestnuts, then the drained, cooked sprouts, plus 1 cup toasted chopped pecans for the final tossing together, keeping some to sprinkle over. And for my Bean Sprouts, as it were, I throw 1/2 pound trimmed green beans, in short lengths, into the big pan once the sprouts have had a minute's bubbling and then carry on as for my basic Christmas Sprouts, but add the zest and juice of a lemon when the sprouts and beans are united with the buttery chestnuts; once the lemon juice has bubbled and reduced by about half, I decant and turn the mix, in the serving dish, in a drizzled tablespoon of best-quality olive oil. So, I like to play sometimes, but it's for pleasure not necessity: the sprouts here simply say Christmas.

❄ Bring a large saucepan of water to the boil for the sprouts, adding salt once it boils.

❄ Cut the stalk-end off the sprouts, just a thin slice, and let the outer blowsier leaves fall away. If you have any large sprouts, cut an "X" in the bottom, so that they cook at the same time as the smaller ones do.

❄ Roughly chop or break the chestnuts so that some are cut in two, some in three; you don't need them whole but nor do you want mealy rubble. Plus, they'll break up further as they get turned in the butter.

❄ Cook the sprouts lightly, in the salted boiling water, for 5 minutes or so, then drain them. You don't want these mushy: you need them tight and nutty.

❄ Melt the butter – either in the pan the sprouts were cooked in, or in a braising pan that you can serve them in – then toss in the chestnuts to warm through and add the cooked, drained sprouts.

MAKE AHEAD TIP:
Trim the sprouts the day before and keep in the refrigerator in a sealable bag.

❄ Add fresh nutmeg and salt and pepper to taste, then coat well with the butter in the pan before turning out into a warmed dish, or serving in your braising pan.

132   THE MAIN EVENT

OPPOSITE: Christmas Sprouts
ABOVE FRONT: Pancetta Sprouts; BACK LEFT: Pecan Sprouts; BACK RIGHT: Bean Sprouts

THE MAIN EVENT **133**

BUTTERNUT ORZOTTO

Serves 10–16 as part of the Christmas feast, or 8–10 if not

1 butternut squash, approx. 2 lbs unprepared weight
1/4 cup olive oil or garlic oil
1 teaspoon ground mace
1 onion, peeled and finely chopped
2 1/2 cups pearl or pot barley
1/2 cup dry vermouth, or white wine
5 cups hot vegetable broth, plus more for reheating
1 cup mascarpone cheese
1/2 cup pine nuts
1 teaspoon finely chopped fresh sage, plus a few small leaves
salt and pepper

MAKE AHEAD TIP:
Leave the cooked squash, mascarpone and barley mixture, covered, in the refrigerator for up to 3 days. Reheat as directed. Toast the pine nuts up to 3 days ahead and keep in a sealable bag.

Let me first explain what I mean by "orzotto": *orzo* is the Italian word for barley; so an orzotto is a risotto that is cooked with *orzo* rather than *riso*.

Now, in the normal run of things, a risotto made with barley rather than rice would have disadvantages, chiefly that you wouldn't get that desirable, stickily binding starch emanating from the grains (due to their relative gluten content), so you wouldn't end up with a squishy risotto texture. But I use the barley for a reason: unlike proper risotto, orzotto can be made in advance and, indeed, seems to benefit from it. Stirring a risotto for visiting vegetarians at the same time as plating up Christmas lunch would be impossible: this one's easy. And it's very, very good: all you need to do is add a little mascarpone to the pan as it reheats, and tinker a little. Although I made this last Christmas for altruistic reasons, it became a truly self-serving exercise: I had three helpings.

❋ Preheat the oven to 425°F and slice the butternut, remove the seeds and cut into approx. 1-inch cubes. I don't peel it, but you do need a big knife and a bit of brute force (and bravery).

❋ Tumble the butternut cubes out onto a shallow sheet pan (I use a jelly roll pan) with 2 tablespoons of the oil and half a teaspoon of the ground mace, and swoosh about to slick all the pieces before roasting for about 40–50 minutes, or until tender. Some of the butternut, chiefly the skin sides, will be scorched and caramelized: this is a good thing.

❋ Meanwhile, gently cook the chopped onion for about 10 minutes in the remaining oil. I do this in my wide, shallow round cast-iron braiser (about 5-quart capacity) that I'm going to serve it in the next day.

❋ Turn up the heat to medium, add the barley to the onion, and stir for about 2 minutes, turning the barley in the mixture, then turn the heat up to high, add the vermouth or wine and let it bubble down a bit.

❋ Add the hot vegetable broth (unlike with a risotto, there is no need to add the liquid gradually and cautiously), put a lid on the pan and let the orzotto cook gently for about 30 minutes, or until done but still nubbly. In a narrower, slightly deeper pan, this could take 40 minutes and you might have to stir midway through.

❋ When the squash is tender, take it out of the oven and put half of it (judging by eye only) in a blender with half the mascarpone, and liquidize. Stir this into

134 THE MAIN EVENT

the cooked barley and season to taste. You can leave for a day or for up to 3 days at this stage.

❄ On reheating (or straightaway if you're not doing any of this in advance), add the remaining mascarpone plus, if needed, some fairly weak vegetable broth (the longer the orzotto stands in advance, the thicker it will be so the more liquid you will need to add), along with the remaining squash cubes and mace. Stir gently but firmly and reheat; this should take about 15 minutes on a gentle heat, with the lid on.

❄ While the orzotto is reheating, or when it is hot (a few minutes on the stove top but off the heat, with the lid clamped on, won't hurt it), toast the pine nuts by tossing them in a hot, dry frying pan until they turn deep gold.

❄ Stir half the pine nuts into the orzotto and scatter the remaining half, along with the chopped sage, on top. Garnish with a few sage leaves.

RED BEET ORZOTTO

This is my favored Christmas orzotto variant, which I wouldn't actually serve with the turkey first time around (though it's fantastic alongside cold turkey and generally breathes glamorous life into any meal of cold leftovers) but have done with goose (perfect, if you're willing to go without the red cabbage) and would love it with pork, too. I put it here simply because the ingredients, but not the method, vary (other than missing out the roasting stage, as cooked red beets are used). It is a satellite recipe and needs to be near the Mother Ship.

❄ Cook the onions and barley as in steps 2 and 3 for the butternut orzotto, opposite; the only point of difference is that you add the teaspoon of dried thyme when the onion has softened.

❄ Liquidize half the beet cubes with half the sour cream in a blender, then stir into the cooked barley. When it is all mixed (and somewhere between puce and

Serves 10–16 as part of a feast, or 8–10 if not

1 onion, peeled and chopped
2 $\frac{1}{2}$ cups pearl or pot barley
2 tablespoons olive oil or garlic oil
1 teaspoon dried thyme
$\frac{1}{2}$ cup Noilly Prat or other dry vermouth, or white wine
5 cups vegetable broth, plus more for reheating
1 lb beets (cooked, not in vinegar), diced into $\frac{1}{2}$-inch cubes
$\frac{2}{3}$ cup sour cream, plus more for serving if wished
$\frac{1}{2}$ cup chopped pecans
3 tablespoons chopped chives

ABOVE:
Red Beet Orzotto (back);
Butternut Orzotto (front)

MAKE AHEAD TIP:
Leave the cooked onion, barley and (half) the beet mixture, covered, in the refrigerator for up to 3 days. Finish and reheat as directed.

magenta) you may put it aside for the time being if reheating later, or carry on.

❋ When reheating (or not), add the remaining beet cubes and sour cream, plus boiling water or weak broth to thin it down if necessary. As this beet variation yields less bulk than the butternut, you may find further liquid unnecessary.

❋ Toast the chopped pecans, as you do the pine nuts on p.135, and, before giving the orzotto one final stir, sprinkle with nuts and chives. If you wanted to, you could let everyone dollop a little sour cream on their serving of bright and sweet orzotto, too.

136 THE MAIN EVENT

ULTIMATE CHRISTMAS PUDDING

I don't deny it: there is something unattractively boastful about calling one's own recipe "ultimate." But having soaked my dried fruit for this pudding in Pedro Ximénez – the sweet, dark, sticky sherry that has a hint of licorice, fig and molasses about it – I know there is no turning back. It's not even as if it's an extravagance: the rum or brandy I've used up till now are more expensive and do the trick less well. This is sensational. I love the same fruits, too, steeped in the magic liqueur (see p.227), but this here is the Queen of Christmas puddings. It has to be tried, and clamors to be savored.

I know that many of you, tradition be damned, are resistant to Christmas pudding, and I do understand why. But you must try this. For until you do, you probably think all that dried fruit is, well, dry, and the pudding heavy. Yet this is far from the case: the fruit is moist and sticky, and the pudding mystifyingly, meltingly light.

A note on Christmas pudding generally, though I admit it's not my first foray into this; traditions, even if not followed to the letter, can't be wholly dispensed with just because they have lost their novelty – that is precisely their point. So, faithful readers, please forgive my ageing-lecturer style repetitiveness here. Traditionally, you should have all the family in the kitchen as you make your pudding, each one giving a stir in turn, the youngest first and going upwards in age. To honor the three kings, you are meant to stir from east to west, but I don't have a compass and am not good enough at geography to work that one out. Stir-up Sunday, when we are supposed to make our puddings, falls near the end of November, on the Sunday before Advent, and is – as I've told some of you before – a religious rather than a culinary injunction, as in "Stir up, we beseech thee, O Lord, the wills of thy faithful people." But personally I have never managed to make my puddings quite so efficiently in advance.

Some cooks like to use only 13 ingredients, symbolizing Jesus and his apostles, but a little bit of superstition enters in as well, since charms were traditionally included in the mix: a thimble, to suggest that whoever found it in their portion would stay a spinster, a coin to indicate riches, a ring to signify a wedding on the horizon, and so on. These days you'd be hard put to find such charms, though I own some pretty ancient ones. Clearly, we're just interested in money, as now it's coins that most of us bury in the pudding. (And some advice here: do clean them first; the best, if alarming way, is to soak them overnight in sugary cola. The Health & Safety recommendation is to wrap the coins in parchment paper even if they have been cleaned, but I unapologetically disobey. You must make up your own mind.)

There is still more than a whiff of the pagan about the pud: not only is each person meant to make a wish – superstition superseding faith – as they stir the mixture in advance; but the flaming of the pudding, as you serve it, is a nod to the pagan winter solstice celebration, in which fire and light and warmth are brought into our chill darkness.

THE MAIN EVENT 137

Serves 10–16 as part of the Christmas feast, or 8–10 if not

¼ cup currants

1 cup sultanas

1 cup roughly chopped pitted prunes

¾ cup Pedro Ximénez sherry (see Suppliers p.267)

¾ cup plus 2 tablespoons vegetable shortening, such as Crisco

⅔ cup all-purpose flour

2⅓ cups fresh breadcrumbs

¾ cup packed dark brown sugar

1 teaspoon ground cinnamon

¼ teaspoon ground cloves

1 teaspoon baking powder

grated zest of 1 lemon

3 eggs

1 medium Granny Smith apple, peeled and grated

2 tablespoons honey

sprig of holly to decorate

½ cup vodka to flame

Eggnog Cream (see p.140) to serve

1½-quart Pyrex mixing bowl

And to reiterate the little English history lesson I gave in *Feast*, actually, the Christmas pudding was once seen as a religious affront. Oliver Cromwell banned it as a "lewd custom," dismissing the rich pudding as "unfit for God-fearing people," and the Quakers magnificently condemned it as "the invention of the scarlet whore of Babylon." I used to fear that the Quakers made Christmas pudding sound more exciting than it is, so I've long done my bit to come up with a pudding that the scarlet whore of Babylon would be truly proud of. I don't recant any earlier recipes, but this one, definitively, is it.

❋ Although I stipulate a capacious 1½-quart bowl, and cannot extol the utter gloriousness of this pud too much, I know that you're unlikely to get through most of it, even half of it, at one sitting. But I like the grand, pride-instilling size of this, plus it's wonderful on following days, microwaved in portions after or between meals, with leftover Eggnog Cream, or fried in butter and eaten with vanilla ice cream for completely off-the-chart, midnight-munchy feasts. But it wouldn't be out of the question – and it would certainly be in the spirit of the season – to make up the entire quantity of mixture, and share between smaller basins – a 1 quart one for you, a ½-quart one to give away. Three hours' steaming both first and second time around should do it; just keep the one pudding for yourself, and give the other to a friend, after it's had its first steaming, and is cool, with the steaming instructions for Christmas Day.

❋ Put the currants, sultanas and chopped prunes into a bowl with the Pedro Ximénez, swirl the bowl a bit, then cover with plastic wrap and leave to steep overnight or for up to 1 week. Put the vegetable shortening in the freezer overnight.

❋ When the fruits have had their steeping time, put a large pan of water on to boil, or heat some water in a conventional steamer, and butter your Pyrex mixing bowl. Grate the shortening on the coarse side of a box grater and return to the freezer while you measure out the other ingredients.

❋ In a large mixing bowl combine all the remaining pudding ingredients and mix either in the traditional manner or any old how, until there are no large lumps of vegetable shortening, though you should see small flecks.

❋ Add the steeped fruits, scraping in every last drop of liquor with a rubber spatula, and mix to combine thoroughly, then fold in cola-cleaned coins or heirloom charms. If you are at all frightened about choking-induced fatalities at the table, do leave out the hardware.

❉ Scrape and press the mixture into the prepared Pyrex bowl, squish it down and wrap in a layer of aluminum foil, followed by a layer of plastic wrap and a second layer of foil, so that the bowl is watertight, then *either* put the bowl in the pan of boiling water (to come halfway up the bowl) *or* in the top of a lidded steamer (this size of bowl happens to fit perfectly in the top of my all-purpose pot) and steam for 5 hours, checking every now and again that the water hasn't bubbled away.

❉ When it's had its 5 hours, remove gingerly (you don't want to burn yourself) and, when manageable, unwrap the foil and plastic wrap. Put a circle of parchment paper over the surface of the pudding then wrap tightly in foil and put the pudding in its basin somewhere out of the way in the kitchen or, if you're lucky enough, a larder, until Christmas Day.

❉ On the big day, rewrap the pudding (still in its bowl) in extra plastic wrap and foil and steam again, this time for 3 hours. Eight hours' combined cooking time might seem a waste of time, but it's not as if you need to *do* anything to it in that time. And by the way, when I give it its Christmas Day steaming, I sit it in the bottom of my pan, in the water, and steam the Chocolate Sponge Pudding (see p.140) in the top part of my steamer.

❉ To serve, remove from the pan or steamer, unwrap and remove the parchment paper, put a plate on top, turn it upside down and give the bowl a little shake to help unmold the pudding. Then remove the bowl – and *voilà*, the Massively Matriarchal Mono-Mammary is revealed. (Did I forget to mention the Freudian lure of the pudding beyond its pagan and Christian heritage?)

❉ Put the sprig of holly on top of the dark, mutely gleaming pudding, then heat the vodka in a small pan (I use my cute little copper butter-melting pan) and the minute it's hot, but before it boils – you don't want the alcohol to burn off before you attempt to flambé it – turn off the heat, strike a match, stand back and light the pan of vodka, then pour the flaming vodka over the pudding and take it as fast as you safely can to your guests. If it feels less dangerous to you (I am a liability and you might well be wiser not to follow my devil-may-care instructions), pour the hot vodka over the pudding and then light the pudding. In either case, don't worry if the holly catches alight; I have never known it to be anything but singed.

❉ Serve with the Eggnog Cream, overleaf, which you can easily make – it's the work of undemanding moments – while the pudding's steaming.

MAKE AHEAD TIP:
Make the Christmas pudding up to 6 weeks ahead. Keep in a cool, dark place, then proceed as recipe on Christmas Day.

FREEZE AHEAD TIP:
Make and freeze the Christmas pudding for up to 1 year ahead. Thaw overnight at room temperature and proceed as recipe on Christmas Day.

EGGNOG CREAM

1½ cups heavy cream
½ cup advocaat liqueur

The traditional sauce for Christmas pudding is a "hard sauce," that's to say, brandy butter (and do make either the brandy butter, rum butter or, even better here, the bourbon butter, on p.190) but I can't help feeling that this corner-cutting Eggnog Cream, devised for my *Express* festivities last year, is best of all.

Actually, Dom, my long-suffering TV director, does a version of this with brandy, which also hits the spot (I think the cool cream factor is key), though you will need to whip in a tablespoonful or two of confectioners' sugar – no more – as you go. And, you know, you might well consider the Cointreau Cream (see headnote p.183) to dollop alongside the pudding as a variation, too.

❉ Put the cream into a bowl and, using an electric whisk, start whipping to aerate and thicken. While it's still floppy, whisk in the advocaat, and once the yolk-yellow, eggnog-flavored liqueur is combined and the cream thick but still soft, stop and spatula into a generous bowl and serve with the pudding.

CHOCOLATE SPONGE PUDDING FOR CHRISTMAS PUDDING HATERS WITH HOT CHOCOLATE SAUCE

Christmas pudding isn't for everyone and, even though I have faith in my pudding's ability to convert, there's no point nagging or, indeed, fighting against real, die-hard antipathies. Besides, I have never met a child who likes Christmas pudding, and it seems unfair not to give a treat to everyone. The joy of this is that you can mix it all up in a processor while the Christmas pudding's in mid-steam (I dash into the kitchen in the middle of lunch to do just that, with ingredients measured out and ready, and bowl prepared) then put it into the top part of the steamer, while the Christmas pud steams in the bottom part. Obviously, you can steam it in a separate pan if you want.

Whatever, don't be put off by having to steam another pudding. It's easier than trying to juggle to find oven space, and, actually, what makes the chocolate pudding Christmassy is that it looks like the traditional pudding (I've never gone in for those round, cannonball molds). Steaming two puddings is really no harder than steaming one. But if you feel you can't be doing with making 2 puddings, keep children happy by providing good store-bought vanilla ice cream and red-white-and-green seasonal sprinkles to be scattered over at gleefully garish will.

THE MAIN EVENT 141

Serves 10–16 as part of the Christmas feast, or 8–10 if not

FOR THE SPONGE:
1 cup plus 2 tablespoons all-purpose flour
1 teaspoon vanilla extract
¼ cup unsweetened cocoa powder
heaping ¾ cup sugar
1½ sticks (12 tablespoons) soft butter
¼ cup buttermilk
3 eggs
2 teaspoons baking powder
½ teaspoon bicarbonate soda
1½-quart Pyrex mixing bowl

FOR THE SAUCE:
¾ cup milk chocolate chips
¾ cup bittersweet chocolate chips
1 cup heavy cream
¼ cup light corn syrup
4 teaspoons vanilla extract

❋ Butter your heat-proof Pyrex mixing bowl. Make sure you have adequate boiling water in a pan (or a conventional steamer) on the stovetop to steam the sponge.

❋ Put the flour and cocoa powder into a processor and blitz to get rid of any lumps.

❋ Add all the remaining sponge ingredients to the processor and blitz, for longer this time, to mix. Take the lid off, scrape it down, then put the lid back on for 3 more long pulses. Scrape the chocolate batter into the prepared bowl, smooth it down (the batter will come only halfway up the bowl) and wrap the bowl, first, in parchment paper, then in a layer of aluminum foil, followed by a layer of plastic wrap and a second layer of foil, so no water could possibly get in. Steam in the boiling water in the pan or steamer for 1½ hours (by which time the sponge will have risen to about 1½ inches below the lip). To cook it for longer will do no harm.

❋ To make the sauce, which can easily be done before you eat, and reheated just before you serve the pudding, put all the sauce ingredients into a saucepan and place over a gentle heat to melt, stirring every now and again and then whisking, off the heat, at the very end, to combine smoothly.

❋ When the sponge is ready, remove it carefully from the pan or steamer without burning yourself, then unwrap from its foil and plastic wrap casing. Put a plate, or a stand, with a slight lip, on top, flip both upside down, so plate and sponge are the right way up, and wiggle off the bowl.

❋ Pour some hot sauce over the sponge, so that it just covers the top and falls in glossy, licking drips down the side, and pour the rest of the sauce into a jug or bowl to be served with a spoon.

MAKE AHEAD TIP:
Measure all the sponge ingredients the day before, ready to whiz together.
Make the chocolate sauce up to 1 week ahead, then cool and chill until needed, reheating gently on the stovetop or in the microwave.

FREEZE AHEAD TIP:
Make and freeze the chocolate sauce for up to 3 months, and reheat as above.

THOUGHTS FOR TURKEY LEFTOVERS

I have already greedily mentioned your options for leftover Christmas pudding; though the chocolate pudding is frankly good for nothing – unless you're truly desperate – once it's grown cold.

But with the turkey, and all those gorgeous bits that go alongside, the possibilities for fabulous leftover meals bring joy to my heart. My first suggestions are obvious, but I can't ignore them all the same. (And remember that your turkey – the carcass or the remaining meat stripped off it – must go in the refrigerator as soon as possible after Christmas lunch.) There are few things that can beat a leftover Christmas lunch sandwich: cold stuffing, cold turkey, cranberry and bread sauces, with some English mustard, and perhaps mayonnaise for those who can't contemplate a sandwich without it, or mango chutney for me, pressed between 2 slices of proper, white bread.

In fact, I relish any meal that's made up of cold cuts: I'll take turkey with ham (hence my insistence on the ham for Christmas Eve supper) and an array of chutneys, a jar of cornichons, some strong cheese, fresh bread and any of the salads from Seasonal Salads (see pp.56–59) or simply some astringently dressed green leaves and a bowl of tomatoes, for people to pluck and slice as they go; and maybe bake some potatoes to go with them, should alcohol consumption seem to demand more carbohydrates. Of course, you can provide one of the soups from pp.50–55 of the same chapter to start with, to ring the changes or to make the meal feel more like a dinner; or produce a sprightly lunch by doing a turkey version of the Tortilla Soup on p.55 (using chicken broth just the same, or making turkey broth if you prefer), complete with its easily assembled accompaniments.

However, there are some recipes – the first new, the others older standbys which have appeared before but can't be missed out here – that I feel I have to suggest less sketchily. Please don't feel bound by the measurements or, indeed, the additional ingredients, in any way: leftover-sourced meals are by their nature provisional.

TURKEY PILAFF WITH POMEGRANATE AND DILL

WILD RICE, TURKEY, CRANBERRY AND PECAN SALAD

TURKEY AND GLASS NOODLE SALAD

ED'S VICTORIOUS TURKEY HASH

THE MAIN EVENT 143

TURKEY PILAFF WITH POMEGRANATE AND DILL

Serves 4–6

2 cups brown basmati rice
2 cups shredded cooked turkey
1/2 cup strong chicken broth (not needed if eating cold as a salad)
1/4 cup chopped dill
seeds from 1 pomegranate, or 1/2 cup pomegranate seeds from a container
2 teaspoons lemon juice
2 teaspoons extra virgin olive, or canola oil
1/3 cup roasted sunflower seeds
salt and pepper (I like to use seasoned salt such as Jane's Krazy Mixed Up Salt, see Suppliers p.267)

❋ Cook the rice either in a rice cooker or in a saucepan according to the instructions on the bag.

❋ Put the shredded turkey in a generous-sized saucepan with the chicken broth. Bring to the boil and bubble gently for 1–2 minutes until piping hot.

❋ Drain the rice and transfer to a large bowl or dish, add the contents of the turkey pan and fork through to mix.

❋ Add the chopped dill and most of the pomegranate seeds, reserving some to sprinkle over the finished dish, and fork through again.

❋ Dress with the lemon juice, and a little oil, then scatter with the sunflower seeds, fork through again, and check for seasoning.

❋ Sprinkle with the remaining pomegranate seeds to decorate.

❋ If you happen to have leftover rice, this makes a great salad, but obviously you won't need the broth component: just mix all the other ingredients, cold, in the same ratio (when cooked, brown basmati increases its volume by $2^{1}/_{4}$, if that helps with the rough math), and serve. Incidentally, this is a perennial possibility if made with leftover chicken; there's not a week I don't roast at least one.

WILD RICE, TURKEY, CRANBERRY AND PECAN SALAD

Serves 6–8

3 cups wild rice
1/2 cup dried cranberries
4 cups cold cooked turkey, diced or shredded
2 tablespoons cranberry sauce or jelly
2 tablespoons lime juice
1/4 cup olive oil
1/2 cup halved pecans or pecan pieces
handful of parsley, chopped

❋ Cook the rice according to the instructions on the bag, and let it go cold. Always cool rice quickly; the best way is to turn it out into a large shallow dish.

❋ Add the dried cranberries and diced turkey to the cold, cooked rice.

❋ Make a dressing by whisking together the cranberry sauce (or jelly), lime juice and oil.

❋ Toss the dressing through the rice, cranberries and turkey. Add the halved pecans (or the pecan pieces) to the salad with most of the parsley, turn out onto a plate or into a serving dish, fork again to mix, then sprinkle with the remaining parsley.

TURKEY AND GLASS NOODLE SALAD

❊ First make the marinade/dressing by mixing all the dressing ingredients together. (This is very useful as a dipping sauce, or just as a dressing even if you're not going in for the glass noodles and so forth.)

❊ To make the salad, marinate the turkey strips in $1/2$ cup of the dressing; while this is going on soak the noodles in freshly boiled water (from a kettle) and, once rehydrated (see instructions on the bag), refresh the noodles in cold water, then drain.

❊ Put the sugar snaps and beansprouts into a colander and pour some more freshly boiled water over them.

❊ Rinse them with cold water and drain – by shaking the colander – so they're not dripping wet.

❊ In a large bowl, mix the marinated turkey strips, and the dressing they're in, with the drained noodles, scallions, sugar snaps and beansprouts.

❊ Dress with the oils and taste to see if you want to add more dressing.

❊ Sprinkle the chopped cilantro over and toss everything together well before arranging on a large plate.

Serves 4–6

FOR THE DRESSING:
2 cloves garlic, minced or crushed
2 fresh long red chiles, seeded and finely diced
2 tablespoons finely minced ginger
$1/4$ cup fish sauce (nam pla)
juice of 1 lime
$1/4$ cup water
2 tablespoons superfine sugar

FOR THE SALAD:
$2 1/2$ cups shredded cold turkey
6 oz glass noodles (also called fine rice vermicelli)
$1 1/2$ cups sugar snap peas
2 cups beansprouts
3 scallions, sliced into thin circles
2 teaspoons peanut oil
1 teaspoon sesame oil
large handful fresh cilantro leaves, finely chopped

Turkey Pilaff with Pomegranate and Dill

Wild Rice, Turkey, Cranberry and Pecan Salad

MAKE AHEAD TIP:
The dressing can be made and kept in a tightly sealed jar in the refrigerator for up to 2 weeks.

THE MAIN EVENT

ED'S VICTORIOUS TURKEY HASH

Serves 2 hungry people as a main course, or 4 with a baked potato and a green salad to go alongside

1/3 cup sliced almonds
1 tablespoon butter
2 tablespoons olive oil
1 onion, peeled and chopped
2 red bell peppers, seeded and chopped into approx. 1/2 x 3/4-inch pieces
1 clove garlic, peeled and minced
2 cups shredded cold turkey
2/3 cup pitted black olives
2 tablespoons sour cream
2 tablespoons leftover turkey broth
1 egg
few dashes of Tabasco sauce, or to taste
heaping 3/4 cup shaved Parmesan cheese
1–2 tablespoons chopped Italian flat-leaf parsley to garnish (optional)

This turkey hash recipe, given to me by my friend and agent, Ed Victor, and in charmingly bossy letter form, has been a recurring feature in my books. Why drop it now of all times? Not least, of course, because it is a real winner.

I've given it here as an actual recipe but, as with all these notions for leftovers, the quantities are meant to be a guide only. They are more of the "a handful of this, a handful of that" school of cookery, and that's how it should be.

Anyway, this is my adaptation of the Victor Original: I've fiddled a bit, but remained essentially faithful, as, indeed, I will always be to him.

❋ Toss the sliced almonds in a hot, dry skillet over a medium to high heat until toasted. Remove to a plate for a while.

❋ Add the butter and oil to the skillet, then throw in the chopped onions and peppers and cook, stirring, over a medium to low heat for about 10 minutes.

❋ Stir in the garlic, then add the shredded turkey and cook until piping hot.

❋ Return the reserved toasted sliced almonds to the pan, add the olives and mix in.

❋ Whisk together the sour cream, turkey broth and egg, then pour into the pan, give a quick stir to combine and shake in the Tabasco sauce.

❋ Finally, add the shaved Parmesan and stir until it begins to melt into the hash.

❋ On serving, sprinkle with chopped parsley, if wished.

THE MAIN EVENT 147

148 THE MAIN EVENT

FOUR ALTERNATIVES TO CHRISTMAS TURKEY

THE GOOSE OPTION

ROAST GOOSE WITH PEAR AND CRANBERRY STUFFING
LIGHT GOOSE GRAVY
BACON-WRAPPED CHIPOLATAS (P.127)
PERFECT ROAST POTATOES (P.128)
CHRISTMAS SPROUTS (P.132)
RED CABBAGE WITH POMEGRANATE JUICE (P.60)
MY MOTHER'S BREAD SAUCE (P.121)
PRODIGIOUS PAVLOVA (P.45)

ROAST GOOSE WITH PEAR AND CRANBERRY STUFFING

It's true that goose has the older pedigree as the traditional British Christmas roast, but if you are assembling in large numbers, it isn't actually feasible. This bird has such a large carcass which means that one only just fits in an oven and won't feed many more than 6, though with all the trimmings, it will probably stretch to 8–10. What the trimmings are, is up to you, of course, though I've suggested a similar line-up to the turkey's. I also suggest, unless there are 6 or fewer of you, that you don't reduce their portions; this way, if you wanted to be sure to feed 10 with a meat-mean goose, you probably could. It's just that I start panicking unless I make too much food for everyone, but I do know in my heart of hearts that 2 small slices of meat is plenty when the plate's piled high with stuffing, roast potatoes, sausages, bread sauce, sprouts and red cabbage.

Nevertheless, the disadvantage of the large carcass yields some positive returns, namely that you can fit in a lot of stuffing. And I do actually stuff the bird, as I no longer do my turkey, not least because a goose is so much easier to stuff than a turkey. And this sharp-sweet mix of grainy-fleshed dried pears and astringent cranberries – which becomes imbued with the flavor-deep juices of the goose as it cooks – is the perfect foil to the gorgeous richness of the dark meat.

If you have vegetarians coming, by all means make the Butternut Orzotto (p.134) to supplement, though I do love this with the Red Beet Orzotto (p.135);

Serves 6–8

FOR THE STUFFING:
1 lb (approx. 22) dried pears
1¾ cups cranberries, fresh or, if frozen, thawed
1 cup dried breadcrumbs
½ teaspoon ground cinnamon
¼ teaspoon ground cloves
1 teaspoon ground ginger
zest and pulpy juice of 1 clementine
1 onion, peeled and chopped
2 tablespoons maple syrup
1 cup pecans
1 tablespoon kosher salt or 1½ teaspoons table salt

FOR THE GOOSE:
1 x 11 lbs fresh goose

MAKE AHEAD TIP:
Make the stuffing up to 2 days ahead and keep in the refrigerator. Then bring to room temperature and stuff the bird as directed.

FREEZE AHEAD TIP:
Make and freeze the stuffing for up to 2 weeks. Thaw overnight in the refrigerator and stuff the bird as directed.

but, as mooted earlier, if you want to serve the beet version, you must be prepared to lose the red cabbage. There's only so much Seventies maroon the eye can appreciate at one table.

❊ Either soak the dried pears overnight in cold water, or pour boiling water over them and leave to cool; this will take 2–3 hours.

❊ Drain the pears and put them into a bowl along with the cranberries and breadcrumbs.

❊ Add the cinnamon, cloves, ginger and clementine zest and pulp.

❊ Stir in the chopped onion, maple syrup and pecans, and add the salt.

❊ Make sure everything is thoroughly mixed before you stuff the goose.

❊ Preheat your oven to 425°F.

❊ Remove any excess fat from the goose cavity – this can go towards your roast potatoes – and remove the neck and giblets, reserving them for the gravy.

❊ Stuff the cavity of the goose with the pear and cranberry stuffing and, once stuffed, wrap the goose skin over, securing with a skewer.

❊ Sit the stuffed goose on a wire rack in a fairly deep roasting pan, as the goose will give off a lot of fat as it cooks and you don't want spillage.

❊ Cook the goose for 3 hours (after about an hour, drain off the excess fat in the pan, and again every half hour or so).

❊ Remove to a board and carve judiciously.

LIGHT GOOSE GRAVY

I'll be honest, my first impulse to make an unthickened gravy came out of my fear of trying to fiddle about with the goose-roasting pan: I didn't think I'd ever be able to skim off the fat and find some intense juice. But once I tasted the goose broth I'd made, I realized it didn't matter. Nothing could improve the taste, and a thicker or richer gravy would be too much for the strong meat. Now, I feel it's almost worth getting a goose just to make this delicate but, at the same time, deeply flavored gravy. In fact, I may have to ask my butcher for as many goose giblets as he can spare, whenever he has them to hand. And don't throw away the liver, even though you don't need it here: unlike the turkey liver, this is well worth frying in butter and a few drops of garlic oil; add a glug of muscat wine (or sweet sherry if that's easier) once the liver's seared, then when it's cooked but still pink inside, wipe the pan out with some good brown toast, and squish the liver on top with a fork.

A final note: because you don't need the juices from the roast goose to make this lightest of gravies, you can make it ahead of the game, which I always find a boon.

Serves 8–10

neck and giblets of the goose (except the liver)
2 carrots, each snapped into 2 or 3
1 unpeeled onion, quartered
5 cloves unpeeled garlic
1 stalk celery, snapped into 4
generous bunch of parsley
1 1/2 teaspoons kosher salt or 3/4 teaspoon table salt
1 tablespoon whole peppercorns (white for choice, though black will do)
2 cardamom pods
5 cups water
1 tablespoon maple syrup

❄ Put all the ingredients into a wide saucepan, and bring to the boil, then turn down and leave on a low simmer for 1 hour.

❄ Taste the broth or, now, gravy; it should be pronounced but delicate. If your saucepan is narrow, the water won't evaporate as quickly, so you may need to give it another 20 minutes. Let taste be your guide.

❄ Strain the gravy, discarding all the solids, then pour some over the carved goose and put the rest in a warmed gravy boat to take to the table.

MAKE AHEAD TIP:
As soon as you have bought your goose, remove the giblets and make the gravy. Cool, cover and keep in the refrigerator for up to 2 days.

THE MAIN EVENT **151**

THOUGHTS FOR GOOSE LEFTOVERS

The most important thing to say is that unless you let any leftover goose sit in any leftover gravy (you may not have the former, but I'd be surprised if you didn't have some of the latter), the goose isn't really worth discussing from this point on. I don't know why it should be so, since goose is so fatty, but it seems to dry incredibly if it's left to get cold untended. But pick off any bits of meat that you possibly can, and bathe them in the broth as it cools, and you have joy ahead.

I'm a fan of the thus-steeped cold goose (taken out of the refrigerator for a while first so it's no longer at refrigerator-temperature) with no more than a cold roast potato or two and a pile of pickled red cabbage from a jar. And although I warned against color pile-up for the Main Event, I'm happy to add my Red Beet and Horseradish Sauce here (see p.68) even if it is tonally too much with the strands of red cabbage. Believe me, I am so grateful to find this gem (think ruby) of a no-cook, no-fuss but still sensational supper for one or two, that I am hardly going to start quibbling about the color palette on my plate.

Otherwise, you can make the Wild Rice, Cranberry and Pecan Salad on p.144, with goose in place of the turkey leftovers, but so rich is this meat that you may want to use much less goose in proportion to the wild rice.

I have only one recipe proper for leftover goose: a cassoulet, though admittedly a corner-cutting, quick-time version, that no doubt would not find favor in the cassoulet and goose region of France, but that keeps me happy on a cold night after a long day at Christmastime.

QUICK CASSOULET

Serves 2–4 (depending on hunger of eaters and what else is being eaten alongside)

smear of goose fat, plus 2 tbsp
2 x 15 oz cans cannellini beans, or any good-quality canned beans, drained and rinsed
2 chorizo sausages, 1/4 lb total
2 cups leftover goose, shredded
scant 1 cup leftover light goose gravy
1 tablespoon Armagnac, or brandy
1 cup fresh breadcrumbs (or enough to cover dish)

❊ Preheat your oven to 400°F and grease an oval gratin dish (approx. 10 inches long) with a little goose fat.

❊ Put the drained and well-rinsed beans into a large bowl.

❊ Cut the chorizo sausages into fat coins, then cut each coin in half, and add to the bowl, along with the goose meat.

❊ Put this mixture into the prepared dish, pour the broth and Armagnac (or brandy) over, and sprinkle with the breadcrumbs to cover the top.

❊ Finally, pour the 2 tbsp goose fat over and bake in the oven for 25 minutes – or until the crumbed top is golden and all is bubbling underneath.

❋ When cooked, the beans should have softened well in the liquid, though they won't have absorbed it: this cassoulet has a spoonable, generously gravied texture beneath the crisp crumb topping.

MAKE AHEAD TIP:
Assemble the cassoulet the day before, cover and keep in the refrigerator. Allow 30 minutes at room temperature before baking as recipe.

THE MAIN EVENT

154 THE MAIN EVENT

THE BEEF OPTION

ROAST RIB OF BEEF WITH PORT AND STILTON GRAVY
PERFECT ROAST POTATOES (P.128)
MAPLE-ROAST PARSNIPS (P.130)
CHRISTMAS SPROUTS (P.132)
BUTTERNUT ORZOTTO (P.134)
RED CABBAGE WITH POMEGRANATE JUICE (P.60)
RED BEET AND HORSERADISH SAUCE (P.68)
PECAN-PLUS PIE (P.205) WITH CRÈME FRAÎCHE AND VANILLA ICE CREAM

ROAST RIB OF BEEF WITH PORT AND STILTON GRAVY

There is something about a big rib of beef sitting proudly on its carving board at the table that makes that table, and those around it, so immediately celebratory. The extravagance of it, the ridiculous vastness of it: this is a proper, stand-up-and-clap feast.

The Port and Stilton Gravy, grapily aromatic and tangy, is the perfect festive foil to the juicy meat. Although its inspiration – the gloriousness of blue cheese melting on top of a steak from an American grill – is not in itself seasonal, port and Stilton are the essence of an English Christmas. Just the words "port and Stilton" make me hear the crackling of logs in the fire, smell the chestnuts roasting there, see twinkling tree lights and hear descanted carols. Too much? Maybe, but isn't that the whole point of this time of the year?

Serves 8 (with leftovers), 14 without

8 1/2 lbs beef standing rib roast (a 4-rib roast)

2 onions, peeled and cut into 1/2-inch rounds

2 tablespoons garlic oil

1 1/2 teaspoons kosher salt or 3/4 teaspoon table salt

1 teaspoon dried thyme

1/2 teaspoon cayenne pepper

❊ Take your beef out of the refrigerator to bring to room temperature, which could take an hour or possibly more, and preheat the oven to 425°F.

❊ Put the onion slices into a roasting pan and sit the rib of beef on top of them. Use the onion slices as props to help the rib sit up on its bones in an "L" shape.

❊ Smear the oil over the white fat of the rib, and sprinkle with the salt, thyme and cayenne pepper.

❊ Cook according to the beef's weight and your taste. I like my beef nice and rare, so I give it 15 minutes per pound, which means, for a roast this size, a cooking time of about 2 hours unless the beef's straight out of the refrigerator, in which case, add another 20 minutes or so. If you want medium beef, give the roast, from room temperature, 20 minutes per pound, and if you like well-done meat, 30 minutes per pound. As for feeding capacity, this size of roast will certainly look after a big tableful, from 8 with lots of leftovers to 14, without the definite promise of them.

❋ When the beef comes out of the oven, remove to a carving board and allow to rest in a warm part of the kitchen under a tent of aluminum foil for 30 minutes before carving; or just leave, tented in its pan, for the same time.

❋ Do not start cleaning up the pan, even if you have taken out the beef, however, as you will need some of the pan juices and onions for the gravy, below.

PORT AND STILTON GRAVY

2 tablespoons fatty juices, from the roast beef pan
1 tablespoon all-purpose flour
1/2 cup ruby port, plus 1 tablespoon
cooked onions from the roast beef pan (optional)
2 cups organic beef broth, from a carton
1 1/4 cups crumbled blue cheese
1 teaspoon red currant jelly
salt and pepper to taste
extra juices from the roasting pan and carving board

I love the mixture between rich, rounded ruby port and sharp, salty cheese. The onions, sweet and soft from the beef's roasting pan, add depth as well as texture if you liquidize them, in a blender (it doesn't work the same way in a processor) with the broth, which, in turn, is then combined with the port and Stilton.

But this Christmas gravy is good enough without, so if you don't feel like blending or your onions are too blackened from the pan, you can dispense with this step without cause for concern.

❋ Make a roux by adding the 2 tablespoons of fatty juices from the roasting pan to a saucepan, whisk in the flour, and then the 1/2 cup of port, and keep heating and whisking over a fairly gentle heat, until thick and bubbling.

❋ If you want to blend the onions and broth, do so now, by putting any but the blackened onions in the blender goblet with the beef broth, and liquidizing. Or leave the broth just as it is, straight out of the carton.

❋ Take the saucepan off the heat, and gradually whisk in the beef broth. When all the broth's added, put the pan back on the heat and cook, whisking to make sure any lumps are banished, over a medium heat for 2 minutes.

❄ Crumble in the blue cheese, then drop in the red currant jelly and turn up the heat to let the gravy bubble for 5 minutes.

❄ Check the seasoning, adding salt and pepper as needed, and then the remaining tablespoon of port, along with any bloody juices – what we called red gravy when I was a child – from the carved beef. Pour into a warmed gravy boat.

THOUGHTS FOR BEEF LEFTOVERS

There is nothing, really, to be done to cold roast beef, and I say that in the best way possible. Cold, it's a dream with the Red Beet and Horseradish Sauce (see p.68), some bitter leaves – spiky endive or a tangle of watercress – and a hot baked potato dolloped with sour cream and chives. In fact, there's not much that doesn't go with cold, sliced roast beef: echo the flavors it came with when it was hot by serving the beef cold alongside a green salad tossed in a dressing of blue cheese whisked with sour cream, a splosh of milk, a few drops of Worcestershire sauce and a spritz of lime; or perhaps add that tang another way by slicing the beef with some char-grilled peppers (out of a jar is fine, if the quality's good) and drizzling the plate with some anchovies whisked to a viscous liquid with olive oil, a squeeze of lemon juice and very finely chopped parsley. Scatter more parsley on top of the divine but murky drizzle on the plate.

    Or you can take this thought further East and drape a platter with slices of red roast beef, and make a dressing by whisking together some freshly grated ginger, brown rice vinegar, a little soft light brown sugar (to temper the vinegar), soy sauce, a scant amount of vegetable oil and a drop of sesame oil, then stir in some sliced scallion, chopped fresh cilantro and pour over the glistening rare beef.

    My mother always made a salad, when any cold beef was coming to an end and what was left was too stubby to carve thinly, by shredding some crisp lettuce, chopping the beef, dicing some cornichons, throwing in a few capers and some small cooked, cooled and halved baby potatoes, and making a thick, oily, Dijon-mustardy dressing. It's a hard one to beat.

THE PORK OPTION

ROLLED STUFFED LOIN OF PORK WITH RUBIED GRAVY
ITALIAN ROAST POTATOES WITH GARLIC AND THYME
CHRISTMAS SPROUTS (P.132)
RED BEET ORZOTTO (P.135)
PANETTONE PUDDING

ROLLED STUFFED LOIN OF PORK WITH RUBIED GRAVY

There is no denying that this is a complete showstopper. There is also no denying this is a fiddly undertaking, but it's worth it. Besides, if a meal isn't worth making a special effort for now, when is it?

The butcher can do a lot of the work for you; you certainly couldn't embark on this using a generic, untailored supermarket joint. So, ask the butcher for a fillet end of pork loin, with the rind and bones removed, but be sure you get to keep the rind and have it scored at the same time: this makes fantastic crackling when roasted separately in its own pan. You can also ask the butcher to open up the pork for you, so that you have a fairly level oblong of meat to stuff and roll up, but otherwise I've tried to show how you can do it yourself.

I like using smoked bacon to wrap round the stuffed roast, but whether the bacon's smoked or not is a matter of taste: what is essential is that it's fairly generously sliced; if the bacon slices are too thin, they will burn before the pork's cooked.

Unlike the goose that is stuffed with fresh cranberries, the spicy filling that swirls its way through the pale pork meat here is studded with dried cranberries. Mixed with the sweet, tart berries, the garlic, cloves and cinnamon make this like a Christmas porchetta, with the bacon and its fat keeping everything juicy; so often, a pork loin is indigestibly lean, but not this one, for just as the stuffing keeps it tender from the inside out, putting the meat in a marinade while the stuffing cooks and cools starts the tenderizing process right away.

Inspired by the notion of a seasonal porchetta, I like to expand on that theme, by making sweet, soft diced Italian roast potatoes instead of the old-fashioned English roasties. But neither would be wrong here.

THE MAIN EVENT 159

Serves 8–10

8 lbs fillet end loin of pork, rind and bones removed and reserved, to give approx. 5 lbs loin

1 lb thick-sliced bacon, plus extra for stuffing (see below)

string to wrap round the rolled loin

FOR THE MARINADE:
1 cup olive oil
1/2 cup white wine or vermouth
2 tablespoons Lea & Perrins Worcestershire sauce
1 teaspoon kosher salt or 1/2 teaspoon table salt

FOR THE STUFFING:
1/4 lb bacon
2 onions, peeled and quartered
4 cloves garlic, peeled
1 teaspoon ground ginger
1 teaspoon ground cinnamon
1/2 teaspoon ground cloves
handful of fresh parsley
3 tablespoons olive oil
2 cups dried cranberries

MAKE AHEAD TIP:
Stuff and tie the loin up to 6 hours ahead. Keep covered in the refrigerator. Allow 20 minutes at room temperature before putting in the oven.

❄ If the butcher hasn't already opened up the loin for you, lay it out in front of you vertically, and then slice partway through the center of the meat laterally to open it out like a book, but without cutting through the "spine" as it were.

❄ Bash the meat (you may want to cover it with plastic wrap first) so that it is as flat and as evenly thick as possible. It should now resemble a rectangle in shape.

❄ Put all the marinade ingredients into a large resealable bag, with the opened, flattened loin. Leave the bag overnight in the refrigerator (in a lasagne-type pan) or just while you are making the stuffing and waiting for it to cool.

❄ Put the 1/4 pound bacon into a processor with the onions and garlic cloves. Add all the spices and parsley, then process until it is pretty well mush.

❄ Heat the oil in a wide, shallow skillet and fry the spiced mush gently for about 10 minutes, then add the dried cranberries and cook for a further 5 minutes before taking off the heat.

❄ Let the stuffing cool completely before you stuff and roll your loin.

❄ Twenty minutes before you want to stuff the pork for roasting, take it out of the refrigerator and preheat the oven to 400°F.

❄ Take the pork out of its bag and marinade, shaking off any excess liquid, and lay it flesh-side up (de-rinded side down) on some parchment paper or wax paper, with the long side facing you, and the short sides at right angles to you.

❄ Spread the stuffing over the pork but leave a good 1-inch border all the way around the edge. Then roll up the loin from the long side to make a long, fat, stuffing-filled sausage. I know it looks, in the pictures, as though I'm rolling from the short side but, believe me, I'm not.

❄ Wrap the 1 pound of bacon slices around the loin to cover the white fat on top.

❄ Cut off lengths of string and, starting from the middle, slide the string under the meat, then tie up the sausage with a tight knot on the top.

❄ Tie the loin at intervals of about 1 1/2 inches so that the meat is secured all the way along. Tuck in any rogue bits of meat or stuffing that may poke out at either end.

THE MAIN EVENT **161**

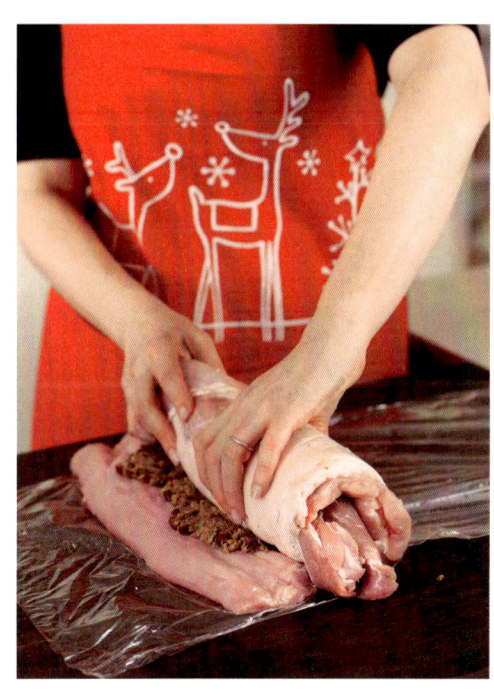

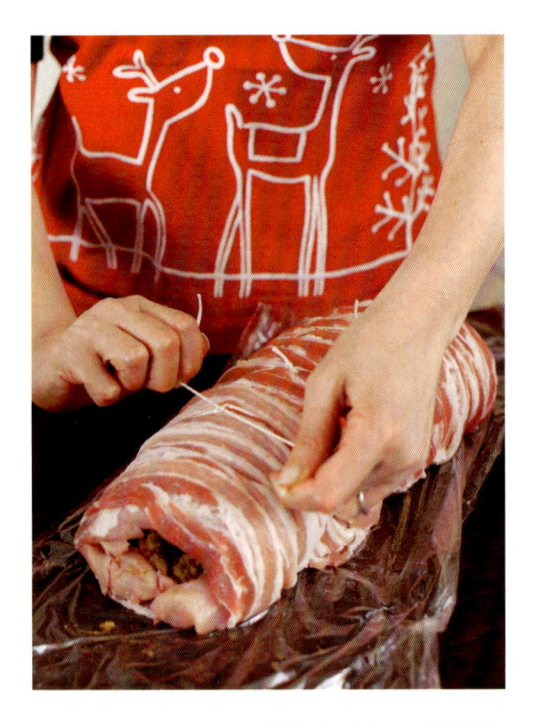

❊ Arrange the bones in a roasting pan so they form a rack to hold the stuffed loin, then sit the loin on top of the bones. Place in the oven for 2¼–2½ hours.

❊ Once you've put the loin into the oven, place the scored rind in a separate shallow roasting pan and sprinkle with salt. Cook alongside the pork on a separate shelf – it will only need about an hour, so your best bet is to put it in the oven halfway through the pork's cooking time.

❊ Insert a meat thermometer, if you have one (and it's advisable), into the pork, to make sure the meat is absolutely cooked all the way through. When the thermometer reads 160°F, the pork's ready. If the bacon has browned too much but the pork needs more cooking time, just cover it with aluminum foil and put it back in the oven for 10–15 minutes before checking again.

❊ Once the pork is cooked, let it rest out of the oven, but leave the crackling in, while you make your Rubied Gravy (opposite).

❊ When the gravy is done and you are ready to carve the pork, cut off the string ties and pull them away from the meat. Then cut the pork into thick slices, about 1 inch, that way each slice gets a good ribboning of stuffing without falling to pieces.

❊ Serve the pork dribbled with the rubied gravy, and break up the crackling to serve alongside.

❊ Should you have any pork left over, know that it is heavenly cold, just as is, or stuffed into a sandwich; mayonnaise and cranberry sauce are both gratifying additions here.

RUBIED GRAVY

The cranberry sauce from a jar or can gives an added fresh tang to the dried cranberries of the stuffing. If you want to go fresher still, make a downsized version of my Redder Than Red Cranberry Sauce on p.119, using ruby port in place of the cherry brandy. You could, indeed, make the regular-sized cranberry sauce and not bother with this gravy; but I'd rather proceed as follows, and unashamedly dollop some cranberry sauce out of a jar to make it.

And this gravy really is rubied: it glints gorgeously like a strange, savory coulis as it's dribbled over the pinkish swirled rounds of pale meat.

2/3 cup cranberry sauce
1 teaspoon Dijon mustard
1/2 teaspoon Lea & Perrins Worcestershire sauce
1 cup chicken broth
1/4 cup ruby port

❋ Place all the ingredients into a saucepan and bring to a boil, stirring a little to dissolve everything.

❋ Let the gravy bubble away for 5 minutes. When it's ready – it should look glossy but still quite runny – pour into a jug, and serve with the pork.

MAKE AHEAD TIP:
Make the rubied gravy up to 3 days ahead. Keep covered in the refrigerator.

ITALIAN ROAST POTATOES WITH GARLIC AND THYME

❋ Preheat the oven to 425°F. Cut the unpeeled potatoes into 1-inch cubes and put them into a large roasting pan, or divide them between 2 pans.

❋ Add the unpeeled garlic cloves and sprinkle the thyme and olive oil over. Move the potatoes around so that they get slick with oil, evenly covered in thyme and dispersed with the garlic cloves.

❋ Roast the potatoes in the oven for 1–1 1/2 hours, depending if they are in one pan or two, or until golden; if they are crowded in one roasting pan they will take longer to crisp up than if they are spread well apart.

❋ When the potatoes come out of the oven, turn them out onto a warmed platter to serve with the pork, sprinkling first with a little salt and a light scattering of fresh parsley.

Serves 8–10

3 lbs (about 8 medium) white potatoes, such as Yukon Gold
cloves from 1 head of garlic (unpeeled)
2 1/2 teaspoons dried thyme
1/2 cup olive oil
kosher salt or table salt to taste
1–2 tablespoons chopped Italian flat-leaf parsley

PANETTONE PUDDING

Serves 8–10

1½ lb panettone

1 x 375ml bottle dessert wine, such as Beaumes de Venise or other reliable muscat

8 eggs

½ cup sugar

2 cups whole milk

2 teaspoons vanilla extract

2 teaspoons confectioners' sugar

I wanted to offer another suitable seasonal alternative to steamed Christmas pudding and since panettone is the sweet, fruited bread of Christmas in Italy, this pudding seemed perfect. It's not quite a panettone version of traditional bread pudding. I wanted something with a little less of the nursery, and more elegantly, but not fussily, partified. This is it: the slices of fruit-studded, warm-spiced bread are baked in a custard made aromatic with muscat, without even a drop of cream to sully its winey clarity. Instead, you can serve some whipped cream (with or without a little Cointreau, Grand Marnier or Triple Sec whisked in), or some vanilla ice cream if you prefer, on the side; and maybe a plate of frozen mixed berries fruits, thawed – with all the vile mushy strawberries removed and a sprinkling of pomegranate seeds in their place – gently stirring in the zest of a clementine/satsuma, so that the orange-oil permeates this Festive Fruit Salad, and dusting with a little confectioners' sugar or dousing with a small slug of Cointreau (or alternative) as you take it to the table with the pudding.

❊ Preheat the oven to 325°F.

❊ Slice the panettone and lay the slices in a large baking dish (about 16 x 10, or 10 inches square, and just over 2 inches deep) that you are happy to bring to the table.

❊ Put the dessert wine into a saucepan and bring to an almost boil, but *do not let it boil*. Take off the heat.

❊ Whisk together the eggs and sugar, then whisk in the warm wine, followed by the milk.

❊ Add the vanilla, and pour the liquid through a strainer over the panettone slices. Let the dish stand for 15 minutes before it goes into the oven.

❊ Bake for 50–60 minutes until the top is golden and the underneath soft but not wet.

❊ Let it cool down until warm, about 20 minutes, though longer would be fine, and then thickly dust the top of the pudding with the confectioners' sugar pushed through a small strainer, before bringing to the table. The glorious puffiness of the pudding will subside once it's out of the oven, so don't worry about that. You can, indeed, make a virtue out of its fall from grace and even bake it in the oven before the pork goes in, so that by the time you serve it, the pudding will be set firm, and you can cut it into squares with neat ease.

MAKE AHEAD TIP:
Assemble the panettone the day before. Cover and keep chilled. Let the panettone stand out of the refrigerator for 15 minutes before going in the oven as directed.

YOU SHALL GO TO THE BALL: THE VEGETARIAN OPTION TAKES CENTER STAGE

CHILE CHEESE CROSTINI (P.17)
SEASONALLY SPICED NUTS (P.21)
ROAST STUFFED PUMPKIN WITH GINGERY TOMATO SAUCE
RED CABBAGE WITH POMEGRANATE JUICE (P.60)
CHRISTMAS SALAD (P.56)
AUSTRALIAN CHRISTMAS PUDDING WITH HOT CHOCOLATE-CHESTNUT SAUCE

ROAST STUFFED PUMPKIN WITH GINGERY TOMATO SAUCE

There is something so magnificent about a whole pumpkin stuffed with jeweled rice, that it doesn't really need too many side dishes to detract: its starchy interior means you can forgo potatoes or the orzotto; and the vibrant sauce precludes the need for a pile-up of condiments. Still, for once I think a couple of nibbly things on the table to start would balance this well, and you could add a sense of munificence and plenty – always important at this time of year – by having either the red cabbage with the pumpkin, or the pomegranate-scattered Christmas Salad (see p.56) after, or both. Indeed, why cut back? At Christmas there must be room, even before the richness of the Australian Christmas Pudding and its thick chocolate-chestnut sauce.

Obviously all pumpkins come in different sizes, and if yours is radically smaller (unlikely, I'd think, to be much bigger and still edible), here is an easy way to work out how much rice you need to stuff it: once you've sliced a "lid" off the top of your pumpkin and taken all the seeds out, put a freezer bag in the hollowed-out cavity. Now fill it with enough rice to come halfway up the cavity. Tip the rice into a measuring jug to see how much you've got, and simply use double the amount of broth to rice. If you're boosting rice quantities, augment the other ingredients accordingly.

You are slightly taking potluck with pumpkin – it's very difficult to tell before you eat one whether the flesh is succulent and sweet or tasteless and grainy – but you should certainly avoid all Halloween pumpkins, and try to buy from a trustworthy greengrocer who takes pride in his, or her, produce.

Serves 8–12

1 x 7–8 lb pumpkin, such as White Lumina or Jarrahdale, unprepared weight
1 onion, finely chopped
1 tablespoon vegetable oil or olive oil
3 cloves garlic, 2 minced plus 1 left whole
1 cup dried cranberries
1 teaspoon ground ginger
1 teaspoon ground allspice
good pinch of saffron strands
zest of 1 clementine
approx. 2 cups basmati rice (but see intro left)
approx. 4 cups hot vegetable broth
salt and pepper to taste

❋ Slice a lid off the top of the pumpkin, and remove the seeds and fibrous flesh from the inside, keeping the top to put back on later.

❋ In a large saucepan with a lid, fry the onion gently in the oil until softened, then add the 2 minced garlic cloves, the cranberries, spices and clementine zest. Stir in the rice, turning till it becomes glossy in the pan.

❋ Pour in the broth and let the pan come to the boil, then clamp on the lid and turn the heat down to the lowest it will possibly go. Cook for 15 minutes.

❋ Cut the remaining clove of garlic in half and rub the inside of the pumpkin with the cut side of each half, then, using your fingers, smear some salt over the flesh inside as well.

❋ The rice stuffing will be quite damp and not very fluffy at this stage, but check it for seasoning – adding more spice, salt or pepper if wanted – and then spoon it into the garlic- and salt-rubbed pumpkin cavity and tamp down well. Press the pumpkin lid back on top and squeeze it down as firmly as you can (it will sit up a bit proud of the top).

❋ Stand the pumpkin on a double layer of aluminum foil, wrapping the foil 2 inches up around the sides and scrunching it there, to keep the pumpkin out of direct contact with the water later.

❋ Place the stuffed, partially wrapped pumpkin in a roasting pan, and pour in freshly boiled water to a depth of 1 inch. Cook the pumpkin for about 2 hours by which time it should be tender when pierced.

❋ Meanwhile, get on with the Gingery Tomato Sauce, overleaf.

❋ Take the pumpkin out of the roasting pan and let it sit for about 10 minutes before you slice it into segments like a cake.

THE MAIN EVENT **167**

GINGERY TOMATO SAUCE

1 onion, peeled and halved
2 cloves garlic, peeled
1 teaspoon dried ginger
1 x 1-inch length fresh ginger, peeled
1 tablespoon butter
1 tablespoon olive oil
3 cups organic tomato sauce (approx. 2 x 14 oz cans)
2 cups water
1 teaspoon sugar
salt and pepper to taste

❋ Put the onion, garlic, dried ginger and fresh ginger into a processor and blitz to a pulp.

❋ Heat the butter and oil in a deep, wide skillet, then add the onion–garlic mixture. Cook over a low heat for about 10 minutes, stirring occasionally so that it doesn't burn.

❋ Add the tomato sauce and water to the pan, and season with the sugar, salt and pepper.

❋ Cook for 15 minutes, at a gentle simmer, then taste for seasoning before decanting into a warmed jug or gravy boat and taking to the table, for people to pour over their slices of stuffed pumpkin.

MAKE AHEAD TIP:
Make the sauce up to 3 days ahead and keep chilled in the refrigerator. Reheat gently before serving.

FREEZE AHEAD TIP:
Make and freeze the sauce for up to 1 month. Thaw overnight at room temperature and reheat as above.

AUSTRALIAN CHRISTMAS PUDDING WITH HOT CHOCOLATE-CHESTNUT SAUCE

My great aunt used to make something called Australian Christmas pudding, which was, in effect, all the ingredients from a Christmas pudding stirred into vanilla ice cream and set in a mixing bowl. It was rather curious, but I have fiddled with it to turn it into something I love. First step: remove the candied peel; for me this is crucial. And I've reduced the bits and pieces, using only mixed dried fruits and chopped glacé cherries. Importantly, for the look and taste, after soaking the fruit in rum, I fold it into chocolate ice cream rather than vanilla. Thus it looks like Christmas pudding – and it tastes divine, even before it's been swathed in the thick, rich, hot chocolate-chestnut sauce.

Serves up to 12

2½ cups luxury mixed dried fruit
¾ cup dark rum
2 x 1 pint containers chocolate ice cream
1½-quart Pyrex mixing bowl

❄ Put the dried fruit and rum into a saucepan and bring to the boil. Turn down the heat and gently simmer for 5 minutes, then take off the heat and allow to cool. Or just pour cold rum over the fruit and leave to steep overnight.

❄ Add the slightly softened, but not runny, ice cream and mix to combine and spoon into your mixing bowl. Wrap tightly with a double layer of plastic wrap and freeze.

❄ When it's almost time to eat, take it out of the freezer and let it stand for 20 minutes or so, to help unmolding, then unwrap, unmold and, if desired, put a sprig of holly on top or scatter shaved or chopped chocolate over on serving.

FREEZE AHEAD TIP:
Make pudding and freeze for up to 1 month. Thaw and serve as recipe.

HOT CHOCOLATE-CHESTNUT SAUCE

This chocolate-chestnut sauce is so divinely rich, I think – unless it's Christmas Day – you don't need more than a quart of good vanilla ice cream to serve with it, which also makes this a fabulous seasonal standby.

¾ cup sweetened chestnut cream (see Suppliers p.267)
¾ cup bittersweet chocolate chips
1 cup heavy cream
2 tablespoons dark rum

❄ Spoon the chestnut cream into a heavy-based saucepan, tip in the chocolate chips and pour in the cream and heat gently to melt together.

❄ Take off the heat, stir in the rum, then take to the table, and let people pour it generously over their pudding. You may have some left over. Don't complain.

MAKE AHEAD TIP:
Make the sauce up to 1 week ahead and keep, covered, in the refrigerator. Reheat gently to serve.

FREEZE AHEAD TIP:
Make and freeze the sauce for up to 3 months. Thaw overnight in the refrigerator and reheat as above.

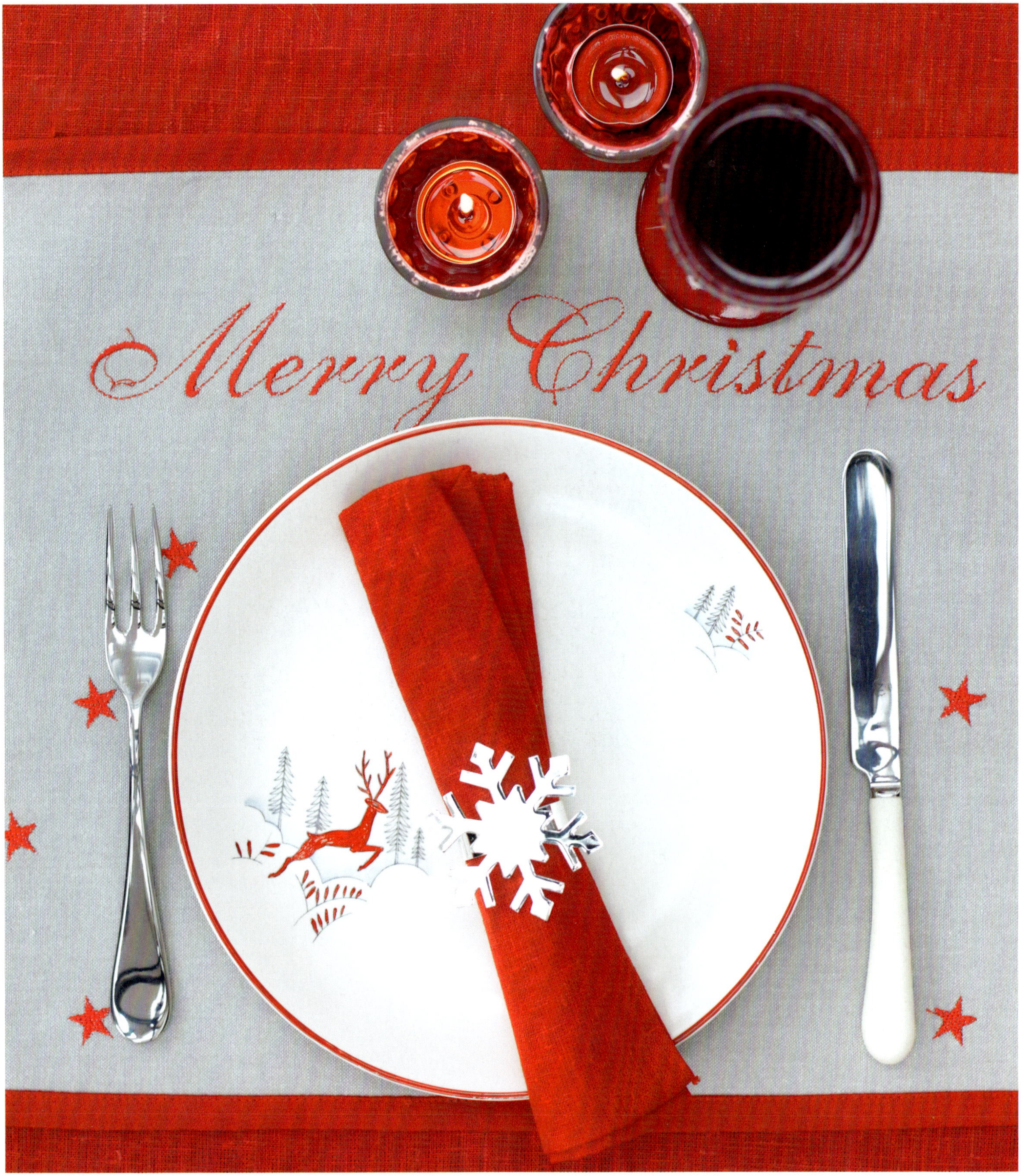
Merry Christmas

JOY TO THE WORLD
CHRISTMAS BAKING AND SWEET TREATS

I AM NOT, I ASSURE YOU, any kind of self-proclaimed Domestic Goddess. True, I conjured her up, but when I did so, it was with gentle irony. It seems cruel to say that she doesn't really exist, and I don't wish to disown her; indeed, I still believe there are times when we need to feel like her. And Christmas, more than any other, is one of those times. In fact, the title of this chapter might easily be "The Return of the Domestic Goddess: This Time It's Personal."

But I stick to "Joy to the World," which is what the mythical Domestic Goddess wants to bring, and which we could all hope for at this time of year. Baking a Christmas cake or a batch of mince pies, mixing up muffins or a meltingly mouthwatering chocolate cake may not carry any moral weight, and it's not going to win you the Nobel Prize, but it makes you, and those around you, feel blissfully immersed in the sort of Christmas we'd like to believe in, all log fires, hushed snowfall and harmony.

Yet, if the picture-perfect Christmas is a dream, or an illusion, baking brings an irrefutable sense of satisfaction, and helps to bridge the wistful gap between fantasy and reality. The edible tree decorations you bake and ice and hang from the tree, the richly fruited pudding you stir up, or the dark, dense sticky gingerbread you give to friends who drop in for tea – these are all real components of that Christmas we want to feel exists beyond the mania which threatens to envelop us at this time of year. I don't promise you can cook yourself calm, but I believe it makes sense to snatch moments when you can quietly busy yourself in the kitchen – frankly doing nothing much more effortful than stirring – and give yourself up to the encompassing warmth that comes from a sense of purpose, the benediction of productivity.

If this book celebrates anything, it is the central, perhaps quintessential, feast of Christmas: it is the time when overindulgence is not just encouraged, it is pretty well ordained. But it also needs to be relished. So don't quibble over cake now: consider, deeply, pie crammed with nuts and gooey with eggy, amber caramel; all that is richly fruited, warmly spiced, luscious with chocolate beckons. Let the scent of Christmas baking fill the air and bring joy, if not to the whole world, then to your world. For Christmas, like charity, begins at home.

TRADITIONAL CHRISTMAS CAKE

Look for almond flour, or almond meal, in cake decorating stores and also natural food stores.

Grateful though I am to Hazel Hook for giving me her foundation-stone recipe for a traditional Christmas cake, with its all-important table for weights, measures and pan sizes, so many Christmasses ago, I have departed somewhat from her strictures. To be honest, I don't always get it together to make a traditional Christmas cake (which needs a bit of time to stand and mellow to be as good as it can be) so I tend to rustle up either the Incredibly Easy Chocolate or Gorgeously Golden Fruitcake (or both) at the last minute. But a traditionally iced and comfortingly decorative Christmas cake is a lovely thing, and if efficiency allows, should be embraced. This version builds on the Time-Honored Christmas Cake of earlier books, but cuts down on varieties of dried fruits, augments alcohol (bourbon for preference, but brandy or sherry will also do), and adds almond flour and chopped pecans. It bakes well, and can be iced beautifully, and is a satisfying way to get Christmas really going in the kitchen.

raisins	2½ cups	5¼ cups	6⅓ cups
currants	1⅓ cups	2½ cups	4¼ cups
candied cherries	¼ cup	½ cup	¾ cup
chopped pecans (or walnuts)	heaping ½ cup	1⅓ cups	2 cups
bourbon (or brandy)	¾ cup plus 1 tablespoon	1⅔ cups	2½ cups
butter	1 stick plus 3 tablespoons	2¾ sticks	4 sticks
dark brown sugar	½ cup packed	1 cup packed	1¾ cups packed
lemon zest, grated	1 teaspoon	2 teaspoons	3 teaspoons
extra large eggs	2	4	6
molasses	1 tablespoon	2 tablespoons	3 tablespoons
almond extract	½ teaspoon	1 teaspoon	1½ teaspoons
all-purpose flour	1 cup	2 cups	3 cups
almond flour	scant 1 cup	1¾ cups	scant 2½ cups
ground cloves	¼ teaspoon	½ teaspoon	¾ teaspoon
ground cinnamon	½ teaspoon	1 teaspoon	1½ teaspoons
ground ginger	¼ teaspoon	½ teaspoon	¾ teaspoon
pan: round springform or deep square	7 inch 6 inch	9 inch 8 inch	10 inch 9 inch
temperature	300°F	300°F	300°F reduce to 275°F after 1 hour
cooking time	1¾ – 2¼ hours	2¾ – 3¼ hours	3¾ – 4¼ hours
yield	approx. 12 slices	approx. 16 slices	approx. 20 slices

❄ Place all the dried fruit in a saucepan, and add the bourbon or brandy. Bring to the boil, then take it off the heat, covering once cooled, and let it steep overnight, covered. And make sure you take your eggs and butter out of the refrigerator so that they will be at room temperature for the making of the cake tomorrow.

❄ The next day, preheat your oven to 300°F, and prepare your pan, see right.

❄ Cream the butter and sugar together, then beat in the grated lemon zest.

❄ Add the eggs one at a time, beating well after each addition, then beat in the molasses and almond extract.

❄ Whisk the dry ingredients together, then mix the soaked fruit alternately with the dry ingredients into the creamed mixture, combining thoroughly. Fold in the chopped pecans.

❄ Put the cake mix into the prepared pan and bake in the oven, following the table opposite, or until a cake-tester or toothpick inserted into the cake comes out cleanish.

❄ When the cake is cooked, brush with a couple of extra tablespoons of bourbon or brandy or other liqueur of your choice. Wrap immediately in its pan – using a double-thickness of aluminum foil – as this will trap the heat and form steam, which in turn will keep the cake soft on top.

❄ When it's completely cold, remove the cake from the pan and rewrap in aluminum foil, storing, preferably in an airtight pan or Tupperware, for at least 3 weeks to improve the flavor. And see the Make Ahead tip, too.

❄ To prepare your pan, line the sides and bottom of a deep, round, springform cake pan with a double layer of parchment paper. The paper should come up a good 4 inches higher than the sides of the pan; think of a lining that's about twice as deep as the pan. Cut out 2 circles of paper, and 2 very long rectangles that will fit along the sides of the pan and rise up above it like a top hat. Before you put the 2 rectangular pieces in the pan, fold one long side of each piece in towards the center by about 1 inch, as if turning up a hem, then take some scissors and snip into this hem, at approx. 1 inch intervals, as if making a rough frill.

❄ Grease the pan, lay one paper circle on the bottom and get one of your long pieces and fit it down one side, with the frilly edge along the bottom, then press down that edge so it sits flat on the circle and holds it in place. Press the paper well into the sides, and repeat with the second rectangular piece. Now place the second circle on top of the 2 pressed-down frilly edges, to help hold the pieces around the edge in place.

❄ If you're making a big cake, it's worth wrapping the outside of the pan with a double layer of brown paper (also coming up about 4 inches above the rim of the tin) but I don't bother if I'm making a normal-sized one (8–9 inches).

MAKE AHEAD TIP:
Make the cake up to 6 weeks ahead and wrap in a double layer of parchment paper and then a double layer of aluminum foil. Store in an airtight container in a cool, dry place. (You could add a bit more bourbon or brandy over this storage time to feed the cake and keep moist.)

FREEZE AHEAD TIP:
Make the cake and wrap as above. Freeze for up to 1 year. To thaw, unwrap the cake and thaw overnight at room temperature. Rewrap and store as above until needed.

CHRISTMAS CAKE ICING AND TOPPINGS

There are a number of ways you can tackle the icing, and I will start with the more traditional; it seems fitting here. Some of the cakes below carry with them their own suggestions for decorating, but any of the methods here can be used for the first 3 cakes.

I love a plain white-iced cake: smooth icing, wrapping the cake almost like a hatbox. I am happy to have this decorated, but I'd just as soon the decorations were also white. I cut out bits of leftover rolled fondant, using my snowflake or star cookie cutter, and perhaps throw a few silver dragees around, too. But play as you wish: red and green rolled fondant can be used to exuberantly Christmassy effect and wherever you buy the blocks of readymade, ready-to-roll fondant or colored sugar paste (see Suppliers p.267) you should be able to get a holly leaf cutter, and it's not difficult to roll little bits into berries. If you are more dextrous than I am (not hard), you can be more adventurous. I long to bake a square cake and ice it like a present, but simple though I'm told this is, I know it's beyond me.

However, I have tried to get a bit artistic and have used white rolled fondant, cutting out a wibbly-wobbly hillscape and some trees and a star with my cookie cutters. The partially iced cake doesn't last as well as a fully covered one, but has a dramatic prettiness, if such is not a contradiction in terms.

If you want icing that gives the traditional snowy effect, I can also accommodate you. You still have to roll out the marzipan – and for what it's worth, I like yellow marzipan under the smooth icing, and white marzipan here – but the icing just needs to be whipped up, slapped on with a spatula and forked around to create the spikey effect that we all accept as snowy. This is the icing to go for if you have Christmas cake toppers – a dinky sleigh, fir trees and reindeer, a red-breasted robin, or the whole, thronging nativity scene – stashed away in a cupboard or in the loft, ready to be brought out each year and put lovingly on top.

Finally, I am very fond of a topping more than an icing, and one that is not particularly British, but is the traditional way of decorating fruit cakes in Italy and America: and this is just a glaze-slicked mounding of nuts and candied fruits (and see p.177). Because the fruit is so sticky, it's not enormously less fiddly than the icing in the first two methods – and is more expensive – but it requires less dexterity and patience, and still looks beautiful. (It won't, however, keep the cake from drying out, as the layers of marzipan and sugar-icing do.) And a cake that has only a topping can look "finished" by having a ribbon tied or pinned around it. Understatement is not the order of the day at this time of the year, after all.

I don't think I ever make my Traditional Christmas cake bigger than 7 inches in diameter, as a little goes a long way, and you really don't want it sitting on a table gathering dust in January. However, the amounts of ingredients for the icings below should be enough to stretch to a 9-inch cake. If you're going big-time with a 10-inch cake or more, then add half again to the ingredients.

Silver dragees should be removed from the cake before eating.

MAKE AHEAD TIP:
The marzipan should have about 1 week to dry out before the icing goes on, otherwise the oils from the fruit cake gradually seep out and stain the icing. It's fine to marzipan and ice together if you're doing it one or two days before eating, but if you want to prepare the cake in the weeks running up to Christmas, the marzipan needs to be done first and dried out.

OPPOSITE:
Variations on Smooth Hatbox Icing (top left, top right and bottom right)
Snowscene Icing (bottom left)

JOY TO THE WORLD **175**

SNOW SCENE ICING

3/4 cup rindless marmalade or smooth apricot jam
18 oz marzipan (2 1/2 cups x 7 oz packs)
1lb box confectioners' sugar plus extra for dusting
3 tablespoons meringue powder (see Suppliers p.267)
approx. 1/3 cup warm water

❄ Follow the method for Smooth Hatbox Icing below only up to the point where the cake is covered with a neat layer of marzipan.

❄ Then make up the royal icing by mixing the confectioners' sugar, meringue powder and the water and whisking until it is thick and gleamingly bulked up, so that it holds its shape if you try to make a peak with a teaspoon. Add an extra tablespoon of the water if the icing is too stiff to spread. Pile the icing over the cake with a spatula, to cover it completely, before forking to leave a rough snowy cover.

❄ Adorn with your treasured Christmas-cake decorations and leave to dry and set.

SMOOTH HATBOX ICING

3/4 cup rindless marmalade, or smooth apricot jam
18 oz marzipan (2 1/2 x 7oz packs)
1 x 24-oz box rolled fondant (more if you want different colorways)
confectioners' sugar for dusting

❄ Warm the marmalade in a small saucepan over a low to medium heat. (If you are not using a rindless marmalade or smooth apricot jam, when it's hot and runny, strain into a bowl to remove rind or pips.) Knead the marzipan into a smooth ball.

❄ Place the cake on a cake board or cake stand and, with a pastry brush, paint the warm marmalade or jam all over the sides and the top of the cake to make a tacky surface.

❄ Dust a work surface with confectioners' sugar, roll out the marzipan till it's about 1/8 inch thick (don't be fanatical; you just want a supple and pliable layer) and drape over the cake. Then press the marzipan cloak against the cake so it covers it smoothly and cut off the excess with a sharp knife. If you find it easier to roll out two lots of 9 ounces marzipan, that's fine, but be sure to smooth over any joins, so the icing will lie smoothly on top.

❄ Dust the work surface again with confectioners' sugar and plonk down your block of fondant. Beat it a few times with the rolling pin, then dust the top with confectioners' sugar and roll out patiently until it's about 1/8 inch thick.

❄ Cover the cake with it, cutting off the excess. If you need to stick bits together to patch up any breaks, sprinkle with cold water first; the water fuses breaks magically together.

❄ Cut out the shapes you want – stars, snowflakes, holly trees or ivy leaves – from leftover bits of fondant and dibble or brush the undersides with cold water to stick them on to the cake.

176 JOY TO THE WORLD

GLOSSY FRUIT AND NUT TOPPING

I tend to order my candied fruits online from France (see Suppliers p.267) but around Christmastime, you tend to find them easily enough in gourmet stores. The range is enormous, and it's up to you to decide how broad to make your choice.

✱ Spoon the apricot jam into a little saucepan, add a tablespoon of water, heat gently, stirring to make a molten glaze, then take off the heat to cool it a little.

✱ Paint the top of the cake with the apricot glaze, and decorate with the fruits and nuts of your choice – I find it easier to cut the fruits into pieces and fit everything together like a jigsaw puzzle.

✱ When the top is completely covered in candied fruits and nuts – although if you're going for a big cake, just pile the fruit and nuts in the center, leaving a frame of plain cake all around – paint a second coat of apricot glaze over the top to give a glossy finish.

8 teaspoons smooth apricot jam

approx. 3 cups (6 oz) assorted candied fruits, about 3 whole fruits plus small handful candied cherries

1/4 cup blanched almonds, whole

1/3 cup pecan halves

MAKE AHEAD TIP:
Decorate the cake with the fruit and nut topping up to 1 week ahead. Wrap a band of aluminum foil or ribbon around the cake to protect the sides. Store in an airtight container.

GORGEOUSLY GOLDEN FRUITCAKE

Makes 10 fat slices

1½ cups roughly chopped dried pears
1¾ cups roughly chopped dried apricots (not Californian)
1¾ cups golden raisins
1½ sticks (12 tablespoons) soft butter
1 cup sugar
½ cup white rum
¾ cup ginger preserve or use marmalade (see Suppliers p.267)
2¼ cups almond flour (meal)
¼ cup sesame seeds or mixture of sesame, sunflower and pumpkin seeds
seeds from 3 cardamom pods
¼ teaspoon ground coriander
3 eggs

FOR THE TOPPING:
½ cup whole blanched almonds

GLUTEN-FREE CAKE

MAKE AHEAD TIP:
Make the cake up to 1 week ahead and wrap in a double layer of parchment paper and then a layer of aluminum foil. Store in an airtight container in a cool, dry place.

FREEZE AHEAD TIP:
Make the cake and wrap as above. Freeze for up to 1 month. To thaw, unwrap the cake and thaw overnight at room temperature. Rewrap and store as above until needed.

This is the fruity blonde sister to the brunette temptress overleaf. It delivers, as promised, a cake of apricot-pear-and-ginger goldenness and goodness, so squidgy and fresh-tasting, which comes perhaps not only from the amount of fruit in it, but also the lack of flour: this is a gluten-free treat for the greedy; fruitcake with the emphasis firmly on the first word.

The lack of flour makes for an exquisitely damp cake, but it does mean that unless you cut it into quite fat slices, it can break into fruity pieces rather than geometrically precise triangles. This is why it tastes so good of course. And, what's more, it makes a fantastic pudding at the end of a seasonal supper.

I do a Dundee cake-type studding of the top with blanched almonds before baking, so there is no need to ice it or adorn further.

❊ Put the pears and apricots into a saucepan with the golden raisins, butter, sugar, rum and ginger preserve, or indeed marmalade.

❊ Simmer for 10 minutes and then leave to stand for about 30 minutes.

❊ Preheat the oven to 300°F. Line the bottom and sides of an 8-inch springform pan with a double layer of parchment paper; the lining should extend about 4 inches above – and see the instructions for the Traditional Christmas Cake on p.172 if you want a more precise, step-by-step guide to the whole lining fandango.

❊ Stir the almond flour, sesame seeds (or a mixture), cardamom seeds and coriander into the cooled saucepan. Beat in the eggs and spoon into the prepared cake pan, smoothing the top.

❊ Starting in the middle, work in concentric circles as you place the skinned almonds on top of the cake batter in decorative rings (see picture opposite).

❊ Bake for 1 hour 40 minutes, then leave to cool completely in the pan. Once cool, take out of the pan, wrap with parchment paper then aluminum foil, before stashing it away in its cake pan or other airtight container. Though, unlike a traditional fruitcake, it doesn't need to stand before being divinely edible.

JOY TO THE WORLD **179**

INCREDIBLY EASY CHOCOLATE FRUIT CAKE

Makes at least 10 generous slices

2 cups (12 oz) roughly chopped prunes
heaping 1 1/2 cups raisins
1 1/3 cups currants
1 1/2 sticks (12 tablespoons) soft butter
1 cup packed soft brown sugar
3/4 cup honey
1/2 cup Tia Maria or other coffee liqueur
juice and finely grated zest of 2 oranges
1 teaspoon pumpkin pie spice
2 tablespoons unsweetened cocoa powder
3 eggs, beaten
1 cup all-purpose flour
3/4 cup almond flour (meal)
1/2 teaspoon baking powder
1/2 teaspoon baking soda

FOR DECORATION (see Suppliers p.267):
about 1/8 cup dark chocolate coffee beans
edible golden decorations of your choice
edible glitter, in Disco Hologram gold

MAKE AHEAD TIP:
Make the cake up to 2 weeks ahead and wrap in a double layer of parchment paper and then a layer of aluminum foil. Store in an airtight container in a cool, dry place. Decorate when needed.

FREEZE AHEAD TIP:
Make the cake and wrap as above. Freeze for up to 3 months. To thaw, unwrap the cake and thaw overnight at room temperature. Re-wrap and store as above until needed.

I think it's hard to improve on this cake: dark, damp, squidgy and luscious; you don't taste the chocolate full-on – the cocoa just leaves a hint of smokey richness. Nor, I should add, do you taste the prunes. When I was making this cake for my TV program, the cameraman, Wee Nev (Neville Kidd, the eminent DOP, for all IMDb-addicts) said with force "Eugh, I HATE prunes!" But when he ate it, later, he proclaimed it to be the best Christmas cake he'd ever had. *And* he asked for the recipe so that he could ask his wife to make it for Christmas. I don't mean to crow; it sounds so undignified. But it's important that you know how universally seductive this cake is, for all that it starts off "2 cups prunes."

I don't know what it is in the prunes that gives the cake its damp bounciness; all I know is that it works. You don't need to make this in advance, although you can, and you don't have to do anything much to make it, either. You just melt everything together, give or take, in a saucepan, pour from saucepan to cake pan and bake. It needs no icing, though I have suggested – see p.267 if you need help with suppliers – a little festive decoration, below.

And there's no reason why you couldn't vary this method to make a Plain Dark Fruit Cake: just replace the Tia Maria with rum (or brandy if you prefer), making up the sweetness by adding a heaped tablespoon of marmalade; take out the cocoa, adding 2 tablespoons of flour to the 1 cup; and decorate with a sprig of holly or any of the suggestions below.

❆ Preheat the oven to 300°F and prepare an 8-inch round, deep springform pan by lining the bottom and sides with a double layer of parchment paper, as for the Traditional Christmas Cake on p.172.

❆ Put the fruits, butter, sugar, honey, Tia Maria, orange juice and zests, spice and cocoa powder into a large, wide saucepan and gently bring to the boil, stirring as the butter melts.

❆ Simmer the mixture for 10 minutes, then take off the heat and leave to stand for 30 minutes.

❆ When the 30 minutes are up – it will have cooled a little, but you can leave it for longer if you want – add the beaten eggs, flour, almond flour, baking powder and baking soda, and stir with a wooden spoon or spatula to combine.

❆ Pour the fruitcake mixture into the prepared cake pan. Place in the oven and bake for 1 3/4–2 hours, by which time the top of the cake should be firm but

180 JOY TO THE WORLD

JOY TO THE WORLD **181**

will have a shiny, sticky look. If you insert a cake tester or toothpick into it, the cake will still be a little gooey in the middle.

❉ Put the cake, still in its pan, on a wire cooling rack – it will hold its heat and take a while to cool; once cool, take it out of the pan and, if you don't want to eat it immediately (like any fruitcake it has a long life), wrap it in parchment paper then in aluminum foil and store in a cake or other airtight tin.

❉ To decorate, though this is optional, place the chocolate-covered coffee beans in the center of the cake and arrange the edible gold decorations on top. Finally sprinkle the edible glitter over the top, not minding that you will be a-glitter yourself for a while.

Gold dragees should be removed from the cake before eating.

CHRISTMAS-SPICED CHOCOLATE CAKE

There are few more popular ways to end a dinner party than with a fallen chocolate cake – the cakes are so called because they are compact and flourless and, when cooling out of the oven, their rich centers drop and dip a little. It is into this dip, not so dramatic as to be called a crater, that you drop or scatter the sticky nut topping.

    I serve this with Cointreau Cream, made simply by whisking 1 cup heavy cream until softly whipped, whisking in about 3 tablespoons of Cointreau (or Triple Sec or Grand Marnier, of course) to taste at the end.

❄ Take anything you need out of the refrigerator to bring it to room temperature. The only truly important thing, however, is that the eggs aren't cold, so if they are, just put them into a bowl (I use the KitchenAid bowl I'm going to whisk them in later) and cover with warm water for 10 minutes.

❄ Preheat the oven to 350°F. Butter the sides (or use a nonstick baking spray) and line the bottom of a 9-inch springform pan with parchment paper.

❄ Melt the chocolate and butter together in a heat-proof bowl, in a microwave according to the manufacturer's instructions, or suspended over a pan of simmering water, and set aside to cool slightly.

❄ Beat the eggs, sugar and vanilla together until thick, pale and moussy. They should have at least doubled in volume, even tripled. If you're using a free-standing mixer, as I do, this is effortless.

❄ Gently fold in the almond flour, cinnamon, cloves, clementine zest and espresso powder, taking care not to lose the air you have whisked in, then, finally, pour and scrape in the melted, slightly cooled, chocolate and butter, folding gently again.

❄ Pour into the prepared pan and bake in the oven for 35–40 minutes, by which time the top of the cake should be firm, and the underneath still a bit gooey.

❄ Remove from the oven, and sit it on a wire rack, draped with a clean tea towel, to cool completely.

❄ To make the topping for the cake, put the clementine juice into a small, preferably non-stick, frying pan with the butter, sugar and cinnamon and melt everything together, then let it sizzle for a minute or so and begin to caramelize before adding the almonds.

Makes 10–12 slices

FOR THE CAKE:
3/4 cup bittersweet chocolate, chopped or chips
1 stick plus 3 tablespoons soft butter
6 eggs
1 1/4 cups superfine sugar
1 teaspoon vanilla extract
1 cup almond flour (meal)
1 teaspoon ground cinnamon
pinch of ground cloves
zest of 1 clementine
4 teaspoons instant espresso powder

FOR THE TOPPING:
juice of zested clementine (above)
1 tablespoon butter
1 tablespoon sugar
1/4 teaspoon ground cinnamon
1/2 cup sliced almonds

GLUTEN-FREE CAKE

MAKE AHEAD TIP:
Make the chocolate cake up to 3 days ahead and store in an airtight container. Make the nut mixture and store, on parchment paper, in small airtight container or wrap in a loose "bag" of foil.

FREEZE AHEAD TIP:
Make and freeze the chocolate cake up to 1 month ahead. Thaw overnight in a cool room.

❋ Stir everything together, and occasionally tip the pan to keep it all moving; what you want is for all the liquid to disappear and the nuts to look shiny and be coated thinly in a fragrant, orange-scented caramel.

❋ Remove to a plate and cool.

❋ Unspring the cake and transfer to a cake stand or plate; I am brave enough to take it off its base sometimes, but don't if you're scared. Remember this cake, however intense and elegant within, has a rather ramshackle rustic appearance on the outside.

❋ Scatter with the almonds, mainly letting them pile up in the center of the cake, but drop a few here and there all over the top, and serve with the Cointreau Cream (see p.183) if wished.

JOY TO THE WORLD **185**

STAR-TOPPED MINCE PIES

Makes 36

1 2/3 cups all-purpose flour
5 tablespoons vegetable shortening, such as Crisco
1/2 stick (4 tablespoons) cold butter
juice of 1 orange
pinch of salt
approx. 2/3 cup mincemeat
confectioners' sugar for dusting

MAKE AHEAD TIP:
Make the mince pies up to 1 week ahead and leave to cool. Store in an airtight container layered up between sheets of parchment paper. Pop into a warm oven for 3–4 minutes before serving, dusted with confectioners' sugar.

FREEZE AHEAD TIP:
Make and pack the pies as above and freeze for up to 3 months. Thaw overnight on a cooling rack and reheat as above.

This is the way I make my mince pies, and there is no changing me or them: they are small, to be popped straight into the mouth in one go; the pastry is plain, the better to contrast with the rich, fruited filling; and they have not full casings but little stars as lids, which makes them look beautiful and taste flutteringly light.

By all means use good store-bought mincemeat if you want (see Suppliers p.267), but I'm hoping you might give my new Cranberry-Studded Mincemeat a go (see p.189): it tastes both rich and boozy and fresh and fruity at the same time; and it makes for a slightly different mince pie, but in a welcome rather than challenging way.

With mince pies, I must have butter of some sort: I'll take brandy butter (my mother's), rum butter or a brown-sugar bourbon butter (see p.190 for butter recipes). Mince pies are to be savored – not just as one of the last truly seasonal foods in England, but also as a home-grown culinary triumph, provoking one delighted Frenchman to exclaim in a letter, as quoted proudly by Agnes Jekyll in her *Kitchen Essays*: "ce que j'adore dans la cuisine anglaise ce sont vos petits mince-pi."

❋ Get out your 12-hole mini muffin pans along with a 2 1/4-inch fluted, round cookie cutter and a 1 3/4-inch star cutter.

❋ Measure the flour into a shallow bowl or dish and, with a teaspoon, dollop little mounds of vegetable shortening into the bowl, add the butter, diced small, shake to cover it, then put in the freezer for 20 minutes. This is what will make the pastry so tender and flaky later.

❋ Mix together the orange juice and salt in a separate small bowl, cover and leave in the refrigerator to chill.

❋ After the 20 minutes, empty the flour and fat into the bowl of your food processor and blitz until you've got a pale pile of cake-like crumbs. Pour the salted juice down the funnel, pulsing until it looks as if the dough is about to cohere; you want to stop just before it does (even if some orange juice is left). If all your juice is used up and you need more liquid, add some iced water.

❋ If you prefer to use a freestanding mixer to make the pastry, cut the fats into the flour with the paddle, leaving the bowl in the refrigerator to chill down for the 20-minute flour-and-fat-freezer session. Add liquid as above. I often find the pastry uses more liquid in the mixer than the processor.

❋ Turn the mixture out of the processor or mixing bowl onto a pastry board or

JOY TO THE WORLD **187**

work surface and, using your hands, combine to a dough. Then form into 3 discs (you'll need to make these in 3 batches, unless you've got enough mini muffin pans to make all 36 pies at once).

❅ Wrap each disc in plastic wrap and put in the refrigerator to rest for 20 minutes. Preheat the oven to 425°F.

❅ Roll out the discs, one at a time, as thinly as you can without exaggerating; in other words, you want a light pastry case, but one sturdy enough to support the dense mincemeat. This is easy-going dough, so you don't have to pander to it: just get rolling and patch up as you need.

❅ Out of each rolled-out disc cut out circles a little wider than the indentations in the tart tins; I use a fluted cookie cutter for this. Press these circles gently into the molds and dollop in a scant teaspoon of mincemeat.

❅ Then cut out your stars with your little star cutter – re-rolling the pastry as necessary – and place the tops lightly on the mincemeat.

❅ Put in the oven and bake for 10–15 minutes: keep an eye on them as they really don't take long and ovens do vary.

❅ Remove from the oven, prying out the little pies straightaway and letting the empty tin cool down before you start putting in the pastry for the next batch. Carry on until they're all done.

❅ Dust over some confectioners' sugar by pushing it through a tea strainer, and serve the pies with one of the butters on p.190.

ABOVE:
Cranberry-studded Mincemeat

188 JOY TO THE WORLD

CRANBERRY-STUDDED MINCEMEAT

I used to be old-school about mincemeat, preferring the sort that is really no more than dried fruits stirred up with some brandy, grated apple and suet and stuffed into a jar. It's certainly easy, since no cooking is involved, but Hettie (who's had more than a walk-on part in every one of my books since *How to Eat*), introduced me to the notion of a suet-free mincemeat, a recipe I used gratefully in *How to be a Domestic Goddess*, and which I've adapted here to make it garnet-glinting and tartly fruity with cranberries.

I know this doesn't make a huge amount, but it is enough to fill a good 50 of my little mince pies. It also happens to be the work – if you call tipping things into a pan and then scraping them out again, work – of moments, so if you need more (and it would be beautiful, in a jar, as a present), it's not going to take much out of you.

I love the louche, old-fashioned mixture of port and brandy (which used to be administered to children for tummy aches) but if you wish to be a little more austere, replace the ruby port with cranberry juice and add another 2 heaped teaspoons to the amount of brown sugar below.

❄ In a large saucepan, dissolve the sugar in the ruby port over a gentle heat.

❄ Add the cranberries to the saucepan.

❄ Then add the cinnamon, ginger and cloves, with the currants, raisins and dried cranberries and the zest and juice of the clementines.

❄ Simmer for 20 minutes or until everything looks pulpy and has absorbed most of the liquid in the pan. You may need to squish the cranberries a little with the back of a wooden spoon to incorporate them.

❄ Take off the heat and, when it has cooled a little, stir in the brandy, almond and vanilla extracts and honey and beat once more, vociferously, with your wooden spoon to encourage it to turn into a berry-beaded paste.

❄ Spoon the mincemeat into sterilized jars (see p.221).

Makes approx. 2 1/2 cups – enough for 50 mince pies

- 1/4 cup ruby port
- 1/2 cup packed dark brown sugar
- 3 cups cranberries, fresh or frozen
- 1 teaspoon ground cinnamon
- 1 teaspoon ground ginger
- 1/2 teaspoon ground cloves
- 1/2 cup currants
- 1/2 cup raisins
- 1/4 cup dried cranberries
- finely grated zest and juice of 1 clementine
- 2 tablespoons brandy
- 1/8 teaspoon or a few drops almond extract
- 1/2 teaspoon vanilla extract
- 2 tablespoons honey

If you want to revert to a more traditional, still suet-free, mincemeat, replace the fresh cranberries with a small grated Granny Smith apple and take out the dried cranberries, adding 2 tablespoons each of currants and raisins.

MAKE AHEAD TIP:
Make the mincemeat and spoon into sterilized jars. Seal with a lid and store in a very cool, dry place for up to 1 month. (An extra splash of brandy on top at this stage helps prevent the mincemeat from going moldy.)
Note: if using cranberry juice in place of port, store the mincemeat in the refrigerator for up to 10 days.

FREEZE AHEAD TIP:
Make the mincemeat and spoon into a freezer-proof container or sealable bags. Freeze for up to 3 months. Thaw overnight at room temperature and use immediately.

RUM AND BRANDY BUTTERS

Makes approx. 1 2/3 cups

1 1/2 cups confectioners' sugar
1 1/4 sticks (10 tablespoons) soft butter
1/2 cup almond flour (meal)
3 tablespoons good dark rum or best brandy, or to taste

MAKE AHEAD TIP:
Make the butter, cover tightly and keep in the refrigerator for up to 2 weeks.

FREEZE AHEAD TIP:
Spoon the butter into a freezer-proof container or wrap in aluminum foil and freeze for up to 3 months. Thaw overnight in the refrigerator and use within 1 week.

I veer between using rum and brandy to flavor this hard sauce, but it remains, essentially, my mother's version, which has – unusually, I've learned – almond flour in with the sugar, giving it a gorgeous, grainy, marzipanny richness.

❉ The easiest way to make this is with a food processor. It means you don't need to sift the sugar: simply put the confectioners' sugar in the processor and process to get rid of lumps.

❉ Add the butter and process again to mix well, then scrape down the sides and add the almond flour and process again.

❉ Now, with the motor running, gradually add the liquor down the feed tube, tasting as you go. You may find one spoonful is all you want; you may find that the suggested three is far from enough.

BOURBON BUTTER

Makes 1 1/4 cups

1 stick (8 tablespoons) very soft butter
1 cup packed soft light brown sugar
2–3 tablespoons bourbon, or to taste

I don't think I've come out of my bourbon phase; it doesn't look as if I'm going to any time soon, either. Still, consider yourself the beneficiary: this is lush.

❉ Cream the butter and sugar either using an electric mixer, a food processor or simply by hand. Don't worry if it looks grainy; the liquor will make it all cohere.

❉ Gradually add the bourbon, depending on how much of a hit you want this to have.

YULE LOG

A traditional French *bûche de Noël* always looks just the right side of cutely enchanting, and there is nothing hard to like about its tender, melting chocolatiness. But I warm to it most of all for the rich pagan symbolism: it is no less than a cake-emulation of the log that the Norsemen would drag home through the streets to burn in celebration of the winter solstice and to honor the gods and hope, thus, to cajole from them a good year to come. But always, too, it is about bringing fire and light to cold and darkness; this, too, is the gift of the winter kitchen.

    I know the recipe looks finicky, and I can't promise it's a doddle, but it works easily and you will soon find you are rolling chocolate logs without a care. In fact, if you have a lot of people coming round, and you can find a serving dish or board long enough, it might be worth making 2 cakes and sitting them end to end, to look like a really long log. But even if you're making just one log, I advise at least a free-standing mixer or a handheld electric whisk: I wouldn't contemplate this by hand.

    Now, it doesn't look anything like a log when it is just a bald roulade, but once you've spread on the chocolate icing, made approximations of wood-markings on it (I use the sharp end of a corn-on-the-cob holder for this) and all, it does look quite impressive. I don't go as far as the French, and make sugar mushrooms to adorn it: this is not only because I lack the talent, but also because a light snowfall of confectioners' sugar is all this yule log really needs to complete its wintry perfection.

❆ Preheat the oven to 350°F.

❆ In a large, clean bowl whisk the egg whites until thick and peaking, then, still whisking, sprinkle in $1/4$ cup of the superfine sugar and continue whisking until the whites are holding their peaks but not dry.

❆ In another bowl, whisk the egg yolks and the remaining superfine sugar until the mixture is moussy, pale and thick. Add the vanilla extract, sieve the cocoa powder over, then fold both in.

❆ Lighten the yolk mixture with a couple of dollops of the egg whites, folding them in robustly. Then add the remaining whites in thirds, folding them in carefully to avoid losing the air.

❆ Line a jelly roll pan with parchment paper, leaving a generous overhang at the ends and sides, and folding the parchment into the corners to help the paper stay anchored.

Makes about 12 fat slices

FOR THE CAKE:

6 eggs, separated

$3/4$ cup superfine sugar, plus extra for sprinkling

$1/2$ cup unsweetened cocoa powder

1 teaspoon vanilla extract

3–5 teaspoons confectioners' sugar to decorate

FOR THE ICING:

scant 1 cup bittersweet dark chocolate, chopped or chips

$1 2/3$ cups confectioners' sugar

2 sticks (16 tablespoons) soft butter

1 tablespoon vanilla extract

MAKE AHEAD TIP:
Make the Yule Log up to 1 week ahead and store in an airtight container in a very cool place.

FREEZE AHEAD TIP:
Make the Yule Log and freeze in a rigid container for up to 3 months. Thaw overnight in a cool room and store in an airtight container until needed.

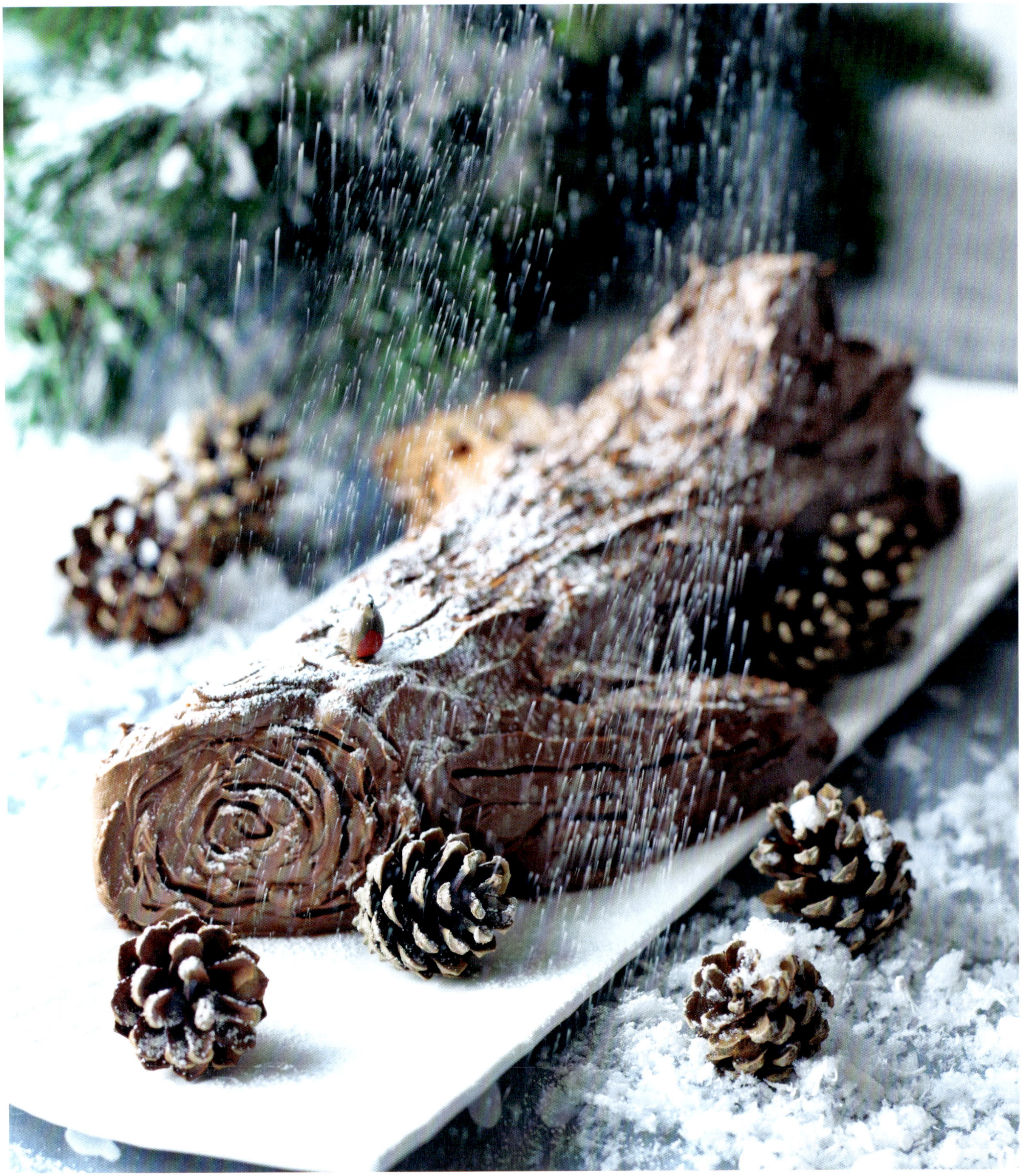

❄ Pour in the cake mixture and bake in the oven for 20 minutes. Let the cake cool a little before turning it out onto another piece of parchment paper. Cover loosely with a clean tea towel. (If you dust this piece of parchment with a little confectioners' sugar, it may help with preventing stickage, but don't worry too much, as any tears or dents will be covered by icing later.)

❄ To make the icing, melt the chocolate – either in a heat-proof bowl suspended over a pan of simmering water or, my preference, in a microwave following the manufacturer's guidelines – and let it cool.

❄ Put the confectioners' sugar into a food processor and blitz to remove lumps, add the butter and process until smooth. Add the cooled, melted chocolate and the tablespoon of vanilla extract and pulse again to make a smooth icing. You can do this by hand, but it does mean you will have to sift the sugar before creaming it with the butter and stirring in the chocolate and vanilla.

❄ Sit the flat chocolate cake on a large piece of parchment paper that has been sprinkled with a little sugar. Trim the edges of the cake. Spread some of the icing thinly over the sponge, going right out to the edges. Start rolling from the long side facing you, taking care to get a tight roll from the beginning, and roll up to the other side. Pressing against the parchment, rather than the tender cake, makes this easier.

❄ Cut one or both rolled cake ends slightly at a gentle angle, reserving the remnants, and place the cake on a board or long dish. The remnants, along with the trimmed-off bits earlier, are to make a branch or two; you get the effect by placing a piece of cake at an angle to look like a branch coming off the big log.

❄ Spread the yule log with the remaining icing, covering the cut-off ends as well as any branches. Create a wood-like texture by marking along the length of the log with a toothpick or somesuch, remembering to do wibbly circles, as in tree rings, on each end.

❄ You don't have to dust with confectioners' sugar, but I love the freshly fallen snow effect, so push quite a bit through a small tea strainer, letting some settle in heaps on the plate or board on which the log sits.

EDIBLE CHRISTMAS TREE DECORATIONS

Makes approx. 35–40

FOR THE COOKIES:
2 cups all-purpose flour, plus more for dusting
pinch of salt
1 teaspoon baking powder
1 teaspoon ground cinnamon
1/4 teaspoon ground cloves
1–2 teaspoons freshly ground black pepper
1 stick (8 tablespoons) soft butter
1/2 cup packed dark brown sugar
2 large eggs, beaten with 1/4 cup runny honey

FOR THE ICING AND TRIMMINGS (see Suppliers p.267):
2 cups confectioners' sugar
2 tablespoons meringue powder
edible gold or silver sprinkles
florists' ribbon for hanging

MAKE AHEAD TIP:
Make the cookies up to 1 week ahead and store in an airtight container. Ice the cookies the day before needed to allow them plenty of time to set.

FREEZE AHEAD TIP:
The raw cookie dough can be made and frozen for up to 1 month. Thaw in the refrigerator overnight. The baked cookies can be made and frozen in sealable bags for up to 6 months.

I couldn't have Christmas without these, or at least, not happily. Rituals are essential to give us meaning, a sense of ceremony, and making these peppery, gingerbready edible decorations is how I have always marked with my children that Christmas has begun.

❋ Combine the flour, salt, baking powder, cinnamon, cloves and pepper in a food processor and, with the motor on, add the butter and sugar, then, slowly, the beaten eggs and honey, through the feed tube, though don't use all of this liquid if the pastry has come together before it's used up.

❋ Form two fat discs and put one, covered in plastic wrap or in a resealable bag, in the refrigerator while you get started on the other.

❋ Preheat the oven to 350°F and line 2 cookie sheets with parchment paper. Then dust a work surface with flour, roll out the disc, also floured, to about 1/4 inch, and cut out your Christmas decorations with cutters of your choice, which could include fir-tree shapes, angels, stars, snowflakes, and so on.

❋ Re-roll and cut out some more, setting aside the dough scraps from this first disc, well covered, while you get on with rolling out the second. When you've got both sets of leftover clumps of dough, roll out and cut out again, and keep doing so till all the dough's used up.

❋ Now take a small piping nozzle and use the pointy end to cut out a hole just below the top of each cookie (through which ribbon can later be threaded).

❋ Arrange the pastry shapes on the lined cookie sheets and bake for about 20 minutes: it's hard to see when they're baked, but you can feel; if the underside is no longer doughy, they're ready. Transfer to a wire rack and leave to cool.

❋ Mix together the confectioners' sugar with the meringue powder and 3 tablespoons water, beating it until it's thick enough to be able to cover the cookies with a just-dripping blanket of white.

❋ Carefully ice the cold decorations, using a teaspoon (the tip for dripping, the back for smoothing), and scatter sparkles or sprinkles as you like. When the icing is set, thread ribbon through the holes and hang on your tree.

JOY TO THE WORLD **195**

PANFORTE

I spent enough of my life in Italy when I was young to feel almost as strongly attached to Italian culinary traditions as I do to my own, home-grown ones. I couldn't have Christmas without a panettone in the house, though I am happy to buy one. Panforte, that other seasonal sweetmeat, is another matter: it's easy to produce, and I love the nougat-chewiness of a homemade version; it tastes rather like a clove-flavored chewy chocolate caramel. Or at least my take on it does – not strictly authentic but recognizably panforte even to Italians.

The original uses candied citron and orange peels; a little crystallized ginger along with the candied peel would work well here, too.

What you're making is not exactly a cake, although it's baked in a cake pan, but rather a fruit-and-nut compacted dark nougat patty. It is wonderful with coffee and with sharp white cheese.

❋ Preheat your oven to 325°F. Line the bottom and sides of a single 8-inch cake pan with aluminum foil.

❋ Mix together the nuts, dried fruits and candied peel in a heat-proof bowl.

❋ Add the cloves, cinnamon, nutmeg, flour, white pepper and cocoa powder.

❋ Put the sugar, honey and butter into a saucepan and melt together gently.

❋ Take off the heat and pour into the dry ingredients in the heat-proof bowl. Stir slowly and patiently to mix everything together well.

❋ Tip into the cake pan and, using wet hands or wearing vinyl disposable gloves, pat and press down on the top to get as smooth a surface as you possibly can.

❋ Bake in the oven for 40 minutes; the top of the cake will be bubbling when it's ready.

❋ Let the cake cool completely in the pan, then remove all the lining and push the confectioners' sugar thickly through a small tea strainer over the top of the cake before removing to an airtight tin.

Makes approx. 20 very thin slices, perhaps even more

1 cup natural almonds, with skins
2/3 cup blanched almonds
1 cup whole shelled hazelnuts
1/2 cup roughly chopped soft dried figs
1 1/4 cups chopped candied orange and lemon or citron peel
1/2 teaspoon ground cloves
1 teaspoon ground cinnamon
good grating of fresh nutmeg
1/3 cup all-purpose flour
good grinding of white pepper
1 tablespoon unsweetened cocoa powder
3/4 cup sugar
1/2 cup honey
2 tablespoons butter
1 tablespoon confectioners' sugar

MAKE AHEAD TIP:
Make the Panforte up to 3 weeks ahead and keep in an airtight pan.

SPRUCED-UP VANILLA CAKE

Makes about 12 slices

2 sticks (16 tablespoons) soft butter, plus more for greasing (or use non-stick baking spray such as Pam)
1 1/2 cups sugar
6 eggs
2 1/3 cups all-purpose flour
1/2 teaspoon baking soda
1 cup plain fat-free yogurt
4 teaspoons vanilla extract
1–2 tablespoons confectioners' sugar

This is a sleight of hand, or a trick of equipment rather than an act of brilliance. True, the cake does look incredibly complicated and seasonally impressive as it comes to the table, but that is all down to the shape of the pan. It's an expense to get a pan that can't be used all year round, but it really is a beautifully Christmassy creation, and a breeze to make.

For the "spruced up" of the cake refers to the Holiday Fir pan I bake it in (see Suppliers p.267); at other times of the year, I call this Eggy Vanilla Cake and cook it in a regular 2 1/2-quart bundt pan, as you can now, too. Whatever the shape, and with either the Antioxidant Fruit Salad on p.254 or the Mixed Berry Compote on p.104, it is one of my proudest creations. And the thing is, it doesn't need just to be brought out as a festive flourish for a supper party, but can be satisfyingly baked and left to preside grandly over the kitchen, commanding anyone to have a slice, damply plain, or toasted, by way of a seasonal treat.

To turn this into Spruced-Up Spice Cake, even more seasonal and just as good, but with less appeal to children, halve the vanilla and add 2 teaspoons each of ground cinnamon and ginger and a half teaspoon of ground cloves.

❊ Preheat the oven to 350°F and put a cookie sheet in at the same time. Butter or spray your large, regular or fir-tree shaped bundt pan very, very thoroughly.

❊ Either put all the ingredients except the confectioners' sugar into the processor and blitz together; or mix by hand or in a free-standing mixer as follows:
– Cream together the butter and sugar in a mixing bowl until light and fluffy.
– Add the eggs one at a time, whisking each one in with a tablespoon of flour.
– Fold in the rest of the flour, and add the baking soda, yogurt and vanilla extract.

❊ Pour and spoon the mixture into your greased pan and spread about evenly.

❊ Place the pan on the preheated cookie sheet in the oven and bake for 45–60 minutes until well risen and golden. After 45 minutes, push a cake tester into the center of the cake. If it comes out clean, the cake is cooked. Let it sit out of the oven for 15 minutes.

❊ Gently pull away the edges of the cake from the pan with your fingers, then turn out the cake, hoping for the best.

❊ Once cool, dust with the confectioners' sugar pushed through a small tea strainer, to decorate: think fresh snowfall on the alps.

MAKE AHEAD TIP:
Make the cake, turn out and leave to cool. Wrap in plastic wrap and aluminum foil and store in an airtight container for up to 2 days.

FREEZE AHEAD TIP:
Make, wrap and freeze the cake for up to 3 months. Thaw overnight in a cool room.

JOY TO THE WORLD **199**

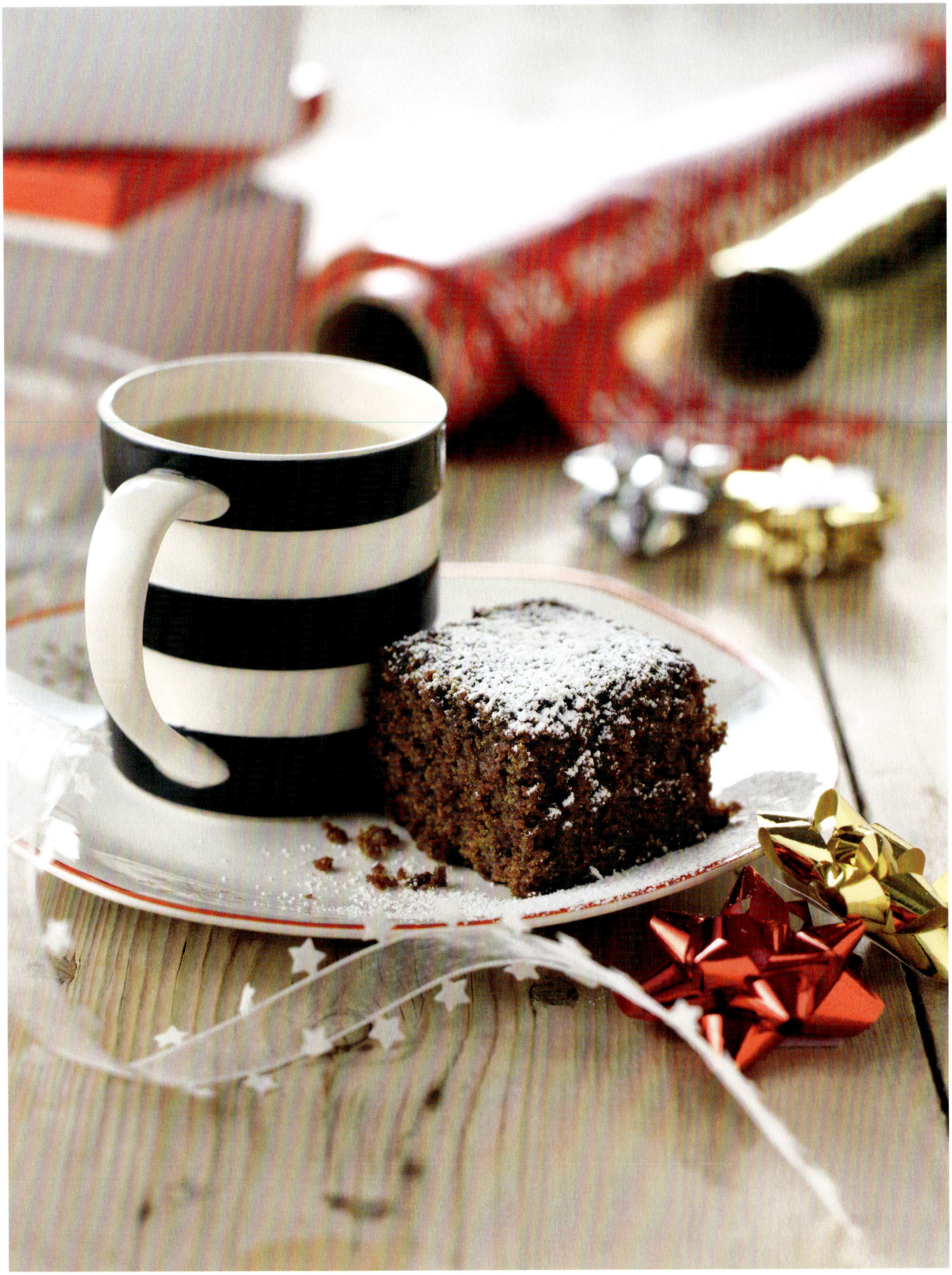

STICKY GINGERBREAD

I can't disentangle the smell of gingerbread from the smell of Christmas: I can think of no better welcome as people come through the door of the kitchen than the waft of it freshly baking in the oven. It is relaxingly simple to prepare, is good at any hour and keeps wonderfully.

I'm happy with it unfrosted, just left plain or perhaps snowily dusted with confectioners' sugar, but if you want you can (as I do if it is for a bake sale) make a sharply contrasting icing by sifting 1¼ cups confectioners' sugar and mixing it till thick and spreadable with a tablespoon of lemon juice and one of warm water. Spread this over the cold slab of gingerbread, and leave to set before cutting.

But it is, perhaps, the simplicity of the gingerbread, sticky with syrup and dark brown sugar, that makes me love it most. A square of it with a nice cup of tea would make even wrapping-up seem less vile, though I'd recommend having a pack of wipes nearby.

❅ Preheat the oven to 350°F and line a roasting pan or ovenproof dish (approx. 12 x 8 x 2-inches) with aluminum foil or parchment paper (if using foil, grease it too).

❅ In a saucepan, melt the butter over a lowish heat along with the sugar, syrup, molasses, fresh and ground gingers, cinnamon and cloves.

❅ Take off the heat, and add the milk, eggs and dissolved baking soda in its water.

❅ Measure the flour into a bowl and pour in the liquid ingredients, beating until well mixed. It will be a very liquid batter, so don't worry. This is part of what makes it sticky later.

❅ Pour it into the prepared pan and bake for 45–60 minutes until risen and firm on top. Try not to overcook, as it is nicer a little stickier, and anyway will carry on cooking as it cools.

❅ Transfer the pan to a wire rack and let the gingerbread cool in the pan before cutting into 20 squares, or however you wish to slice it.

Makes 20 squares

- 1 stick plus 3 tablespoons butter
- ¾ cup dark corn syrup
- ¾ cup molasses
- ⅔ cup packed soft dark brown sugar
- 2 teaspoons finely grated ginger
- 1 teaspoon ground ginger
- 1 teaspoon ground cinnamon
- ¼ teaspoon ground cloves
- 1 teaspoon baking soda, dissolved in 2 tablespoons warm water
- 1 cup whole milk
- 2 eggs, beaten to mix
- 2 cups all-purpose flour

MAKE AHEAD TIP:
Make the gingerbread up to 2 weeks ahead, wrap loosely in parchment paper and store in an airtight container. Cut into squares as required.

FREEZE AHEAD TIP:
Make the gingerbread, wrap in parchment paper and a layer of aluminum foil then freeze for up to 3 months. Thaw at room temperature for 3–4 hours and cut into squares.

SCARLET-SPECKLED LOAF CAKE

Makes 10–12 slices

1 large uncooked red beet, approx. 7 oz
2¼ sticks (18 tablespoons) soft butter
finely grated zest and juice of ½ lemon
1 cup superfine sugar
4 eggs
1 cup dried cranberries
½ teaspoon ground nutmeg
2 cups all-purpose flour
1 teaspoon baking powder

Simple loaf cakes are grossly underrated in the unspoken hierarchy that exists in baking. They don't have the show-off credentials of a frosted layer cake or glazed torte, but they are unassumingly, unfailingly good. Hettie, my assistant and so much more, calls them the pumps rather than the high heels of the cake world.

This one here is not exactly plain, however, but more of a festively hued fruit loaf – the kind you eat thickly sliced for tea, maybe with some cream cheese spread over it. I had the idea straightforwardly enough. If you can make a cake from grated carrots – and I've made one with grated zucchini, too – why not from grated beet? Well, it works, and although its color is distinctive, the taste is not emphatic, though the lesser amount of lemon does sing through with refreshing clarity; I doubt anyone could guess the cake had beets in it. I advise not advertising the fact: too many people who would adore the cake in reality, might let their prejudices hold sway, as prejudices will.

❋ Preheat the oven to 350°F.

❋ Butter and line a 2-pound loaf pan (10 x 4 x 2½-inches) with parchment paper or greased aluminum foil, or use a store-bought paper insert (my preference) to drop into the pan.

❋ Peel the beet, and grate it using the finer grating blade of a food processor. It's as well to wear vinyl or rubber gloves for this, or you'll have a touch of the Lady Macbeths.

❋ In a large bowl, cream together the butter, lemon zest and superfine sugar, then beat in the eggs, one at a time.

❋ Stir in the grated beet, cranberries, lemon juice and nutmeg. Then, finally, stir in the flour and baking powder and spoon the mixture into the loaf pan, spreading it out evenly.

❋ Bake in the oven for 1 hour, or until a cake tester or toothpick inserted into the cake comes out clean. Let it cool in the pan, before turning it out onto a wire rack.

MAKE AHEAD TIP:
Make the loaf up to 3 days ahead. When cool, wrap in parchment paper and store in an airtight container.

FREEZE AHEAD TIP:
Make the loaf, wrap in parchment paper and a layer of aluminum foil, then freeze for up to 3 months. Thaw at room temperature.

JOY TO THE WORLD **203**

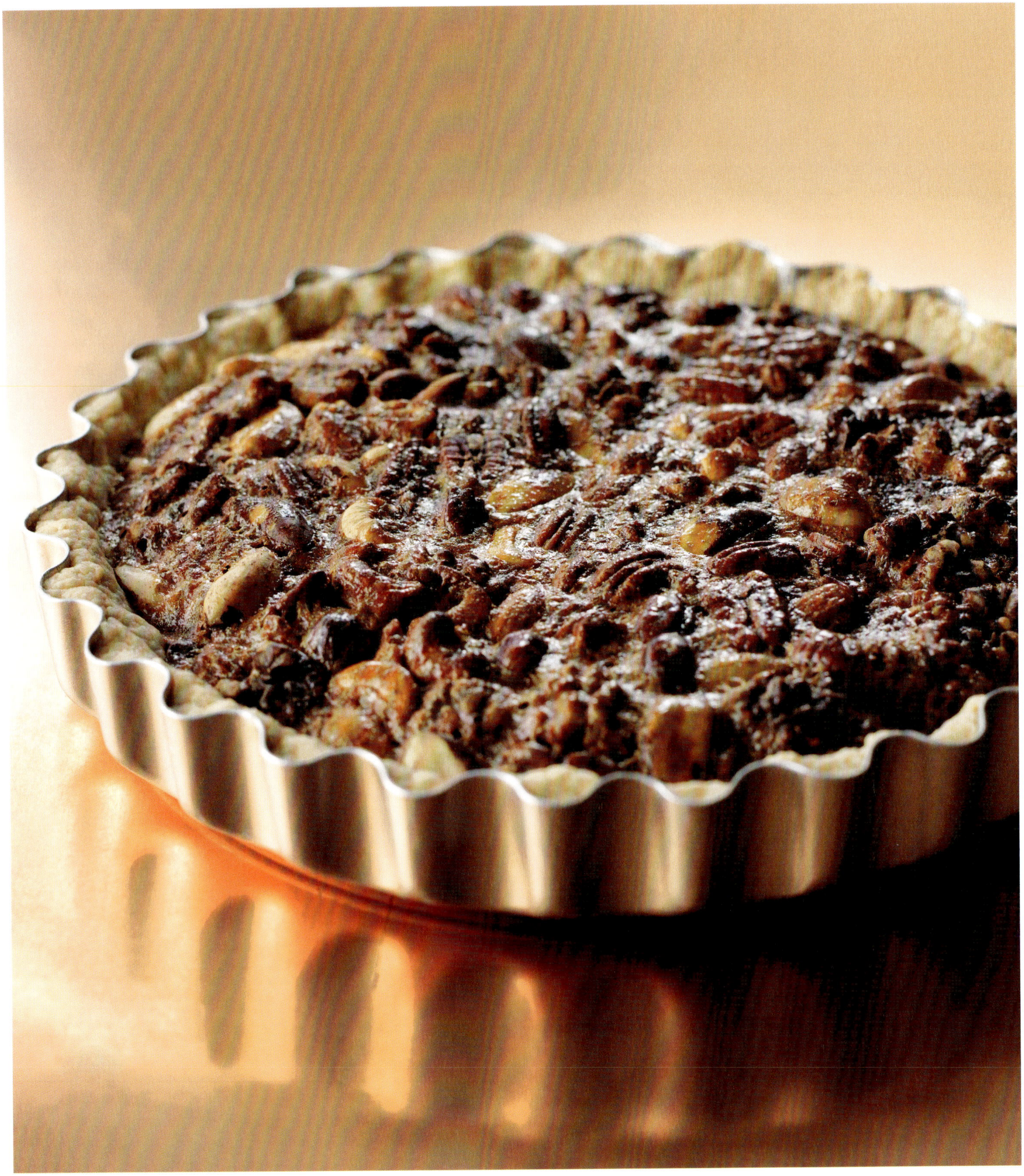

PECAN-PLUS PIE

This is somewhat of an Anglo-American enterprise. I have taken a pecan pie, and added other nuts, simply because for me, an English Christmas means bowls of mixed nuts and the memory of my grandfather being able to crack them, pressing two against each other, in his bare hands.

I don't crack them myself here even with a nutcracker, I'm afraid. But I do make sure I buy good fresh (check the dates on the packet) natural ones – that's to say unsalted and free of additives – that come together in a pack comprising Brazils, almonds, hazelnuts, pecans and walnuts.

If you eat this while it's still warm, then it's hard to put up a good argument against having a scoop of vanilla ice cream with it; when cold, I like it with a little cream, whipped or poured.

There is something so gloriously festive about this gleaming, golden, nut-laden pie, I wouldn't even rule it out for Christmas Day itself. The pastry couldn't be simpler: it's very plain, as the filling is so rich, and you don't roll it out, but press it down into the tin; I aim to ease.

❅ Preheat your oven to 350°F. In a large bowl, mix the flour, salt, oil and milk to form a rough damp dough.

❅ Tip out into a fluted tart pan 10 inches wide and around 2 inches deep, and press the dough patiently over the base and the sides of the pan, slightly coming up over the top if possible. Put in the freezer.

❅ Melt the syrup, butter and brown sugar over a lowish heat in a saucepan.

❅ Add the vanilla, stir, then take off the heat and let it stand for 10 minutes.

❅ Take the pastry-lined tart pan out of the freezer, and arrange the nuts on it.

❅ Whisk the eggs into the slightly cooled sugary syrup until it looks like a caramel mixture, then pour it over the nuts.

❅ Bake in the oven for 40 minutes, or until the filling has set and the pastry is golden.

Makes approx. 12 slices

1 1/2 cups all-purpose flour
1/2 teaspoon salt
1/2 cup flavorless vegetable oil
1/4 cup whole milk
1/2 cup golden syrup or light corn syrup
1 stick (8 tablespoons) soft butter
1 cup packed soft light brown sugar
1 teaspoon vanilla extract
3 cups (3/4 lb) mixed nuts
3 eggs

MAKE AHEAD TIP:
Make the pie up to 2 days ahead and keep in an airtight container.

CHRISTMAS CHOCOLATE COOKIES

Makes approx. 24

2 1/4 sticks (18 tablespoons) soft butter
3/4 cup sugar
1/3 cup unsweetened cocoa powder
2 cups all-purpose flour
1/2 teaspoon baking soda
1 teaspoon baking powder

FOR THE FESTIVE TOPPING:
2 tablespoons unsweetened cocoa powder
1 1/2 cups confectioners' sugar
1/4 cup boiling water, from a kettle
1 teaspoon vanilla extract
Christmas sprinkles (see Suppliers p.267)

I love these dark, fat patties of chocolate shortbread exuberantly topped with festive sprinkles. There's something so cheering about the sight of them, but they have more in their favor than looks: they are a doddle to make, and meltingly gorgeous to eat.

❄ Preheat the oven to 325°F and line a cookie sheet with parchment paper.

❄ Cream the butter and sugar in a bowl and, when you have a light, soft, whipped mixture, beat in the 1/3 cup cocoa powder (sifting if it is lumpy) and, when that's mixed in, beat in the flour with the baking soda and baking powder. Or just put everything in the processor and blitz, if you prefer.

❄ This mixture is very soft and sticky and I find it easiest to form the cookies wearing my disposable vinyl gloves, so pinch off pieces about 1 tablespoon in size, roll them into balls, then slightly flatten into fat discs as you place them, well spaced, on your cookie sheet; you should get about 12 on at a time.

❄ Bake each batch for 15 minutes; even though the cookies won't feel as if they've had enough time, they will continue to cook as they cool. They will look slightly cracked on top, and it's this cosy, homespun look I love.

❄ Remove the cookie sheet to a cold surface and let it sit for 15 minutes before transferring the cookies to a wire rack, with a sheet of newspaper under it (to catch drips while topping them).

❄ To make the topping, put the cocoa powder, confectioners' sugar, water and vanilla extract into a small saucepan and whisk over a low heat until everything's smoothly combined. Take off the heat for 10 minutes.

❄ When the cookies are cool, drizzle each one with a tablespoonful of chocolate glaze – to glue the sprinkles on in a minute – using the back of the spoon to help spread the mixture, though an uneven dribbly look is part of their charm. After you've iced 6 cookies, scatter with some of the Christmas sprinkles, and continue thus until all the cookies are topped. If you ice them all before sprinkling, you will find the cocoa "glue" has dried and the sprinkles won't stick on.

MAKE AHEAD TIP:
Bake the cookies up to 5 days ahead. Cool and store in an airtight container between sheets of parchment paper.

FREEZE AHEAD TIP:
Freeze the cooled cookies in sealable bags or rigid containers for up to 3 months. Thaw at room temperature.

JOY TO THE WORLD **207**

CRANBERRY AND WHITE CHOCOLATE COOKIES

Makes 30

1 cup all-purpose flour

1/2 teaspoon baking powder

1/2 teaspoon salt

1 cup quick-cooking oats

1 stick (8 tablespoons) plus 1 tablespoon soft butter

1/2 cup packed dark brown sugar

1/2 cup sugar

1 egg

1 teaspoon vanilla extract

1/2 cup dried cranberries

1/2 cup roughly chopped pecans

3/4 cup white chocolate chips

This is yet another recipe to make use of dried cranberries, and it is not an accident. I can't help feeling that their inclusion in a cake, muffin or cookie confers instant Christmassiness, despite their all-year-round availability.

I also love their spicy tartness, which balances perfectly with the intense sweetness of the white chocolate morsels, though you can use darker, meaner chips, if you want. Still, even if you are not usually a white chocolate eater, you will, I think, find these persuasive, perhaps even having to eat a second one straightaway just to make perfectly sure.

❈ Preheat the oven to 350°F and line a cookie sheet with parchment paper.

❈ Measure the flour, baking powder, salt and oats into a bowl.

❈ Put the butter and sugars into another bowl and beat together until creamy – this is obviously easier with an electric mixer of some kind, but otherwise you just need to put some muscle into it – then beat in the egg and vanilla extract.

❈ Beat in the flour, baking powder, salt and oat mixture, then fold in the cranberries, chopped pecans and chocolate chips.

❈ Roll tablespoonfuls of dough into balls with your hands, then place them on your prepared cookie sheet and squish the dough balls down with a fork. (You may need 2 cookie sheets or be prepared to make these in 2 batches.)

❈ Bake for 15 minutes; when ready, the cookies will be tinged a pale gold, but be too soft to lift immediately off the sheet, so leave the sheet on a cool surface and let the cookies harden for about 5 minutes. Remove with a spatula, or similar, to cool fully on a wire rack.

MAKE AHEAD TIP:
Bake the cookies up to 5 days ahead. Cool and store in an airtight container between sheets of parchment paper.

FREEZE AHEAD TIP:
Bake and then freeze the cooled cookies in sealable bags or rigid containers for up to 3 months. Thaw at room temperature.

JOY TO THE WORLD **209**

CHRISTMAS CORNFLAKE WREATHS

Makes 22

1 stick (8 tablespoons) soft butter
4 cups mini marshmallows
½ teaspoon almond extract
½ teaspoon vanilla extract
4 cups cornflakes
⅓ cup sesame seeds (optional)
Christmas sprinkles to decorate

I try to rein myself in, but not always successfully, and here's evidence of my bolting from the constraints of good taste. That's not to say these don't taste good: they are crunchy and chewy and (very) sweet, and the almond and vanilla come through strongly. As you might expect, children especially, though not exclusively, adore them. And, what's more, they can help you make them or even, after a certain age, make these wreaths themselves – so well worth bearing in mind for the school Christmas Bake Sale. My office children, Zoe and Anzelle, made the ones here.

❉ Put a piece of wax paper or parchment paper on a surface for the wreaths to sit and set on later.

❉ In a generous-sized saucepan, over a gentle heat, melt the butter then add the marshmallows, stirring until both are smoothly combined.

❉ Take the pan off the heat, and stir in the almond and vanilla extracts.

❉ Add the cornflakes, and sesame seeds (if you like them), gently crushing the cornflakes as you go and mixing well so that all are covered in creamy goo.

❉ Pull out a clump of sticky cornflakes the size of a small clementine, squish it down into a disc on the wax paper, then make a hole in the middle to form a wreath of about 2½ inches in diameter. After you've made 3 wreaths, scatter with your Christmas sprinkles; if you leave it any longer, they won't adhere. Continue until all your cornflake mixture is finished.

❉ Leave – for at least 2 hours – to cool and firm up out of harm and small hands' way.

MAKE AHEAD TIP:
Make the wreaths up to 1 week ahead. Store in an airtight container between sheets of wax paper or parchment paper.

FREEZE AHEAD TIP:
Make the wreaths and freeze in a rigid container for up to 3 months. Thaw in a cool room.

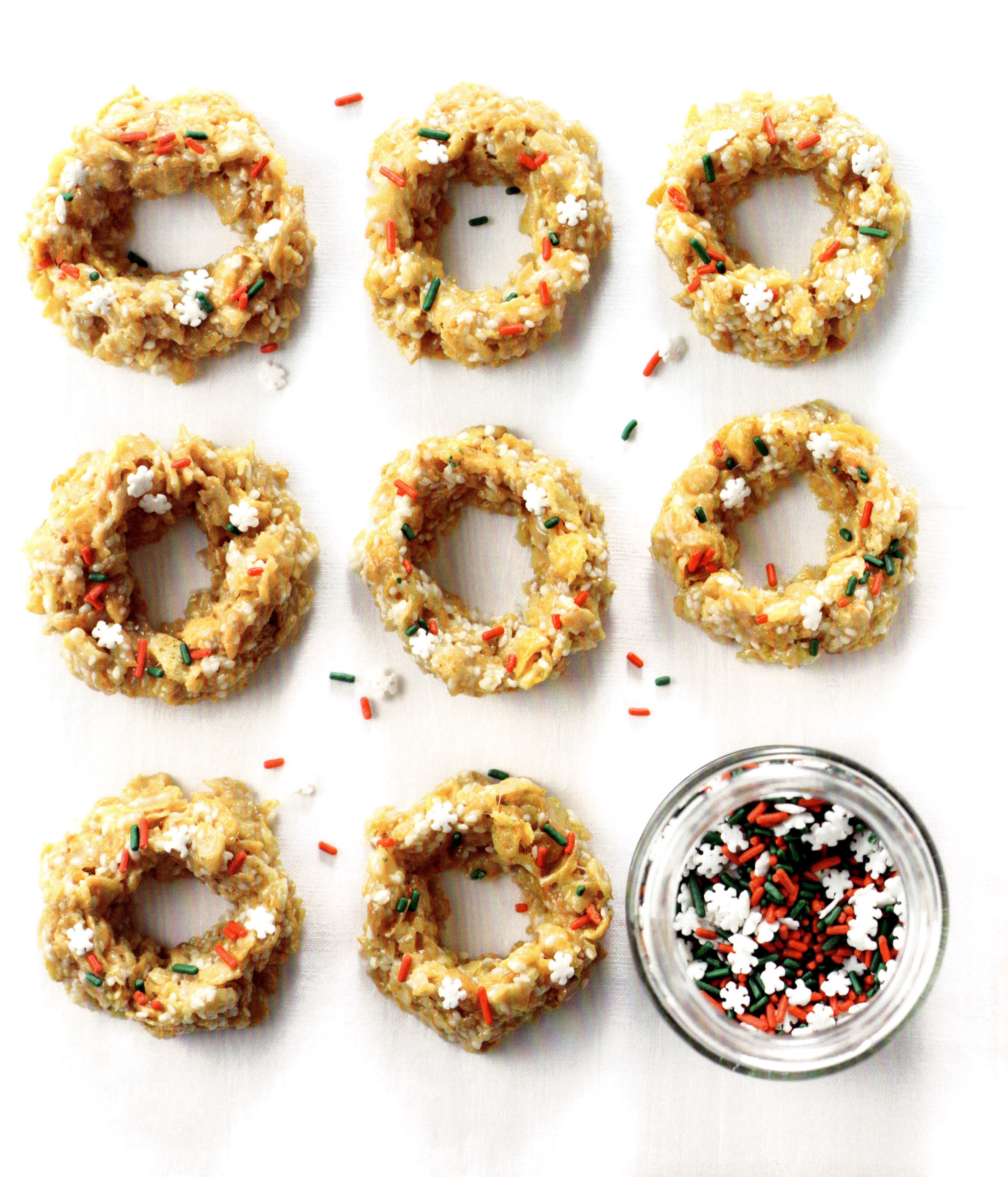

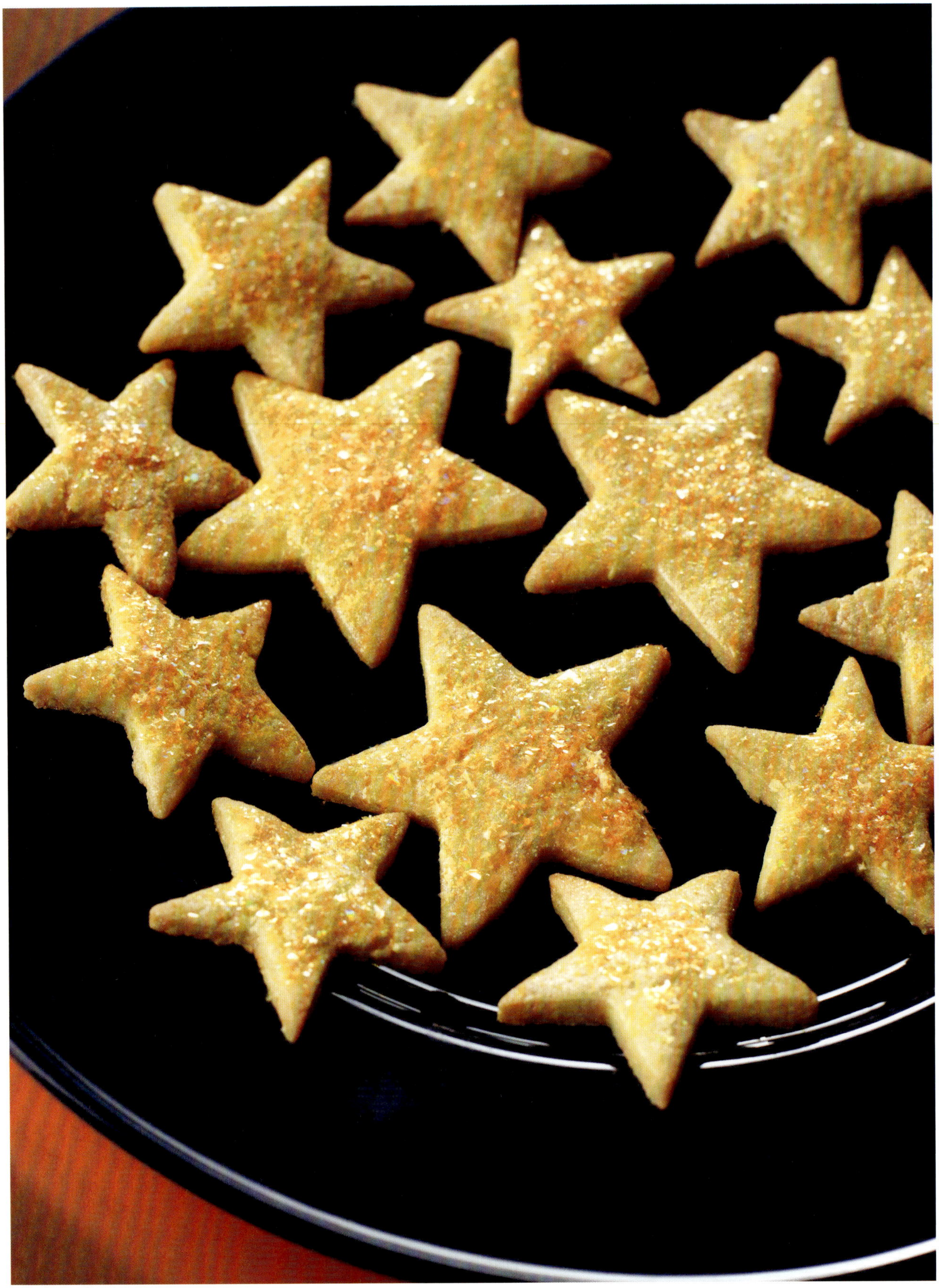

GOLD-DUST COOKIES

I freely acknowledge there is a place for the jauntily vulgar at Christmas, as is evidenced by – not least – the previous recipe, but sometimes quietly smouldering elegance can do the trick, too. These gold-dust cookies certainly have that: they are simple, ginger-seasoned (if I'm making them for the children I use vanilla instead) butter cookies cut into pretty shapes – I am a sucker for stars – and, when baked and cooled, brushed with edible gold dust or glitter flakes. You need a specialist supplier for this (see Suppliers p.267) but the actual gilding is easy, and since the cookies are not otherwise iced, you can get them done and dusted in no time. They're beautiful as a present, offered up after dinner with coffee or to keep in your festive cookie jar or biscuit pan for any eventuality.

Makes about 30, depending on size

3/4 stick (6 tablespoons) soft butter
1/2 cup superfine sugar
1 large egg
1 teaspoon ground ginger (or vanilla extract)
1 1/3 cups all-purpose flour, plus more for sprinkling
1/2 teaspoon baking powder
1/2 teaspoon fine salt
edible gold dust cluster or glitter flakes (see Suppliers p.267)

❄ Cream the butter and sugar together until whipped soft and pale, then beat in the egg, followed by the ginger (or vanilla), flour, baking powder and salt and continue mixing until it all comes together to make a soft dough.

❄ Form into two discs, wrap each one in plastic wrap and let it rest in the refrigerator for 20–30 minutes.

❄ Preheat the oven to 350°F and line a cookie sheet or two with parchment paper.

❄ Sprinkle a suitable surface with flour, place a disc of dough on it and sprinkle a little more flour on top. Then roll it out to a thickness of about 1/4 inch.

❄ Cut into shapes, dipping the cutter into flour as you go, and place the cookies a little apart on the lined cookie sheet/s. Keep the scraps of the first disc, to mix with the scraps of the second and roll and cut, re-roll and cut, until you've used up the mixture. This is a wonderfully pliable dough, which makes it an unstressful joy to work with.

❄ Bake in the oven for 8–12 minutes: this depends on their shape, how many sheets are in the oven at the same time, and whether on the upper or lower shelf, though you can swap them around after about 5 minutes. When they're ready, expect them to be tinged a pronounced pale gold around the edges; they'll be softish still in the middle, but will harden on cooling.

❄ Take the sheets out of the oven, remove the cookies, with a flat, preferably flexible, spatula to a wire rack and let cool.

❄ Using a small (unused) paintbrush or eyeshadow brush, dip in the edible gold dust – I use Pearl – or glitter flakes, and give each cookie its gilded coating.

MAKE AHEAD TIP:
Bake the cookies up to 5 days ahead. Cool and store in an airtight container between sheets of parchment paper.

FREEZE AHEAD TIP:
Bake and then freeze the cooled cookies in sealable bags or rigid containers for up to 3 months. Thaw at room temperature.

CHRISTMAS MORNING MUFFINS

Makes 12

1 2/3 cups all-purpose flour
2 1/2 teaspoons baking powder
1/2 teaspoon baking soda
1/2 cup superfine sugar
1 teaspoon ground cinnamon
good grating of fresh nutmeg (or 1/4 teaspoon ground nutmeg)
2 clementines
approx. 1/2 cup whole milk
1/3 cup vegetable oil (or melted butter left to cool slightly)
1 egg
1 1/2 cups dried cranberries

FOR THE TOPPING:
1 tablespoons turbinado sugar

MAKE AHEAD TIP:
Bake the muffins up to 3 days ahead. Cool and pack in an airtight container between layers of parchment paper. Pop into a warm oven for 5 minutes just before serving.

FREEZE AHEAD TIP:
Make and then freeze the muffins in a rigid container for up to 3 months. Thaw at room temperature. Pop into a warm oven for 5 minutes just before serving.

I have never quite understood how people can go in for vast, rich breakfasts on Christmas morning. I am hardly a modest eater by anyone's standards, but even I can't quite accommodate a platterful of buttery scrambled eggs with smoked salmon before the gargantuan Christmas feast. And I speak as cook and eater on this one.

I do, however, see the need to make breakfast special in some way, and these muffins do that. What's more, if you measure out the dry ingredients the night before and put the paper liners in the muffin pan, you don't need to do anything more labor-intensive on Christmas morning itself than preheat your oven, whisk up a few runny ingredients in a jug and stir them into the waiting bowl. Then dollop the batter into the prepared muffin pan and all's sweet – and smelling of cinnamony, orange-scented Christmas.

A last, heartfelt, note: Christmas, as I've said often, is about ritual and tradition; we inherit some, we invent others. But even those we invent are not sacrosanct. These muffins were my way, years back, of establishing a Christmas routine as a grown-up, and I have no desire to change things – essentially – now. But I've improved the recipe, and give you its new, evolved form here. In the kitchen, as in life, it is possible to play with tradition, without turning away from the past.

❋ Preheat the oven to 400°F. Line a 12-hole muffin pan with paper liners or (as I have here) silicone inserts.

❋ Measure the flour, baking powder, baking soda, superfine sugar, cinnamon and nutmeg into a large bowl; grate the zest of the clementine over, and combine. If you are doing this in advance, leave the zesting till Christmas morning.

❋ Squeeze the juice of the clementines into a measuring jug, and pour in the milk until it comes up to halfway between the 3/4 cup and 1 cup marks.

❋ Add the oil (or slightly cooled, melted butter) and egg, and lightly beat until just combined.

❋ Pour this liquid mixture into the bowl of dried ingredients and stir until everything is more or less combined, remembering that a well-beaten mixture makes for heavy muffins: in other words a lumpy batter is a good thing here.

❋ Fold in the cranberries, then spoon the batter into the prepared muffin pan and sprinkle the turbinado sugar on top.

❄ Bake in the oven for 20 minutes, by which time the air should be thick with the promise of good things and the good things themselves golden brown and ready to be eaten, either plain or broken up and smeared, as you go, with unsalted butter and marmalade.

CHRISTMAS CUPCAKES

Makes 12

FOR THE CUPCAKES:
1 stick plus 1 tablespoon soft butter
1/2 cup plus 1 tablespoon sugar
2 eggs
3/4 cup all-purpose flour
1/2 teaspoon baking soda
2 teaspoons baking powder
2 teaspoons vanilla extract
2–3 tablespoons whole milk

FOR DECORATION (see Suppliers p.267):
1/2 x 1 lb box confectioners' sugar
1 1/2 tablespoons meringue powder
Christmassy sprinkles
red and green rolled fondant (optional)
seasonal sugar decorations (optional)

MAKE AHEAD TIP:
Make the cupcakes the day before and store in an airtight container.

FREEZE AHEAD TIP:
Make and freeze the cupcakes for up to 3 months. Thaw on a wire rack. Use on the same day.

These are what I make – biggest batch to date 96 in one morning – when required to provide something for the cake stall at the school Christmas Bake Sale. I double the recipe, put 2 pans of cupcakes in the oven at a time and then blitz on and on (4 double batches all told) until my whole kitchen table is covered. When they're cool, I ice and decorate – all white, but some scattered with sprinkles, some with holly and berries made from bought rolled fondant icing, some with sugar poinsettia (expensive but enchanting) and other seasonal delights – and a more beautiful sight is hard to imagine.

But a simple, single batch of 12 is all you need under normal Christmassy conditions. The thing about sponge is that it is best the day it's made, although if covered thickly and completely with the royal icing, you might buy yourself an extra day.

❆ Take everything you need out of the refrigerator in time to come to room temperature – this makes a huge difference to the lightness of the cupcakes later – and preheat the oven to 400°F. Fill a 12-hole muffin pan with paper liners.

❆ Put all the ingredients for the cupcakes except the milk into a food processor and blitz until smooth.

❆ Pulse while adding the milk down the funnel – try one tablespoonful at a time – to make a smooth dropping consistency.

❆ Divide the mixture in your prepared muffin pan, and bake in the oven for 15–20 minutes. They should have risen and be golden on top.

❆ Let them cool a little in their pan on a rack, and then carefully take them out of the pan to cool in their papers, still on the wire rack.

❆ To ice, mix together the confectioners' sugar, meringue powder and 1/4 cup warm water and using a tablespoon, dollop over the cupcakes, so that each one is thickly covered.

❆ Adorn with sprinkles (don't let the icing dry before scattering) or sugar decorations, or roll out the fondant icing and cut out Christmassy shapes of your choice to go on top.

JOY TO THE WORLD **217**

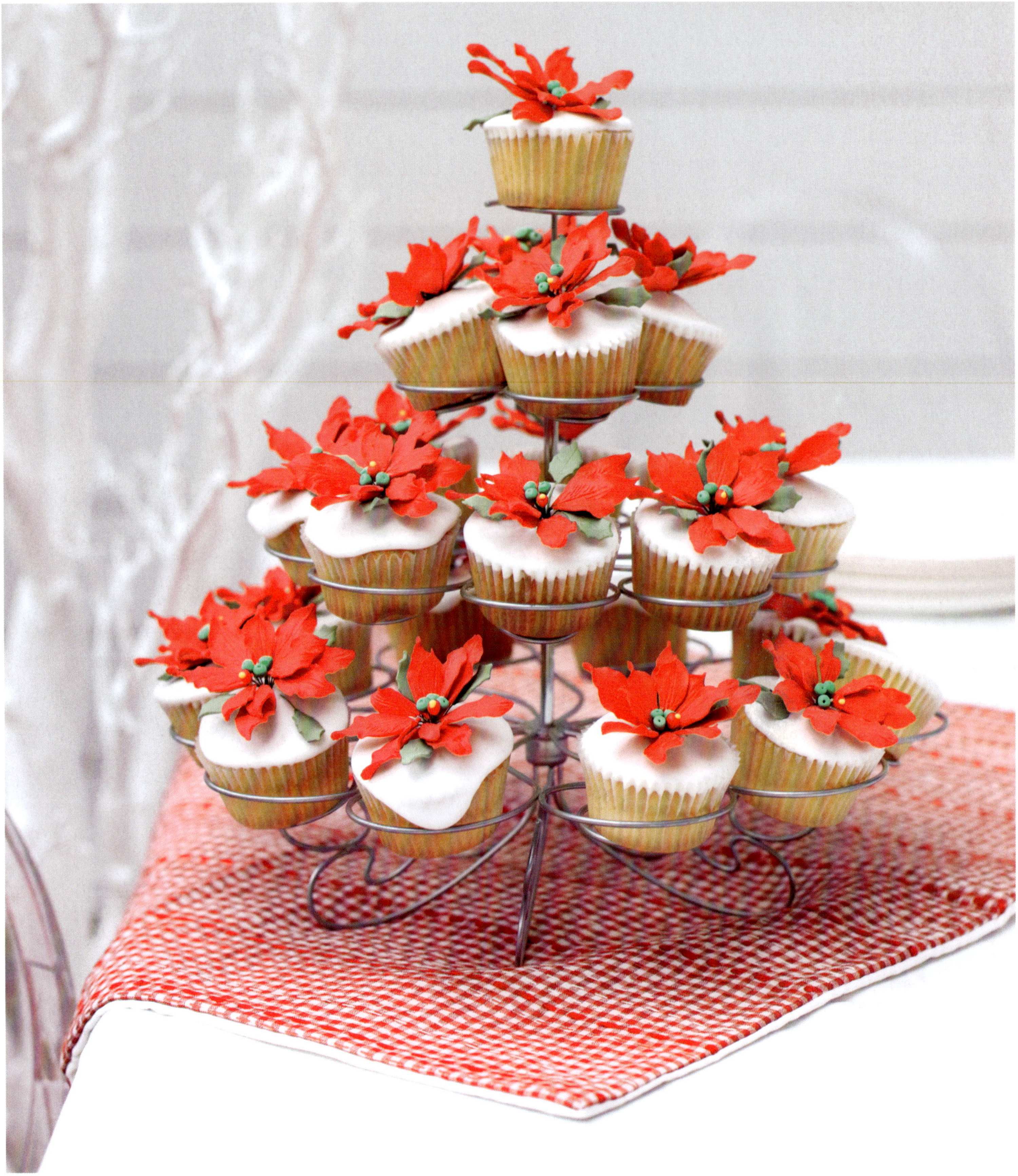

ALL WRAPPED UP
EDIBLE PRESENTS AND PARTY PRESERVES

I AM AWARE THAT it sounds almost affectedly homespun to advocate the return of handmade presents, but my fervor here makes me indifferent to any accusation of winsomely retro fancy. There is a wonderful German adjective, *rechthaberisch* – to denote someone who always thinks they're right – that describes me, at least on this issue, with delicious Teutonic accuracy. I am beyond doubt; no contemporarily faddish self-questioning or equivocation can diminish my zeal. I know I'm right. It's not that I feel such an overwhelming drive to be stirring pots, and clipping lids and getting labels ready – though I do – but that the other choices, the Christmas-present game as it is currently played out, seems vulgar, grotesque, idiotic by comparison.

Of course, this is not essentially new: people have been tut-tutting about the crass commercialization of Christmas ever since I was a child and, I'm willing to believe, long before that. I don't doubt it has been getting steadily worse, but then, after a certain age it seems that most things do. And perhaps at this time of year, nostalgia bites in a little too sharply. Christmas can't ever match up to our childhood memories of it. Even now – and I am a person without a sentimental bone in her body – I can remember the ecstatic excitement of waking up in the early hours of dawn with the leg-deadening weight of my Christmas stocking at the end of my bed. And it's also true that if I filled my children's stockings with what my childhood stockings were stuffed with – a book or two, several clementines, a pomegranate and a lucky dip sweetie bag, hair clips and transfers – they would probably not take it in good part. But still, I am too committed a consumer to feel able to complain about rampant commercialism with a clear conscience or good heart.

Nevertheless, even for me, there comes a moment, a long, protracted, sanity-busting moment, when it all seems just too much. And it is too much: too much money, too much shopping, too much wrapping, too much to worry about, and just too out of control. Wrapping paper costs more than presents used to. And there are so many presents to get. I don't say that because I'm mean or because I have anything against the exchange of gifts. Actually, giving presents is one of the few pure pleasures in life. I relish and savor it, and delight in getting it right. But that requires thought, honest selection and time for a proper unpanicked, focused search. Can you tell me that any of this is possible at Christmas? No, I didn't think so. It's too easy to feel the mania and the raging impatience come over you in the bustle of the shops, and then you end up with presents that cost too much and aren't even right. According to my history teacher at school, Churchill once apologized for the length of a memorandum, saying that if he'd had more time, he'd have made it shorter. Present buying is a bit like that: it takes time to find the right thing, and when you don't have that, you just spend more to lesser effect.

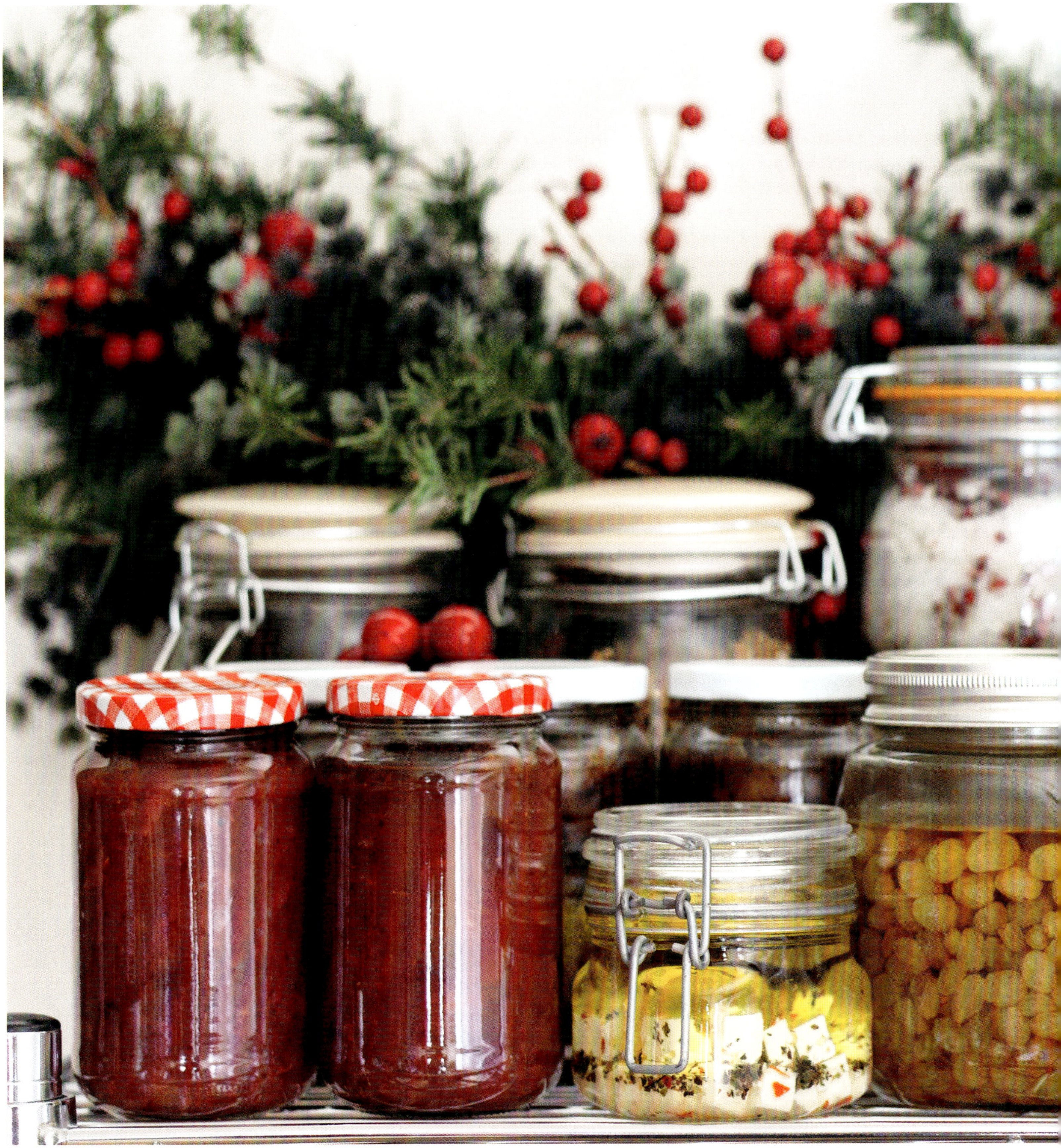

ALL WRAPPED UP 223

224 ALL WRAPPED UP

VANILLA SUGAR

I start with an idea, rather than a recipe, as I want to emphasize (even to the point of hectoring repetition) that you don't have to be a master culinary craftsperson in order to make an edible Christmas present. You don't, as you will see, even need to cook.

This is probably the most basic of homemade edible gifts, but it is no less lovely, and will be none the less appreciated, for all that. I love the snow-whiteness of the sugar in the jar, just as it is, but I have nothing against tying on festive ribbons and bows: the season gives license for exuberance.

To denote what's in the jar, however, I feel a no-nonsense brown luggage label or parcel tag looks best, and it has the advantage of giving you space to suggest uses for the vanilla sugar – which are that it brings an exotic yet nursery-comforting scent to mugs of coffee or hot chocolate, warm milk, cakes, cookies, pies and muffins and anything else that takes your or the recipient's festive fancy. Be sure to make clear, too, that the sugar can be replaced as it is used, keeping the jar as a permanent source of aromatic sweetness.

I think it's best to make the sugar up – and it's hardly arduous to tip some sugar into a jar and snip in a vanilla pod – at least a week before you're giving it, but you could do it months ahead. I keep a jar permanently in my kitchen.

Makes enough to fill 1 x 2½ cup jar

1 x 1 lb box superfine sugar
1 vanilla pod

1 x 2½ cup sealable jar, or whatever permutation of sizes you prefer

---

❄ Sterilize your jar, following the instructions on p.221, and leave to cool.

❄ Pour the sugar into the cooled jar.

❄ With the point of a small, sharp knife, cut into the vanilla pod lengthways, so its black and densely aromatic seeds are revealed, then cut this spliced and splayed stick into 3 short lengths and drop them into the sugar, embedding most of them well.

❄ Seal the jar and leave in a cool, dark place for at least a week before giving to some lucky person.

MAKE AHEAD TIP:
Vanilla sugar can be stored in a cool, dark place for about 1 year. If you make it 1 month before using or giving, add a label to say it can be kept for a further year and topped up as the sugar is used. After 1 year, replace the vanilla pod.

CHRISTMAS-SPICED SALT

Makes enough to fill 1 x 2 cup jar

2 cups good-quality sea salt or kosher salt
2 teaspoons red or pink peppercorns
2 teaspoons crushed red pepper flakes
4 star anise

1 x 2 cup sealable jar

You could call this the savory version of the Vanilla Sugar on the previous page: an idea, simply achieved, with the ingredients gathered in the course of your normal supermarket shop. Not all supermarkets stock red peppercorns, it's true, but plenty do, and a scour around a local specialty store should easily yield a supply (or if you're a mail order queen like me, turn to p.267 for Suppliers).

But do make sure you get red peppercorns, as it's the little red cheeks peeking through the salt, like holly berries in the snow, that make this so Christmassy.

And maybe scrawl on a piece of red card that this salt is good sprinkled on steak or roast chicken or to add a little oomph to the table and plate whenever desired.

❈ Sterilize your jar, following the instructions on p.221, and leave to cool.

❈ Put the salt into a bowl with the peppercorns, red pepper flakes and star anise.

❈ Toss everything about, then carefully tip into your cooled, prepared jar and seal tightly.

MAKE AHEAD TIP:
Spiced salt can be stored in a cool, dark place for about 1 year. If you make it 1 month before using or giving, add a label to say it can be kept for a further year and topped up as the salt is used.

STEEPED CHRISTMAS FRUITS

Many of you will know that this is not a new enthusiasm, but an undimmed one, which I think speaks more for it anyway. The first of the options, the Mixed Fruits steeped in Pedro Ximénez – that Spanish sherry tasting of raisin and muscovado sugar – truly is Christmas pudding in a jar; as you open it, the thick scent of molasses-dark sherry and rich fruit hits you. I love it, as I do the other fruits here, the golden raisins suspended in and swollen with the deeper golden Grand Marnier and the dark-red dried cherries in the equally dark-red syrupy, clove-scented cherry brandy – spooned over vanilla ice cream to make an instant dessert. But I'm not just finding an excuse to satisfy my own greed, unapologetic though I am about such an instinct: these are my seasonal no-wrap standbys. There are some people I wouldn't dare not give a jar to at Christmas, but then these liquor-steeped fruits make the perfect present: simple to make; luxurious to receive.

❄ Sterilize your jar (or jars), following the instructions on p.221, and leave to cool.

❄ Add the dried fruit to its cooled, prepared jar and then pour in the liqueur, which should just cover the fruit if it is a jar that isn't too roomy for it. Clamp on the lid, or seal tightly, and leave to stand in a cool, dark place.

❄ It is preferable to keep these for at least 4 days before giving away, but you could, if in a hurry, give them away instantly. However, as the fruit stands in the liqueur, it will absorb it and swell; after 4 days of steeping, you may want to top up with about 1/2 cup more liqueur.

Each batch makes enough to fill 1 x 2 cup jar

FOR THE MIXED FRUITS IN PEDRO XIMÉNEZ:
2 cups mixed dried fruits (raisins, sultanas, currants and candied cherries)
1 cup Pedro Ximénez, plus 1/2 cup for topping up if needed (see Suppliers p.267)

1 x 2 cup sealable jar (or 2 x 1 cup jars)

FOR THE GOLDEN RAISINS IN GRAND MARNIER:
1 3/4 cup golden raisins
1 cup Grand Marnier, plus 1/2 cup for topping up if needed

1 x 2 cup sealable jar (or 2 x 1 cup jars)

FOR THE DRIED CHERRIES IN CHERRY BRANDY:
2 cups dried cherries
1 cup cherry-flavored brandy (not kirsch), such as Bols, plus 1/2 cup for topping up if needed

1 x 2 cup sealable jar (or 2 x 1 cup jars)

MAKE AHEAD TIP:
Make the steeped fruits up to 1 month before eating or giving, and keep the alcohol level topped up. Store in a cool, dark place and use within 1 year. Once opened, keep in the refrigerator and use within 1 month.

ALL WRAPPED UP

MARINATED FETA

1 1/4 lbs drained feta cheese, cut into 1/2-inch cubes
1 teaspoon crushed red pepper flakes
1 teaspoon dried mint
1 teaspoon dried oregano
2 cups regular (not extra virgin) olive oil

2 x 1 cup and 2 x 1/2 cup sealable jars

There's something rather lovely about giving the sunny taste of the Greek hillside as a Christmas present. And I can't help relishing that, despite the Aegean sunshine conjured up by the promise of salty feta in its herb-sprinkled oil, the sight of the white cubes, speckled with the dark green of the mint and oregano and the red of the crushed chillies does, in fact, look Christmassy in the extreme.

This is another bung-in, rather than cook-up, present. And, to make your life even easier, you could buy the feta that comes ready cubed in little tubs of brine. But if you do so, be aware that about half of the tub's weight is made of the liquid the feta's sitting in.

❄ Sterilize your jars, following the instructions on p.221, and leave to cool.

❄ Put the cubed feta into a bowl and add the red pepper flakes, mint and oregano, gently tossing the cubes about to get even coverage, keeping in mind that you don't want to bash the feta about too much.

❄ Fill the cooled, prepared jars loosely with the herb- and pepper-sprinkled cubes to just below the rim, and pour oil over to cover. Seal the jars and keep in the refrigerator. Don't forget to scribble storing notes on the label.

MAKE AHEAD TIP:
Prepare the marinated feta up to 1 week before eating or giving, and store in the refrigerator. Use within 1 month, keeping the cheese topped up with olive oil.

OLIVES 'N' PICKLED THINGS

This is, I suppose, a hybrid of a recipe, if putting pickled vegetables and spices in a jar counts as an actual recipe. I wanted to make a jar of the sort of pickles you might be given over a glass of Bandol rosé or pastis if you're in the south of France, but which would be just as nice with a hunk of good bread and cheese or a post-Christmas meal for anyone lucky enough to get it in their stocking.

The nigella seeds, borrowed from Indian cooking, are here to add their sour oniony taste, their sooty black coloring (*nigella* denoting little and black) and for obvious egomaniacal gratification; the rice vinegar, which is plucked from my Southeast Asian shelf, is here for no other reason than that it is as clear as water and I didn't want even the pale straw color of cider or white wine vinegars to interfere with the sombre preserved beauty of the pickles. A distilled white vinegar would work on this principle, but might be a bit rough on the palate.

1 cup drained black pitted olives
1 cup drained cornichons (baby dill pickles, about the size of a child's little finger)
3 tablespoons capers
3/4 cup drained cocktail or pearl onions
1 teaspoon cumin seeds
1 teaspoon whole coriander seeds
1 teaspoon nigella seeds
3 fresh red chiles
3/4 cup rice vinegar

1 x 3 cup sealable jar (or 3 x 1 cup jars), with vinegar-proof lid, such as a French hermetic seal jar or reusable pickle jar

❈ Sterilize your jar (or jars), following the instructions on p.221, and leave to cool.

❈ Drain the olives, cornichons, capers and cocktail (or pearl) onions of any liquid they may be in.

❈ Tip them into your cooled, sterilized jar (or jars), and spoon in the cumin, coriander and nigella seeds.

❈ Halve and seed 2 of the chiles, tucking the 4 halves into the jar.

❈ Now seed and finely chop the remaining chile, sprinkling the Christmas-red confetti into the jar as well.

❈ Top up the jar with the rice vinegar, so that everything is covered, then screw on the lid.

Nigella seeds may also be labeled as kalonji or black onion seeds (see Suppliers p.267).

MAKE AHEAD TIP:
Make the pickles up to 1 month before eating or giving. Store in a cool, dark place for up to 3 months. Once opened, store in the refrigerator and use within 1 month, keeping the pickles topped up with vinegar.

WINTER-SPICED VODKA

Makes 2 cups

1 teaspoon whole coriander seeds
3 cardamom pods, bruised
½ teaspoon whole cumin seed
1 cinnamon stick
1 whole dried red chile
2 cups vodka

1 x 2 cup sealable bottle

It's true, a shot of vodka is warming enough, but this makes a real present out of doing little more than opening a bottle and some spice jars. I love how beautiful it looks, with the dried chile, the cinnamon stick, the seeds and pods captured in the vodka, and imbuing it with fireside warmth and glowing pale amber color.

You may suggest, as you hand it over, that it be knocked back in shots, used to make a festively spiced martini or, with the addition of some tomato juice, a sprinkle of salt and a dash of Worcestershire sauce, a particularly memorable Christmassy Bloody Mary.

❋ Sterilize your bottle (see p.221) and leave to cool.

❋ Pop all the spices into your cooled, prepared bottle.

❋ Preferably using a miniature funnel (see p.267 for Suppliers of such arcane kitchenalia, as well as of bottles and jars, and so forth), pour in the vodka, seal the bottle and put it to steep, in a cool, dark cupboard, or anywhere away from the light.

MAKE AHEAD TIP:
Make the spiced vodka up to 1 month before drinking or giving. Store in a cool, dark place and use within 1 year.

POMEGRANATE VODKA

I concede: there is no occasion in your or anyone's life when Pomegranate Vodka will be a pressing need. But that is why it makes such a wonderful present. It's out of the ordinary, but eminently usable, in an indulgent, uplifting kind of a way.

For me, pomegranate is the quintessential Christmas fruit, bringing back memories of a time when it appeared only at Christmas, bulging in my stocking, and I'd spend captivated hours winkling the seeds out with a pin and a kirby grip. And I say this even though I find packets of the seeds, freshly popped out for me, in the supermarket pretty well all year round now.

You don't have to be as lazy as I am: by all means buy the whole fruit and seed it yourself, but make sure you drain them (and you can drink the juice) before putting in the vodka bottle.

I defy anyone to look at the pretty pale-pink vodka and not to smile: it is indisputably happy-making. The steeping pomegranate seeds don't, it's true, make as emphatic a difference to the taste as to the color, but that floral sour-sweet fragrance does make itself delicately, mysteriously felt. I don't think anyone drinking this would be able to say exactly what the flavor was, but it's plainly not straight vodka: perhaps it's more accurate to think of it as scented rather than flavored with pomegranate. But, whatever, you can tell the lucky recipient that it lends itself, iced, to petal-colored shots, or fragrant martini-mixing or even the building of long, pink drinks.

Makes 3 cups

1 cup pomegranate seeds
3 cups vodka (1 x 750ml bottle)

1 large sealable jar, approx. 1 quart for steeping
1 x 3 cup sealable bottle for presenting

❊ Sterilize your jar (see p.221) and leave to cool.

❊ Add the pomegranate seeds to the cooled, prepared jar, followed by the vodka. Seal and give the jar a safe shake before putting it in a cool, dark cupboard, or anywhere out of the light.

❊ Leave it for 4 days, shaking it any time you remember to, before sieving it into a measuring jug. Sterilize your bottle (or indeed the original vodka bottle with the label freshly soaked off), pour in the steeped vodka and put the lid on tightly before storing.

MAKE AHEAD TIP:
Make the fragrant vodka. Store the bottle in a cool, dark place and use within 1 year.

HONEYED FIG VINEGAR

Makes 1 quart

1 quart white wine vinegar
1 1/2 cups finely chopped soft dried figs
1/3 cup runny honey
2 teaspoons dried thyme
1 teaspoon white peppercorns

1 large sealable jar, approx. 2 quarts, with vinegar-proof lid, such as a French hermetic seal jar or reusable pickle jar
2 x 2 cup sealable bottles

I have to confess, I have never been one for flavored or fruity vinegars, which became such a cliché of the late Eighties – when I first started going to restaurants, and even reviewing them – that I developed something of an aversion.

But in the right circumstances I can reconsider. And am humbly happy to do so now: the mellowness and warm depth that the honey and figs bring to the vinegar make this perfect, with nothing more than a little oil and salt added, for dressing a seasonal salad; and in terms of flavor and present presence, so to speak, you really do get a lot of bang for your buck.

❋ Sterilize your jar (see p.221) and leave to cool.

❋ Pour the vinegar into the cooled, sterilized jar, then add the figs, honey, thyme and peppercorns, seal tightly and give a good shake.

❋ Put the fig-steeping vinegar into a cupboard, or anywhere out of the light, and leave for 4 days. It will begin to look like some strange specimen jar, the sort of freak-show medical curiosities collected by the tzars and now stored in that spooky museum in St Petersburg, the name of which I'm too traumatized to remember. But try not to let this put you off.

❋ Strain into a large measuring or batter jug, taking care that no dusty spikes of thyme get through the net.

❋ Now, sterilize your 2 bottles, let them cool, then pour the vinegar in. Seal tightly and set aside in a cool, dark place until you present them.

MAKE AHEAD TIP:
Make the fig vinegar. Store the bottles in a cool, dark place and use within 1 year.

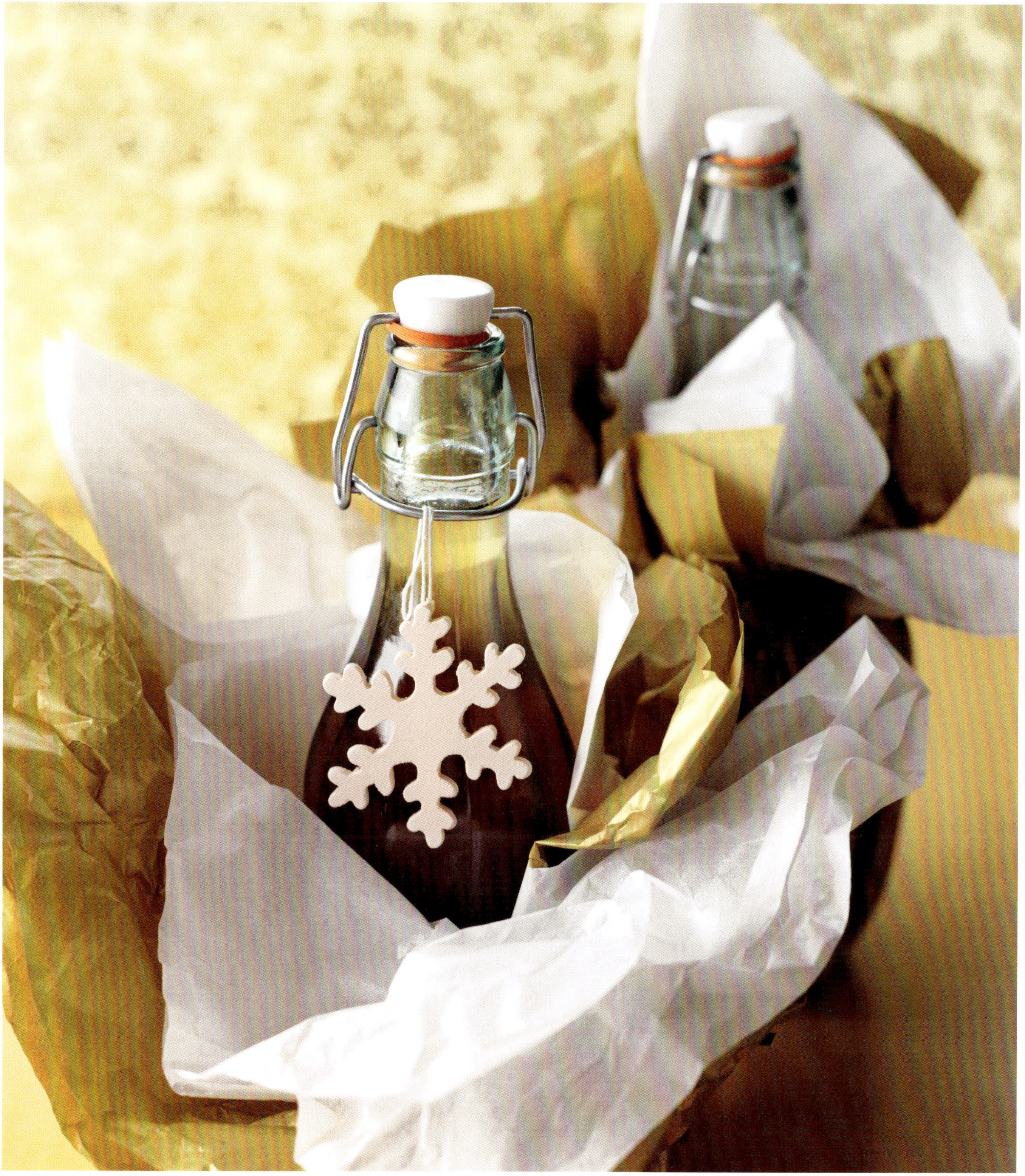

234 ALL WRAPPED UP

CHRISTMAS CHUTNEY

Chutney is not the most obviously festive, seasonally indulgent, must-have foodstuff, but it is the cornerstone of my Christmas pantry. I begin to hyperventilate, now as I write, even at the idea of not having a stock of it. My need is threefold: cold cuts and Christmas Day leftovers are impossible to contemplate without chutney (and the Christmas ham first-time-out must have it as well); it is what I make, annually, and with very, very little effort for the children's school Christmas Fair; and since it is easy to prepare a lot at one time, you can get a tidy number of presents seen to out of one under-an-hour stint in the kitchen, too.

Four of my favorite chutneys are recorded here, but this first, unsubtly named Christmas Chutney, is the one – in jars decorated as they are here, with squidgy, cut-out snowflake ribbon – that I box up and heave over to the Christmas Fair, along with as many cupcakes as I can muster.

Of course, any of the chutneys in this chapter would do, and gloriously, but this one is just so full of Christmassiness, crammed as it is with dates, cranberries and clementines, and spiced with cloves and cinnamon.

❆ Sterilize your jars (see instructions on p.221). You get about 2¼ quarts from this recipe, so you can either fill 9 x 1 cup/¼ ltr jars or go (as I do) for a variety of jars of differing sizes, amounting, give or take, to the total volume.

❆ Put the apples, onion, cranberries and dates into a large pan.

❆ Zest the clementines over the top, then squeeze in the juice and scrape in the pulp.

❆ Add the sugar, ground cloves, ginger, cinnamon and cayenne pepper, then pour the vinegar over and sprinkle in the salt.

❆ Now all you have to do is give a good stir, turn on the heat, bring to a boil, then turn down the heat and let it bubble cheerfully, uncovered, for about an hour or until you have a pulpy mass.

❆ Spoon into your warm, prepared jars and seal.

Makes approx. 2¼ quarts

5 cups peeled, cored and finely chopped Granny Smith apples (approx. 1¾ lbs unprepared weight)
1 medium onion, peeled and roughly chopped
4½ cups fresh or frozen cranberries, thawed if frozen
2 cups chopped pitted soft dates
zest, pulp and juice of 2 clementines
2 cups sugar
½ teaspoon ground cloves
1 teaspoon ground ginger
1½ teaspoons ground cinnamon
¼ teaspoon cayenne pepper
2 cups white wine vinegar
2 teaspoons kosher salt or 1 teaspoon table salt

9 x 1 cup sealable jars, with vinegar-proof lid, such as French hermetic seal jars or reusable pickle jars

MAKE AHEAD TIP:
Make the chutney up to 2 months before using or giving (the longer it has to "mature" the better). Store in a cool, dark place for up to 1 year. Once opened, store in the refrigerator and use within 1 month.

RICH FRUIT CHUTNEY

Makes 1½ quarts

2 cups dried apricots (8 oz, not Californian)
heaping 2 cups pitted dried dates
2 cups dried pears (8 oz)
2 cups dried cranberries (8 oz)
¾ cup packed soft light brown sugar
1¼ cups cider vinegar
1¼ cups water
1 teaspoon kosher salt or ½ teaspoon table salt
zest of 1 lemon, finely grated
¼ teaspoon ground cloves
½ teaspoon ground allspice
1 teaspoon ground cinnamon
1 teaspoon ground ginger

3 x 2 cup sealable jars (or 6 x 1 cup jars), with vinegar-proof lid, such as French hermetic seal jars or reusable pickle jars

MAKE AHEAD TIP:
Make the chutney up to 2 months before using or giving (the longer it has to "mature" the better). Store in a dark, cool place for up to 1 year. Once opened, store in the refrigerator and use within 1 month.

This could be described as a soft-set, savory take on Christmas pudding. But as someone who has always liked a slab of un-iced fruitcake with a slice of sharp cheese, I see that as a good thing. What gives the richness, and the reminder of the Christmas pudding, is that this chutney is made with dried fruits. What you end up with is a rich, dark, fruity, deeply-spiced chutney with a slightly more luxurious taste and texture than you might expect. This, of course, makes it an ideal present.

It also happens to be the easiest of the chutneys to make (not that it would be possible to find one that's difficult) because you don't have to peel or chop anything: all the dried fruit goes, as is, into the pan, and then, only when cooked, is gently processed to turn it into a sticky, spoonable preserve.

❊ Sterilize your jars (see p.221). The amount of chutney you're making here is enough to fill 3 x 2 cup/½ ltr jars (as I've done) or 6 half that size, or, indeed, any permutation in the middle.

❊ Put all the ingredients into a decent-sized saucepan and bring to the boil.

❊ Once it has begun to bubble in earnest, turn down the heat, partially cover the pan (unlike the other chutneys, this one has no fresh fruit to give off liquid as it cooks) and simmer for 15–20 minutes or until all the fruit is soft.

❊ Take the pan off the heat for about 10 minutes to let it cool a little, before scraping it into a food processor fitted with the double-bladed knife.

❊ Process for approx. 3 seconds, then open the lid to scrape down the chutney before pulsing again in short bursts. You want this chopped but not like untextured pulp or mush.

❊ Fill your warm, prepared jars and seal.

RED BEET AND GINGER CHUTNEY

Some people of my generation were put off prunes at school; I developed an antipathy to beets. For those of us who grew up eating them at their worst, beets can conjure up an almost putrid sweetness and corrosive vinegariness. But to borrow, almost, a famous phrase: the past is another country; they cook things differently there.

So now I find myself on the verge of becoming a born-again beet lover: I admire the beauty (and the taste) of them raw; I look for ways to celebrate them in my cooking. This chutney, which marries the earthy sweetness of the beet with the pepperiness of fresh ginger – the sourness of the apple, like a useful go-between, providing balance – is a triumph of prejudice overcome.

You need give nothing but a small jar of this gorgeous stuff as a present, but if you wanted to pair it with anything to amplify the gift, may I suggest a snowy log of sharp but creamy fresh goat's cheese.

❈ Sterilize your jars (following instructions on p.221).

❈ Take a large saucepan and tip in the beets and apple – the beets take a lot longer than the apple to cook, so the latter doesn't have to be chopped as small. Add the red onion.

❈ Grate in the fresh ginger, tumble in the chopped crystallized ginger and sprinkle the brown sugar, salt and ground allspice over.

❈ Pour the vinegar over and stir to mix.

❈ Turn on the heat, bring to the boil, then turn down the heat and let the pan simmer steadily for approx. 1 hour, stirring every now and again, until the pieces of beet are tender. The apple will have turned to mush long before this.

❈ Spoon into your warm, prepared jars and seal.

Makes approx. 1 1/2 quarts

- 3 2/3 cups peeled and finely chopped red beets (approx. 1 1/4 lbs unprepared)
- 4 1/2 cups peeled, quartered and finely chopped Granny Smith apples (approx. 2 1/2 lbs unprepared)
- 1 large red onion, peeled and finely chopped
- 1 x 1-inch piece fresh ginger
- 1/2 cup finely chopped crystallized ginger
- 1 3/4 cups packed soft light brown sugar
- 2 teaspoons kosher salt or 1 teaspoon table salt
- 1 teaspoon ground allspice
- 3 cups red wine vinegar

6 x 1 cup sealable jars, with vinegar-proof lid, such as French hermetic seal jars or reusable pickle jars

MAKE AHEAD TIP:
Make the chutney up to 2 weeks before using or giving. Store in a cool, dark place for up to 6 months. Once opened, store in the refrigerator and use within 1 month.

238 ALL WRAPPED UP

CRANBERRY AND APPLE CHUTNEY

Apple is – generally – the basis of a chutney, as it's the sourness and pectin-rich nature of a Granny Smith, or indeed all sour apples, that gives chutney its soft set and its sour-sweet tang. The Rich Fruit Chutney, on p.236, is an exception, but deliberately so. Apple can be used, therefore, as a binding vehicle for other ingredients but it can, indeed, be the only fruit. The cranberries that dot this chutney are dried, so they stand in for raisins, providing punctuation rather than adding flesh, as the fresh ones do in the Christmas Chutney on p.235.

I add dried cranberries in preference to any other dried fruit, simply because their redness, their celebratory seasonality, makes this feel more Christmassy; the whole of the chutney's cheery hue does its festive bit, too.

❇ Sterilize your jars (see p.221).

❇ Take a medium-sized (not too big) saucepan and chuck into it all the ingredients. Stir with a wooden spoon and then put the pan on the heat.

❇ Bring to the boil, then turn down the heat a little to let the pan cook, uncovered, on a fast simmer for about 45 minutes, or until the chutney has thickened slightly and the fruit is soft.

❇ Spoon into your warm, prepared jars and seal them.

Makes about 1 quart

5 cups peeled, cored and finely chopped Granny Smith apples (approx. 1 3/4 lbs unprepared)
2 cups dried cranberries
1 onion, peeled and finely chopped
1 1/3 cups cider vinegar
1 cup sugar
1 teaspoon ground ginger
1 teaspoon ground turmeric
1 teaspoon ground cumin
1 teaspoon ground coriander
2 teaspoons kosher salt or 1 teaspoon table salt

4 x 1 cup sealable jars, with vinegar-proof lid, such as French hermetic seal jars or reusable pickle jars

MAKE AHEAD TIP:
Make the chutney up to 2 months before using or giving (the longer it has to "mature" the better). Store in a dark, cool place for up to 1 year. Once opened, store in the refrigerator and use within 1 month.

240 ALL WRAPPED UP

CHILE JAM

Although I call this chile jam, I don't mean that it's the sort of thing you'd spread on your toast at breakfast (though smeared inside a bacon sandwich, it could be a real help one hungover morning) but rather a chile jelly – chelly? – that glows a fiery, flecked red and is fabulous with cold meats or a cheese plate. And just a small pot of it makes a gorgeous present.

In the traditional run of things, jellies are incredibly hard work to make, or at least I find them so. If I tell you that jelly-making tends to involve tying jelly bags or cheesecloth to the leg of an upended stool and straining stuff through the fine cloth into a bowl sitting in the underside of the stool's seat for at least 12 hours, you'll get the picture.

But don't worry. I don't strain – in either sense of the word – myself, but leave the orange-glowing, red jelly cheerfully freckled with the bits of chile and sweet bell pepper, and, instead of getting my jelly set from preparing, cooking and sieving bucketloads of high pectin fruit, I simply cook the chiles in vinegar and sugar with added pectin, an essential ingredient I buy from canning suppliers (see Suppliers p.267). It could scarcely be easier.

I make the "chelly" with equal weights of hot and sweet peppers, but if you wanted a bit more fire in your jelly, you could up the amount of chile peppers and reduce the amount of bell pepper. But this proportion provides enough tingle for those who like it hot, but without burning more sensitive palates.

Makes 1½ quarts

1 cup seeded and roughly chopped fresh red serrano chiles (5 oz unprepared)

1 cup cored and seeded roughly chopped red bell pepper (5 oz unprepared)

5 cups sugar

1 x 1.75 oz box powdered fruit pectin, such as Ball's original fruit pectin

2½ cups apple cider vinegar

6 x 1 cup sealable jars, with vinegar-proof lid, such as French hermetic seal jars or reusable pickle jars

❄ Sterilize your jars (see p.221) and leave to cool.

❄ Put the cut-up chiles into a food processor and pulse until they are finely chopped. Add the chunks of bell pepper and pulse again until you have a vibrantly red-flecked processor bowl.

❄ Dissolve the sugar and pectin in the vinegar in a wide, medium-sized pan over a low heat without stirring.

❄ Scrape the chile pepper mixture out of the bowl and add to the pan. Bring the pan to the boil, then leave it at a rollicking boil for 15 minutes.

❄ Take the pan off the heat and allow it to cool. The liquid will become more syrupy, then from syrup to viscous and from viscous to jelly-like as it cools.

❄ After about 40 minutes, or once the red flecks are more or less evenly dispersed in the jelly (as the liquid firms up, the bits of chile and pepper start being suspended in it rather than floating on it), ladle into your jars. If you want to stir gently at this stage, it will do no harm. Then seal tightly.

MAKE AHEAD TIP:
Make the jam up to 1 month before using or giving. Store in a cool, dark place for up to 1 year. Once opened, store in the refrigerator and use within 1 month.

CHRISTMAS KETCHUP

Makes about 2 quarts

3 x 12 oz bags fresh or frozen cranberries, thawed if frozen
2 long cinnamon sticks, or 4 short ones
3 star anise
1 x 2-inch piece unpeeled fresh ginger, sliced into thin coins
1 fresh long red chile, seeded and finely chopped
1 orange
1 teaspoon ground cloves
2 cups cider vinegar
2 cups water
3 cups packed light brown sugar
2 teaspoons salt
1 x 14 oz can diced tomatoes
½ cup sugar

4 x 2 cup sealable bottles

MAKE AHEAD TIP:
Make the ketchup up to 1 month before using or giving. Store in a cool, dark place for up to 6 months. Once opened, store in the refrigerator and use within 4–6 weeks.

I've made a lot of chutneys in my life, but very few ketchups. I love homemade brown sauce (and the one I made in *Domestic Goddess* really came about as a way of rectifying a rhubarb chutney I'd attempted and overcooked), but I think that tomato ketchup is so loved in its industrial form, that I have never been able to face the sneer and snub of my children were I to offer my own version. This is a red sauce, but a deep, garnet red, a ketchup that's made primarily with cranberries and just begs to be added to the Christmas-leftover table. It's also – for what it's worth, and I think a tip in the right direction is always good for a slight detour – fantastic dribbled over some seared scallops, or mixed with mayonnaise to make a dip or dressing for cold pink prawns. It's a strangely gratifyingly, versatile little number.

You will need a Mouli or food mill for this ketchup; you could always push it through a strainer, but a food mill is easier and faster (and it's not an expensive piece of equipment).

❋ Sterilize your bottles (see p.221), and make sure you've got a funnel.

❋ Put the cranberries into a wide, medium-sized saucepan, and add the cinnamon sticks, star anise, ginger and chile.

❋ Finely zest the orange over cranberries and spices, then squeeze out the juice from the orange and pour that in.

❋ Add the ground cloves, cider vinegar, water, brown sugar, salt and diced tomatoes.

❋ Stir well with a wooden spoon, then put on the heat and bring to the boil.

❋ Once it's started boiling, turn down the heat to let it simmer, uncovered, with steady gusto, for 30 minutes, then take the pan off the heat and let the contents cool a little.

❋ Work the mixture through a Mouli, or other food mill, into a fresh pan. Or mouli it into a jug and then into the washed-out pan.

❋ Add the white sugar to the smooth ketchup, stir well, then reheat till it comes back to the boil and let it boil vigorously for about 10 minutes or until it becomes thick and glossy. Stir occasionally to ensure an even heat.

❋ Pour, through a funnel, into your warm, prepared bottles and seal well.

CORN CHOW-CHOW

Just in case you're wondering, this bears no resemblance to the sugary, vinegary corn relish you find in burger joints. Or perhaps that's not quite accurate: it bears a resemblance, but tastes so much better.

The term chow-chow comes from the Pennsylvania Dutch (those Low German speakers who settled in America) but the relish has its counterpart, too, in American cooking of the South. I've slightly made it my own by using hot English mustard rather than the milder one that would be used Stateside.

It isn't as set as the store-bought stuff, but I prefer it this way, and I find the tumbling beads of corn, sweet, sharp and glossed in its dressing, utterly addictive; moreover, its sunny yellowness is an uplifting sight on a winter's day.

I use frozen corn, since you need plenty and it makes more sense than canned, but if you forget to thaw it, just sit it in a large strainer over a bowl and pour boiling water from the kettle over it.

❇ Sterilize your jars, following the instructions on p.221. (I favor a 12-ounce wide-necked bottle, so I use 5 of those plus a 1-cup jar, but 8 of the smaller jars might be wiser.)

❇ Take the corn out of the freezer and let it begin to thaw in a strainer over a bowl. If you need to speed the process, pour boiling water over it.

❇ Put the mustard, honey, vinegar, salt and sugar into a saucepan, and place it on a low heat, stirring with a wooden spoon to help everything dissolve.

❇ Stop stirring, and turn up the heat so that the mixture comes to the boil, then let it boil for 5 minutes.

❇ Check the corn is thawed and drained, tip it into a bowl, and add the scallions and diced bell peppers.

❇ Once your liquid has boiled for 5 minutes, take it off the heat and pour through a sieve (so you get a smooth syrup) onto the corn, scallion and pepper mixture.

❇ Ladle equal amounts of corn mixture and liquid into your warm, prepared jars. The syrup should cover the chow-chow; or rather, no corn should sit above the syrup but it doesn't matter if the syrup comes up over the corn a bit.

❇ Seal the jars or screw on the lids, and store in the refrigerator.

Makes 2 quarts

6 cups (2 lbs) frozen corn, thawed
8 teaspoons hot English mustard, from a jar
1 cup honey
2 cups cider vinegar
1 tablespoon celery salt
1/4 cup sugar
8 scallions, sliced into 1/4-inch rounds
4 red bell peppers, seeded, cored and cut into 1/2-inch dice

8 x 1 cup sealable jars, with vinegar-proof lid, such as French hermetic seal jars or reusable pickle jars

MAKE AHEAD TIP:
Make the chow-chow and store in the refrigerator for up to 2 months before using or giving. Once opened, use within 1 month.

PEANUT BRITTLE WITH ART AND SOUL

Makes approx. 10 oz.

1 cup sugar
1/4 cup water
1/2 cup light corn syrup
1 cup salted peanuts
1 1/2 teaspoons vanilla extract
1 tablespoon soft butter
1 1/4 teaspoons baking soda

This title isn't a boast, but a name to denote provenance. It's a recipe given to me, at my greedy request, by the cook-and-a-half, Art Smith. True, I've slightly simplified it, but only because I don't have his deserved confidence, so I make my batch smaller, and leave out the difficult technical bits.

But even so, what this makes is fabulous: you really have to steel yourself to give it away.

❈ Get out a large sheet of parchment paper or aluminum foil, place on a cookie sheet, and butter or oil it. Sit it by the stove, waiting to receive the brittle once it's ready to pour.

❈ Put the sugar, water and syrup into a saucepan, bring to the boil gently, then turn up the heat and let it boil for 8–10 minutes, swirling (but not stirring) the pan a couple of times, until the syrup has turned gold in color. It will be smoking by then, so be warned!

❈ Take the pan off the heat and, with a wooden spoon, stir in the nuts, followed by the vanilla, butter and baking soda. You will have a golden, frothy, hot and gooey mixture.

❈ Pour this briskly onto the waiting parchment or foil, using your wooden spoon to coax and pull it to make a nut-studded sheet, puddle-shaped though it may be, rather than a heap.

❈ Leave it to cool, then break into pieces and store in an airtight container or box; or bag up to give at once as presents. You'll get about 1 pound in total, and it's up to you how much you want to put in each bag, really. I find it easier to do several small batches like this, rather than multiplying quantities as I cook.

MAKE AHEAD TIP:
Make the brittle up to 1 week before eating or giving. Store in airtight bags or containers in a dry, non-humid environment. Once opened, eat within 7 to 10 days.

ALL WRAPPED UP 245

246 ALL WRAPPED UP

CHRISTMAS PUDDINI BONBONS

I know there aren't many sweet things in this chapter – strictly speaking only two – but that is mainly because, as I suggested in the introduction, there are lots of sweet treats, just waiting to be wrapped and beribboned (see pp.194–215). And the truth is, apart from baking, making sweets is a lot harder than making savory edible presents. These bonbons, however, are almost alarmingly easy. I was inspired by a picture I saw in *The Australian Women's Weekly*, fell in love with their cuteness and had to have a go myself. This isn't quite their recipe, but the idea – and the decoration – is the same, which is to say, these are delectable little truffley bonbons made by mixing up cold Christmas pudding, liquor, syrup and melted chocolate, rolling them into small balls, then melting white chocolate over them and arranging small pieces of red and green glacé cherries on top to make them look like miniature Christmas puddings themselves.

I made this just after last Christmas, using some leftover pudding, foil-wrapped and waiting to be gratifyingly recycled (though you could buy a mini one, microwave it and leave it to get cold) and adding a slug of my beloved Pedro Ximénez – since that was the alcohol I'd originally put into the pudding – and an ooze of golden syrup before compacting it with melted dark chocolate, but you could just as easily add rum or brandy and, as the original recipe also does, 3 tablespoons confectioners' sugar.

The hard part – in the sense that you need superhuman patience, rather than any special skills – is dripping over the melted white chocolate and snipping the cherries and arranging them to evoke a sprig of berried holly. I am not really cut out for this work, and you will curse my name as you do it, but, afterwards, you will be thrilled with what you've done.

And, although they look like baby Christmas puddings, they taste like meltingly rich, spiced chocolate truffles. These babies have got everything going for them.

❋ Line a baking sheet (that will fit in the refrigerator) with plastic wrap, parchment paper or aluminum foil, and set it to one side while you make the bonbons.

❋ Melt the bittersweet chocolate in a heat-proof bowl suspended above a pan of simmering water, or in the microwave according to the manufacturer's guidelines.

❋ Put the cold crumbled Christmas pudding into a bowl, add the Pedro Ximénez sherry and golden syrup and stir briskly till all is incorporated.

❋ Pour in the melted dark chocolate and stir again: this will make the mixture much more cohesive.

Makes about 30

2/3 cup best-quality bittersweet chocolate, finely chopped or chips

2 3/4 cups crumbled cooked and cooled, Christmas pudding or rich fruitcake (see Suppliers p.267)

1/4 cup Pedro Ximénez sherry (see Suppliers p.267)

2 tablespoons golden syrup, such as Lyle's

FOR DECORATION:

1/2 cup white chocolate, finely chopped or chips

6 red candied cherries

6 green candied cherries

MAKE AHEAD TIP:
Make the bonbons up to 2 weeks before eating or giving. Pack in boxes and store in a very cool place. If made 2 weeks ahead, add a label to say "keep cool and eat within 1 or 2 days".

❄ To make this step easier, put on a pair of those disposable vinyl gloves sold in hardware stores and supermarkets, pinch out small lumps of mixture and roll so that you have little rounds about the size of a chocolate truffle. You should get about 30 out of this mixture; fight the impatient urge to make these balls larger as you go.

❄ Cover with plastic wrap and slot into the refrigerator to firm up.

❄ To decorate, melt the white chocolate either in a heat-proof bowl suspended over a pan of simmering water, or in the microwave according to the manufacturer's guidelines, then let cool for about 5 minutes, to make it easier to work with, while you chop the red cherries into small pieces (to evoke berries), and snip the green cherries (or angelica) into miniature lengths, to represent leaves.

❄ Using a teaspoon, drip a little of the melted but slightly cooled white chocolate on each bonbon, then arrange the infuriatingly sticky pieces of cherry on top.

❄ Place in boxes to give away – if you use small boxes that will fit 6 bonbons each, you will get 5 adorable presents out of this – or on a plate to hand round with coffee, instead of dessert, after a post-Christmas dinner.

A CHRISTMAS BRUNCH FOR 6–8

MUCH AS I LOVE COOKING, and derive perhaps more pleasure from feeding people than is altogether decent, at this time of year it can make sense to think of how to curtail kitchen activity. I don't wish to sound lacking in seasonal cheer or sociability, but I know from experience that if you overstretch yourself, it's hell for everyone: you suffer, growing more resentful by the meal; your family ditto, as they bear the brunt of your probably self-imposed martyrdom. Sometimes – and I know I shouldn't project on to all of you my flaws, inherited with almost ironic precision down the maternal line – the domestic overload is an unavoidable feature of the festivities. But a little mealtime merging can lessen the load. And this is where brunch comes in.

Not, I hasten to add, that I intend my Christmas brunch to be for the big day itself. I have no desire to bust a gut – infelicitous as that sounds – on Christmas Day: there's enough cooking and eating as it is, without adding more of either. But around that time, whether you have family staying or friends visiting, brunch can be the answer. This isn't just about streamlining the schedule: the essential uneverydayness of this hybrid of a meal makes it feel like a holiday hoolie from the off.

Cooking a good breakfast for people really requires you to be a short-order chef; my brunch is designed to free you from stoveside captivity or last-minute frenzy. Yes, there are eggs, but the strata – which is a cross between a savory bread pudding and a toasted sandwich – is assembled the night before, left in the refrigerator to steep and merely popped in the oven to bake mid-morning. The pumpkin in the pancakes means they can be made ahead of time and kept warm, or reheated, without drying out or going limp. I have been known to make the Antioxidant Fruit Salad with ready-cubed mango; and the Christmassy Cranberry, Almond and Honey Granola, well, that can be done ages ahead, in quantity, to be stored in a jar and brought out whenever needed.

Not that anything needs adding, but if at any time there's some Spruced-Up Vanilla Cake (see p.198) knocking around, slice and toast it and present people with golden triangles of what tastes like French toast, but requires no soaking or frying.

But the final step here is really my first: that's to say, if there's a better kick-start than is provided by the Espresso Martini on p.250, I've yet to discover it. I don't even drink coffee in the normal run of events, and yet I can knock this back. You could, of course, partner it with a matching jug of Marteani or cut a little slack for those who want to start the day less boldly by mixing up – see p.3 for the recipe – a pitcherful of Poinsettia, a festively red and knock-backable drink made of fizzy wine, orange liqueur and cranberry juice.

ESPRESSO MARTINI

Makes 1 quart

1 cup espresso or very strong coffee, left to cool

1 cup Kahlúa or other coffee liqueur

1 cup vodka, chilled

1 cup caramel vodka (see Suppliers p.267) or butterscotch schnapps

ice cubes to serve

It's not too much of an exaggeration to say that this magnificent creation – a full fabulous jugful of it – is the rock on which this whole brunch rests.

I am unashamed to boast about it, as it is a filch rather than a fully-fledged offspring of mine. That's to say, I once had a sip of the espresso martini at the restaurant Locanda Locatelli in London, and I knew, just knew, I had to make it mine. I own, too, that my version isn't quite as virtuoso as theirs. Order one there, and it comes whizzed to perfection, with that pale frothy head of foam – the authentic *crema* – and a trio of coffee beans on top. I just mix the ingredients together, but it tastes no less fabulous.

The only thing to bear in mind is that you should make your espresso the night before so it's properly cold, chilled if possible, before you start.

❋ To make a pitcher, mix the ingredients together and serve over ice.

❋ To make just 1 cocktail, remember that this martini is made up of equal parts, so 1 x 1-ounce bartenders' measure of each component is enough, with a pile-up of ice, for a gratifying martini-glassful.

MAKE AHEAD TIP:
Make the espresso the day before, cool, cover and chill. Next day, mix all the ingredients together up to 4 hours ahead. Cover and leave in a cool place.

MARTEANI

Makes 1 quart

1 cup strong Earl Grey tea, left to cool

1 cup Cointreau, gin, or Triple Sec

1 cup vodka, chilled

As already mooted, this is an obvious partner for the coffee-cocktail, above. As with that, remember to get the crucial component – here tea, rather than the espresso above – brewed the night before so it's cold and ready to be mixed into a cool drink for your brunch.

❋ To make a pitcher, mix the ingredients together and serve over ice.

❋ To make just one drink, replace the 1 cup amounts with a 1-ounce shot each.

TRIPLE CHEESE AND ONION STRATA

A strata is, in effect, a savory bread pudding and this one is a particularly shining model of its kind. It's the easiest way to make an egg dish for breakfast when you've got a tableful of people, as it's composed in advance and you don't need to stand at the stove like a harassed, short-order cook.

I tend to let the bread stale in the day, and put the strata together before I go to bed, removing it from the refrigerator and cooking in the oven the next morning, which makes for a very unstressful way of having people over.

I kept this meatless on purpose, as a veggie-pleasing brunch dish is always a consideration, but of course a panful of sizzling bacon served alongside would keep me most awfully happy.

❄ Arrange the stale baguette slices in a baking dish measuring approx. 9 inches square.

❄ Put the scallions, mozzarella, Parmesan and cheddar into a food processor.

❄ Add the sour cream and eggs, then process to make an eggy-cheese sauce. Pour this over the stale bread, cover with plastic wrap, and leave it to soak overnight. If you want to do this by hand, simply whisk together the eggs and sour cream, then finely chop the scallions and mozzarella and add them to the eggs. Add in the cheddar and Parmesan and stir to combine before pouring over the bread pieces.

❄ In the morning, preheat your oven to 350°F. Take the strata out of the refrigerator and uncover it.

❄ Bake for 30 minutes, though the strata may need longer in the oven if it is really f-f-f-fridge c-c-c-cold when it goes in.

❄ Once it's out of the oven, scissor the chives finely over the strata and spoon onto serving plates.

1 baguette or French loaf (both elbow-ends discarded), cut into 1/2-inch slices and allowed to go stale (this is about 1/2 lb of stale bread slices, in case you want to substitute other loaves or types of bread)
6 scallions, roughly sliced
1/4 lb fresh mozzarella cheese, roughly chopped
3/4 cup shaved Parmesan cheese (I like to make this in the processor, so it's easier to use shaved Parmesan, but if you're grating, do use proper block Parmesan.)
1 cup grated cheddar cheese
1/2 cup sour cream
6 eggs
small bunch of chives to garnish

MAKE AHEAD TIP:
Assemble the strata the evening before. Cover with plastic wrap and leave to soak overnight in the refrigerator. Next day, take the strata out of the refrigerator and uncover. Allow to come to room temperature while you preheat the oven. Cook as directed.

A CHRISTMAS BRUNCH

PUMPKIN PANCAKES WITH STICKY MAPLE PECANS

Although these pancakes are perfect for a brunch with a party feel, to be honest, I feel they can be eaten at any time. Add a little ice cream or whipped cream and you have a pretty fantastic supper-party pudding, too.

What I like about them particularly is that without too much of an initial shopping expedition you can be sure you have the wherewithal to make these as and when: maple syrup and canned pumpkin purée are stashed in the store cupboard; buttermilk has a pretty long life in the refrigerator, or you could simply add a teaspoon of vinegar to ordinary milk and let it stand, souring, for 5 minutes or so before proceeding.

And these are special. Pumpkin pancakes are to ordinary breakfast pancakes as a comforter is to a blanket. The sweet puréed flesh blends with the sour tang of buttermilk to make a pancake that is fleshy and downy and supersoft. You could, of course, eat these any way you so wish, but topped with pecans that have been tossed in a hot pan with maple syrup and doused with more maple syrup, is the best way I can think of.

It's probably easiest to make these before people appear and just stash them, covered loosely with foil and interleaved with parchment paper, in a low oven (say 250°F), for 45 minutes to an hour.

❈ Whisk together the eggs and buttermilk until frothy, then add the pumpkin purée and whisk again.

❈ Beat in the flour, sugar, baking powder, baking soda and salt, whisking until you have a smooth batter. Or just put everything into the blender, together, and liquidize.

❈ Heat a heavy-based skillet or flat griddle, and pour in the oil. Wipe away any excess with kitchen paper, taking care not to burn your fingers, so that the pan is very lightly oiled. Any more than that, and the pancakes will burn.

❈ Using a 1/4-cup measure, pour small amounts of batter into the pan or onto the hot griddle, gently coaxing them into 3-inch diameter circles.

❈ When bubbles form on the top of the pancakes, flip them over. (You'll have to do this in batches, depending on the size of your skillet or griddle. I get 4–5 on my griddle comfortably at any one time.)

❈ Cook for another 1 1/2–2 minutes, then transfer them to a plate, and keep warm with a layer of aluminum foil over the pancakes.

❈ This amount of batter does make a lot, but the pancakes are not very big,

---

Makes approx. 30

FOR THE PUMPKIN PANCAKES
2 eggs
1 1/2 cups buttermilk (see margin note below)
1 x 15 oz can pumpkin purée (or 2 cups homemade)
1 3/4 cups all-purpose flour
3 tablespoons sugar
1 teaspoon baking powder
1/2 teaspoon baking soda
1/4 teaspoon table salt
1 teaspoon vegetable oil

FOR THE STICKY MAPLE PECANS
1 1/2–1 3/4 cups pecans
2 tablespoons maple syrup, plus more for pouring over pancakes

Be sure to use plain canned pumpkin and not pumpkin pie filling.

MAKE AHEAD TIP:
Make the pancakes the day before and stack on a heat-proof plate. Cover with a "tent" of aluminum foil and keep in a cool place. To reheat, keep them on the plate under the foil and pop in a warm oven, about 325°F, for 20 minutes.

FREEZE AHEAD TIP:
Make the pancakes and cool as above. Stack them interleaved with parchment paper. Wrap securely in aluminum foil and freeze for up to 1 month. Thaw overnight at room temperature. Reheat as above.

OPPOSITE:
Espresso Martini, Triple Cheese and Onion Strata, Pumpkin Pancakes with Sticky Maple Pecans

and will keep well under the foil until you have finished making all of them. And they're so good for when you've got people staying that it seems a pity to make fewer (and you can always freeze any leftover pancakes).

STICKY MAPLE PECANS

❊ Toast the pecans in a large, hot, dry frying pan.

❊ When the pecans are warm and smelling nutty, spoon the maple syrup over, stir to coat them and keep sautéeing them in the pan until they are stickily, glossily coated.

❊ Take the pan off the heat, and as you serve the pancakes, sprinkle each plate with a few sticky pecans and pour some maple syrup over the top.

ANTIOXIDANT FRUIT SALAD

4 cups mango cubes (I buy containers of ready-diced mango, totalling 1³/4 lbs in weight, but if you're using whole mango, you'd probably need 3 large or 4–5 small ones)

2 cups blueberries

1 cup pomegranate seeds (I buy pomegranate seeds in containers, you need 5 oz in weight; otherwise, we're probably talking 2–3 pomegranates here.)

4 teaspoons lime juice

This combination of mango, pomegranate and blueberries – named not entirely ironically to take account of fashionable medico-dietary concerns – is probably my favorite fruit salad of all time. It is sensational, at any time, and I often serve it alongside the Spruced-Up Vanilla Cake on p.198 as a dinner party dessert. But it is a crucial part of this or, I rather think, any brunch. I'm certainly not suggesting you make everything altogether every time, but I'd never leave this out.

If you're using a whole mango, to dice, stand the mango on its end in front of you and, using a sharp knife, score vertically through the skin all round. It should then be easy to peel off the skin from one half. Now, cut through the peeled half of the mango, right to the pit, in lines down, about $1/2$ inch apart; do the same across. Then, take your knife and press it down, sliding it right against the pit so you feel it scrape the pit, thus letting the dice you've scored through tumble out. Do the same – messily – with the other side. If I can do this, it really doesn't require any great dexterity, trust me.

❊ Put the mango cubes into a bowl and tumble the blueberries and pomegranate seeds in after them.

❊ Squeeze the lime juice over the fruit, mix everything together gently, and taste to see if you want to add more lime juice before serving.

MAKE AHEAD TIP:
If using whole mangoes, prepare the mango cubes the day before and put into a non-metallic bowl. Squeeze the lime juice over, cover and chill. When ready to serve, add the blueberries and pomegranate seeds.

A CHRISTMAS BRUNCH **255**

256 A CHRISTMAS BRUNCH

CRANBERRY, ALMOND AND HONEY GRANOLA

Granola is really nothing more than extra-crunchy muesli. And this seasonal variant provides texture and a gorgeous cinnamony honeyed taste, best savored – both taste and texture – with a luscious dollop of yogurt. By all means, though, eat it with milk like regular breakfast cereal if you prefer. I am permissive in these matters; besides, I concede that the granola-flavored milk at the end of a bowlful is always a treat worth looking forward to.

❄ Put everything except the dried cranberries into a large mixing bowl and mix well. Two spatulas are probably the best tools for the job here – or use your own two hands, wearing vinyl disposable gloves.

❄ Spread this mixture on a lined cookie pan and bake in a 325°F oven, turning over the mixture with a spatula about halfway through baking and redistributing the granola evenly during the baking process. The object is to get the granola evenly golden without toasting too much in any one place. If you have a convection or fan oven, you may need to turn it to a lower heat as well as keeping a sharp eye on it.

❄ This should be ready – golden enough and dried out like a crunchy breakfast cereal rather than the sticky mess that went into the oven – in anything from 40–50 minutes.

❄ Remove from the oven and let cool, taking it off the hot cookie pan, before mixing with the dried cranberries. Store in an airtight container.

Makes enough to fill a 1.2-litre tin or jar

2 1/4 cups quick-cooking oats (not instant)
1/2 cup sunflower seeds
heaping 1/4 cup white sesame seeds
2 teaspoons ground cinnamon
1/2 cup honey
1/3 cup packed light brown sugar
1/2 cup whole raw almonds
1/2 cup blanched almonds
pinch of table salt
1 tablespoon Canola oil
1 cup dried cranberries

MAKE AHEAD TIP:
Make the granola, cool and store in an airtight container for up to 1 month.

A CHRISTMAS BRUNCH

A BEVY OF HOT DRINKS

THERE ARE FEW THINGS BETTER THAN COMING in from the cold and wrapping your hands around a cup of warm cheer. All these drinks do the trick, raising your spirit levels in every sense, and imbuing all and sundry with festive feeling.

MULLED CIDER

Makes 1 1/4 quarts, enough for about 6 servings

- 1 quart apple cider
- 1/4 cup dark rum
- 1 cup apple cinnamon tea, made up from a herbal teabag
- 1/4 cup packed dark brown sugar
- 2 clementines
- 4 whole cloves
- 1 stick cinnamon
- 2 fresh bay leaves, preferably Turkish
- 2 cardamom pods, bruised
- 1 x 1-inch piece unpeeled ginger

Much as I adore the *vin chaud* on p.261, I think there is room to expand the repertoire of warm punches to get a Christmas party started, or to warm body and soul after a brisk walk or a bout of carol singing (not that I could ever inflict my voice on anyone). This mulled cider is mellow and fruity and, despite the rum sploshed in as well, mild to the taste and all too drinkable. Just make sure you don't swig while it's still mouth-burningly hot.

❋ Pour the cider, rum and herbal tea into a wide saucepan, add the sugar and put over a low heat to mull.

❋ Halve the clementines, stick a clove into each half, and add them to the pan.

❋ Break the cinnamon sticks in half, and tip into the pan. Add the bay leaves, bruised cardamom pods and whole piece of ginger, and let everything infuse as the pan comes almost to the boil.

❋ Once the pan is near to boiling, turn down the heat, so that it just keeps warm, and ladle into heatproof glasses with handles to serve.

❋ To make this into a non-alcoholic warmer, replace the cider and rum with 1 quart of apple juice and 1/4 cup freshly squeezed lemon juice. You probably won't need the sugar, but taste when warm to see if you want a little and then add as you like.

MAKE AHEAD TIP:
Make the cider, strain and cool. Remove the cloves at this point otherwise the flavor will become too overpowering as the drink sits. Cover and keep in a cool, dark place for up to 2 days until needed. When ready to serve, return the mulled cider to the saucepan and reheat gently without boiling.

A BEVY OF HOT DRINKS

Hot Honeyed Vodka (back left and front right); Mulled Cider (centre); Vin Chaud (back right and front left)

VIN CHAUD

Yes, this is simply the French for mulled wine, but this is how I like to think of it, as drunk from paper cups at the beautiful Christmas market in Brussels or in Francophone alpine regions – I love snow-peaked mountains, so long as I don't have to ski down them.

Serves 6–8

1 x 750ml bottle good robust red wine, such as Beaujolais
4 cinnamon sticks
1 x 5-inch curl orange zest, shaved off the orange with a vegetable peeler
1/3 cup sugar
1 star anise
5 whole cloves
1/3 cup cognac

❄ Pour the wine into a large saucepan and add the remaining ingredients.

❄ Bring to an almost boil, *don't* actually let it boil, then turn down the heat and let it simmer gently.

❄ The mulled wine is ready when the sugar has dissolved, though you can leave the pan on a very low heat so that your *vin chaud* stays *chaud*. This is best served in small cups or heatproof glasses with handles.

❄ To make an approximate, non-alcoholic version, replace the 750ml bottle of wine with 2 cups pomegranate juice and 2 cups cranberry juice, and dispense with the cognac.

MAKE AHEAD TIP:
Make the *vin chaud*, strain and cool. Remove the cloves at this point otherwise the flavor will become too overpowering as the drinks sit. Cover and keep in a cool, dark place for 1 day until needed. When ready to serve, return it to the saucepan and reheat gently without boiling.

HOT HONEYED VODKA

This is a warmed-up version of *Krupnik*, the Polish honey vodka – and none the worse for that. Indeed, you can make this and drink whatever's left (in that unlikely instance) cold. It's all good.

Makes 1 1/4 quarts, enough for about 25 double-shot glasses

2 cups sugar
2 tablespoons cold water
1 quart boiling water, from a kettle
10 allspice berries
1 cinnamon stick
2 whole cloves
1 lemon, zest and juice
1 cup honey
2 cups vodka

❄ Put the sugar into a large, heavy-based saucepan with the cold water and dissolve over a low heat.

❄ When the sugar has dissolved and started bubbling, leave to bubble for a few seconds until it turns a pale caramel color. Carefully pour in the boiling water, standing well back as you do so, as it will splutter.

❄ Add the allspice berries, cinnamon stick, cloves and lemon zest (shaved off with a vegetable peeler) and bring to the boil – *never* stir – and let it bubble for 5 minutes.

MAKE AHEAD TIP:
Tie the allspice berries and cloves in a small cheesecloth bag. Follow the recipe as directed (adding the bag of spices along with cinnamon stick and lemon zest), up to, and including, adding the honey. Remove the bag, cool the mixture, cover and keep in a cool, dark place for up to 2 days until needed. To reheat, return the mixture to the saucepan, bring to the boil, then take off the heat and pour in the vodka. Continue as directed.

❊ Add the honey, stir, and keep stirring until the honey has dissolved into the spiced caramel.

❊ Bring to the boil again, then take off the heat and add the vodka, stirring well, and the juice of the peeled lemon.

❊ Strain into a jug and pour into waiting shot glasses; it should be invigoratingly warm, rather than burningly hot, so that it can be knocked back with relish. *Na zdrowie!*

HOT SCHNOCOLATE

Makes enough for 2 cups

2 cups whole milk
½ cup best-quality bittersweet chocolate, chopped or chips
4 teaspoons sugar
1 x 1 oz measure peppermint schnapps (see Suppliers p.267)

FOR SERVING:
½ cup heavy cream
3 peppermint candy canes

Well, how could I resist? A friend gave me this gorgeously named concoction – hot chocolate with peppermint schnapps in it, of course – a Christmas or so ago, and I have had to appropriate it. She couldn't remember where she got the name or the idea, so whoever created it, thank you. The recipe below, however, is mine, from distant, delicious memory.

❊ Whip the cream and put aside. Put the milk and chopped chocolate into a pan and slowly warm, until the chocolate has melted.

❊ Add the sugar, stir well, and bring to almost boiling point, though *at no time* must it boil.

❊ Off the heat, stir in the peppermint schnapps, and leave while you crush one of the candy canes or your boiled sweets: you just need enough beautiful pink splinters to adorn the top of the hot schnocolates; leave aside for one moment, though.

MAKE AHEAD TIP:
Follow the recipe up to, and including, stirring in the peppermint schnapps. Cool, cover and keep in the refrigerator for up to 2 days until needed. To reheat, return the schnocolate to the saucepan, heat to a gentle simmer, then finish with whipped cream and candy canes as directed.

❊ Pour the hot schnocolate into 2 mugs and top with the whipped cream, sprinkle the crushed candy cane (or sweets) on top and, if wished, put a whole candy cane into each before drinking one and handing out the second to a lucky other.

❊ If you want this to be a non-alchoholic, but still pepperminty hot chocolate, replace the schnapps with a drop or two of natural peppermint flavoring, which is generally how the best-tasting peppermint essence is labeled.

A BEVY OF HOT DRINKS **263**

DR LAWSON PRESCRIBES ...

EVEN BOWING UNDER THE WEIGHT of this season of over-indulgence, I will never be a nil by mouth kind of a person. I go with the Ancient Greeks on this: let food be your medicine. So here is a brace of recipes to help you through the festivities.

CUBAN CURE BLACK BEAN SOUP

Serves 2

1/4 lb chorizo sausage (not the salami sort)
2 scallions
1/2 teaspoon ground cumin
1 x 15 oz can black beans, drained
1 fresh tomato
2 cups chicken broth/stock (I do not intend for you to make your own stock for this; I use a good quality carton or canned one)
juice of 1 lime, or to taste (feel free to squirt in lime from a plastic bottle)
2–4 tablespoons chopped fresh cilantro

This is the perfect antidote to an evening soured by too much office-party wine. A clanging head finds solace in fire and fat, and this bean stew of a soup provides both, with ease and speed.

❋ Cut the chorizo sausage into slices roughly 1/8 inch thick. Then cut each coin in half or quarters, as you wish.

❋ Cook the chorizo pieces in a dry saucepan for about 5 minutes, or until they give up their orange oil and crisp up a little. Remove them with a slotted spatula to a bowl or plate.

❋ Cut off the green parts of the scallions and reserve for slicing later, then finely slice the white part and add this to the pan slicked with orange oil, along with the ground cumin, stirring everything together for a couple of minutes over a gentle heat.

❋ Tip the black beans into the pan and roughly chop the tomato, adding the pieces – peel, seeds and all – along with the chicken stock. Stir the pan and let it simmer, uncovered, for 10 minutes.

❋ Ladle the soup into 2 bowls; add the reserved chorizo pieces, then give each bowl a good squirt of lime juice and sprinkle with the finely sliced green part of the scallions and some chopped cilantro.

MAKE AHEAD TIP:
Make the soup up to 3 days ahead. Cool, cover and store in the refrigerator. When ready to serve, return the soup to the saucepan and bring slowly to the boil. Reduce the heat and simmer very gently for 5 minutes until piping hot. Ladle the soup into bowls and finish as directed.

A PANACEA FOR SEASONAL AND SELF-INFLICTED ILLS

I love any sort of chicken soup, known in its original form as "Jewish penicillin." This version is rather different: hot with ginger, which is warming, soothing and exotically aromatic. It's been recently "proved" – whatever that means – that chicken soup really does inhibit infections and clear the tubes, so those Jewish matrons weren't actually wrong… Not that they ever thought they were.

A clementine mixed with lime gives sour punch and provides some very necessary vitamin C.

Chicken wings, I find, make for the best chicken soup, and a gratifyingly economical one. You can eat this soup plain, or spiked with any or all of the suggestions, right.

❋ Put the chicken wings, carrot, onion and cinnamon stick into a large saucepan. (I never bother to peel onions for broth as I feel the skin adds to the deep gold of your eventual broth.)

❋ Pour in the water, stir in the salt, and add the piece of ginger left whole.

❋ Finally add the mixed clementine and lime juices.

❋ Bring to a boil, then turn down and let simmer for $1^{1}/_{2}$–2 hours, until the liquid has reduced by about half. Taste to see if the chickeniness has come through: when it has, the broth is reduced enough and ready.

❋ Strain into a wide-necked measuring jug or bowl and leave to cool (you should have about $1^{1}/_{2}$ quarts) and when cold, chill in the refrigerator overnight to let all the fat rise to the surface, so it becomes a solid layer you can easily remove.

❋ When you want salvation in the form of this soup, scrape off the fat, and wipe over the surface with paper towel to degrease efficiently, then ladle as much as you want to cook at each time into a saucepan and bring to a boil.

❋ Drink from a mug if you want this clear; or spoon from a bowl, first adding some beansprouts and, after ladling in, scatter with chile, scallions and fresh cilantro as you wish.

Makes 4–6 bowls or mugs

3 lbs chicken wings (you can use a couple of chicken carcasses or a fresh, uncooked small chicken instead)
1 carrot, peeled and halved
1 unpeeled onion, cut in half
1 cinnamon stick
3 quarts water
1 tablespoon kosher salt or $^{1}/_{2}$ tablespoon table salt
approx. 1 x 3-inch piece ginger, peeled
juice of 1 clementine mixed with juice of $^{1}/_{2}$–1 lime, to taste

FOR SERVING (OPTIONAL):
handful of beansprouts
1 small red chile, seeded and cut into fine wheels
2 scallions, finely sliced
chopped fresh cilantro

MAKE AHEAD TIP:
Make the chicken stock up to 3 days ahead. Cool, cover and store in the refrigerator. When ready to serve, remove the fat, ladle into a saucepan and bring slowly to the boil. Finish as directed.

FREEZE AHEAD TIP:
Cool and freeze the chicken stock, in handy portions, for up to 3 months. Thaw overnight in the refrigerator, then reheat as above and finish as directed.

DR LAWSON PRESCRIBES …

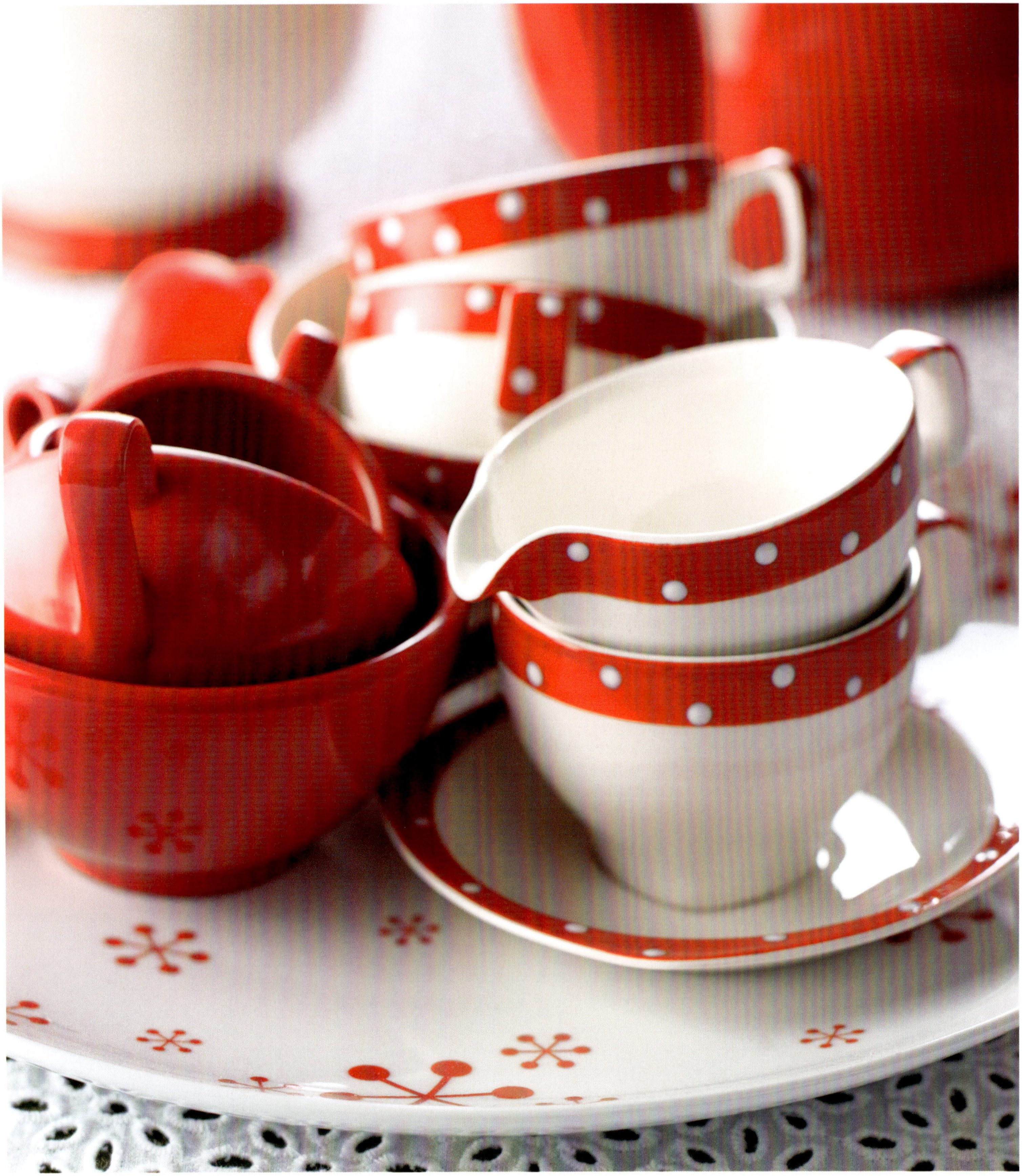

SUPPLIERS

Not all the ingredients or items below will be hard for you to find, but some could be, so – being an internet shopping addict myself – I feel it only right to give a short list of online suppliers to help you source something I've mentioned in the text but that might elude you on the main street. For a wider range of suppliers, see **www.nigella.com**.

LIQUORS, WINES, BEVERAGES AND SYRUPS

Lychee liqueur, Pedro Ximénez sherry
www.morrellwine.com

Tuaca, butterscotch schnapps
www.sendliquor.com

Monin syrups
www.coffeeam.com

British ginger beer
www.cameronsbritishfoods.com
www.popsoda.com

Bitter Lemon
www.fever-tree.com
(for list of retail outlets)

Cherry brandy
www.wallywine.com

Caramel vodka, peppermint and butterscotch schnapps, Parna
www.internetwines.com

MEAT

Uncooked hams
www.smithfieldhams.com
www.smithfieldfarms.com

Chipolata sausages
www.britishdelights.com
www.jonesdairyfarm.com
(breakfast links)

FOODS AND SPICES

Tiptree preserves (including ginger preserve and little scarlet preserve), mincemeat, Christmas pudding, Christmas cake, and marzipan.
www.britishdelights.com

Chestnut puree and sweetened chestnut cream
www.caviar-line.com

Sweetened chestnut cream
www.agferrari.com

Lychee puree
www.funkin.us

Jane's Krazy Mixed-Up Salt
www.janeskrazy.com

Passion fruit
www.melissas.com

Pink/red peppercorns, white peppercorns
www.bulkpeppercorns.com

Nigella seeds
www.ishopindian.com

Powdered pectin
www.canningpantry.com

Glazed (candied) cherries and fruits, almond flour, and marzipan
www.nutsonline.com

CAKE DECORATING AND OTHER SPECIALIST EQUIPMENT

Edible cake decorations, gold dust (luster), edible glitter, rolled fondant, crystallized rose petals, cookie cutters, instant read thermometers, gold and decorative paper baking cups, and related paraphenalia
www.fancyflours.com

Rolled fondant and meringue powder
www.wilton.com

Cast iron braisers
www.williams-sonoma.com

Rectangular paper mini loaf molds
www.bakedeco.com

Holiday Tree bundt pan
www.nordicware.com
(item #57648)

Jars, bottles, French hermetic seal jars, funnels, gift bags, wrapping paper and boxes
www.containerstore.com
(plus stores nationwide)

ACKNOWLEDGMENTS

This is the first time, since I began with *How to Eat* in 1998, that I have published a book two years running. I don't feel it's something I should make a habit of, but nor can I regret it. Writing and making a book is something I love above all else and, besides, self-denial has never been my strong suit. I just feel grateful that I have work I enjoy so much. But such gratitude is really owed to the raft of people whose hard work allows me to enjoy myself, and whose support and encouragement are crucial. Thanks – heartfelt and enduring – to (in alphabetical order) Olivia Antolik, Jan Bowmer, Louise Dennys, Mary Gibson, Vivienne Gill, Poppy Hampson, Caz Hildebrand (the *sine qua non* of any enterprise I embark on), Julie Martin, Lis Parsons, the inspirational and pitch-perfect Gail Rebuck, Alison Samuel, the most elegant and erudite of editors, and Caroline Stearns: without all these, it wouldn't be as much fun; indeed, it wouldn't even be possible.

The same is true of those whose names follow (again, alphabetically) and who make up what I think of as my work family, and who, teasingly I think, call themselves Team Nigella: Kate Bull, Elisabetta Grillo, Francesca Grillo, Mark Hutchinson, Rose Murray, Hettie Potter, Ed Victor, Zoe Wales and Anzelle Wasserman. I know how fortunate I am to be thus surrounded by those I love and trust.

Over the last year my home has looked like a cross between Santa's Grotto and Miss Havisham's apartments. Much of this agreeable clutter I provided myself, but as much again was gratefully harvested especially for this project and I owe thanks to those who have so generously helped furnish the pictures in this book, even if simultaneously feeding my addiction for seasonalia, in particular B&Q, Best Season, Big Tomato Company, Cath Kidston, Ceramica Blue, Cherubim, ChristmastimeUK and the ever helpful Alfred Rose and his elves, The Conran Shop, The General Trading Company, Heals, Jane Asher Party Cakes & Sugarcraft and the fabulous David Trumper, John Lewis Partnership, Krebs International Glass, Laura Ashley, Marks & Spencer, Merchant Gourmet, Nordicware, Ocean Spray, Papstar, Peter Harvey, Star Trading, Steelite International, Sur la Table (notably Olivia and her staff at the Dallas branch), VV Rouleaux, Wedgwood and Wild Card.

This book is subtitled "Food, Family, Friends, Festivities," and it remains only for me to say that the food and festivities would mean nothing without those other two components; it is to my family and my friends that my deepest gratitude are owed, not just – as the RSPCA admonitory poster used to say – for Christmas, but for life.

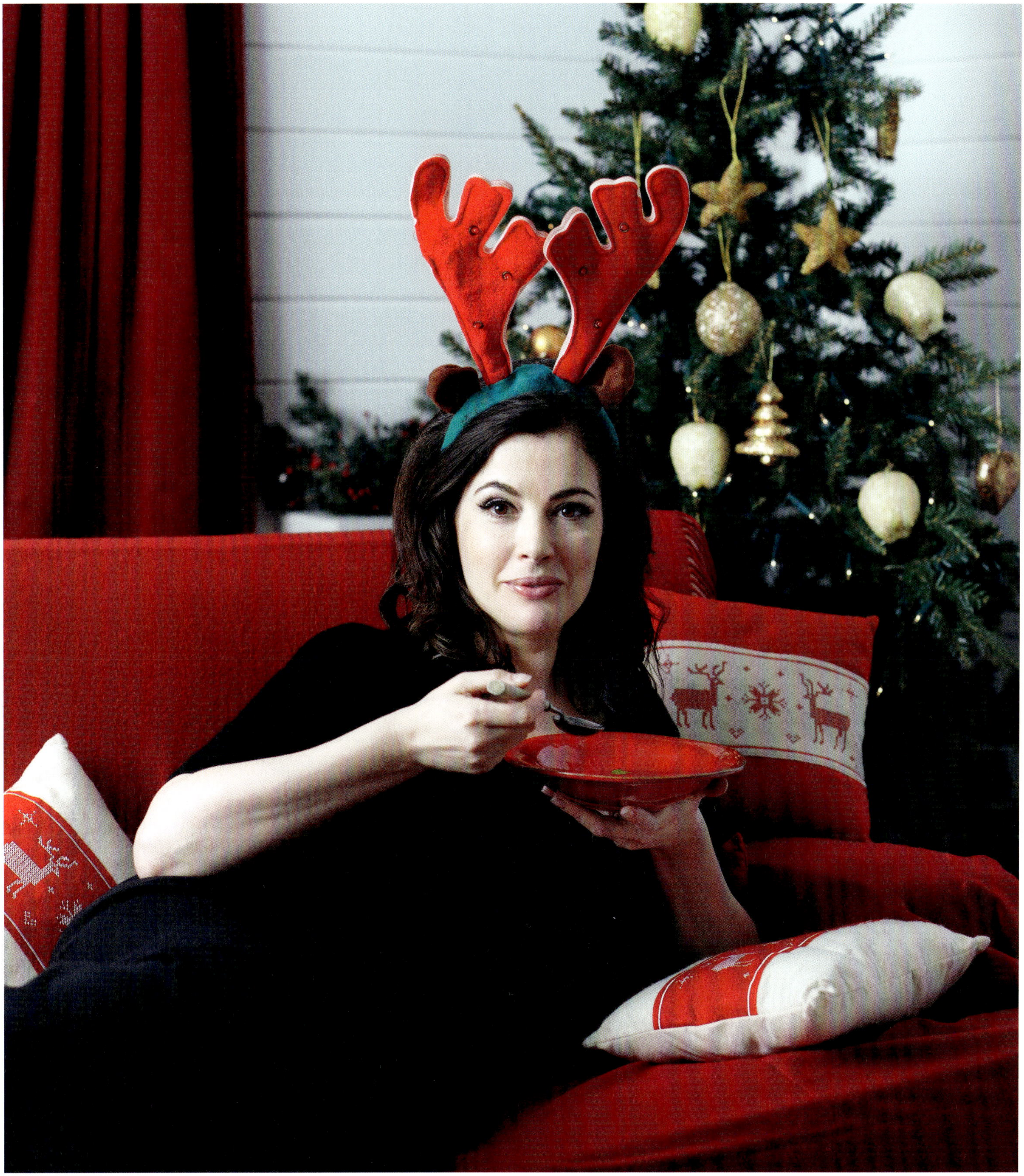

INDEX

allspice gravy 118
almonds
    cranberry, almond and honey granola 257
amaretto sour 7
Amis, Kingsley 3
antioxidant fruit salad 254–5
apple juice
    seasonal breeze (mocktail) 11
apples
    apple and onion gravy 89, 91
    Christmas chutney 235
    cranberry and apple chutney 239
    Australian Christmas pudding with hot chocolate-chestnut sauce 169
avocados 15
    guacamole 25

bacon
    bacon-wrapped chipolatas 127
    drunken devils on horseback 22
    see also pancetta
barley
    red beet orzotto 135–6
    butternut orzotto 134–5
beans, black
    Cuban cure black bean soup 264
beans, cannellini
    quick cassoulet 152–3
beans, green
    beans with Brussels sprouts 132
beans, haricot
    Boston baked beans 61
beans, kidney
    red salad 58
beef
    choc chip chili 38
    roast rib of beef with port and stilton gravy 155–7
    leftovers 157

beets
    red beet and ginger chutney 237
    red beet and horseradish sauce 68
    red beet orzotto 135–6
    Christmas coleslaw 37
    scarlet-speckled loaf cake 202
cookies
    Christmas chocolate cookies 206
    cranberry and white chocolate cookies 208
    edible Christmas tree decorations 194
    gold-dust cookies 213
black beans
    Cuban cure black bean soup 264
Black Forest martini 6
blissful blueberry (mocktail) 12
bloody Mary, Christmassy 230
blueberries
    antioxidant fruit salad 254–5
    blissful blueberry (mocktail) 12
boozy British trifle 42–4
Boston baked beans 61
bourbon butter 190
bourbon-glazed ribs 82
bread sauce, my mother's 121–2
butter x
butternut squash
    butternut orzotto 134–5
    roast squash and sweet potato soup with buttermilk-blue cheese swirl 53
    spiced squash 96
butters
    bourbon butter 190
    rum and brandy butters 190
butterscotch topping 87

cabbage, red
    Christmas coleslaw 37

    red cabbage with pomegranate juice 60
cakes
    Christmas cake with icing and toppings 172–7
    Christmas cupcakes 216
    Christmas-spiced chocolate cake 183–4
    easy chocolate fruitcake 180–82
    golden fruitcake 178
    tiramisu layer cake 88, 93–4
    plain dark fruitcake 180
    scarlet-speckled loaf cake 202
    spruced-up spice cake 198
    spruced-up vanilla cake 198
    sticky gingerbread 201
    Yule log 191–3
    see also panforte
canapés 1, 15–24
    chile cheese crostini 17
    crab crostini 17
    cranberry and soy-glazed cocktail sausages 23
    double-blue crostini 15
    drunken devils on horseback 22
    party Parma ham bundles 20
    seasonally spiced nuts 21
    smoked salmon soda breads 18
    wasabi crab cakes 24
cannellini beans
    quick cassoulet 152–3
    see also kidney beans
cassoulet, quick 152–3
champagne cocktail, Cornish 8
champagne cocktail, Tuscan 8
char-grilled peppers with pomegranate 58–9
cheese
    chile cheese crostini 17
    double-blue crostini 15
    fully loaded potato skins 40–41

macaroni cheese deluxe 102–3
marinated feta 228
party Parma ham bundles 20
pumpkin and goat's cheese lasagne 34–6
triple cheese and onion strata 251
cheesecake, gleaming maple 70, 74–6
cherries, dried
dried cherries in cherry brandy 227
chestnuts
beans with Brussels sprouts 132
chestnut chocolate pots 98
chestnut soup with bacon crumbles 50–51
chestnut stuffing 122–3
Christmas Brussels sprouts 132
hot chocolate-chestnut sauce 169
pancetta Brussels sprouts 132
pecan Brussels sprouts 132
chicken 49
chicken soup 265
see also party poussins
chicory
Christmas salad 56
chile/chili
chile cheese crostini 17
chile jam 241
choc chip chili 38
chocolate
chestnut chocolate pots 98
chocolate–peanut butter cups 25
Christmas chocolate sponge pudding with hot chocolate sauce 140–42, 143
Christmas chocolate cookies 206
Christmas pudding bonbons 247–8
Christmas rocky road 28
Christmas-spiced chocolate cake 183–4
cranberry and white chocolate cookies 208
easy chocolate fruitcake 180–82
girdlebuster pie 87
hot chocolate-chestnut sauce 169
hot schnocolate (drink) 262
tiramisu layer cake 88, 93–4
Yule log 191–3
chorizo sausages
choc chip chili 38
Cuban cure black bean soup 264
Christianity vi
Christmas brunch 249–57
Christmas cake ix, 172–3
icing and toppings 174–7
Christmas chocolate cookies 206
Christmas chutney 235
Christmas cornflake wreaths 210
Christmas cupcakes 216
Christmas Eve supper 100–4
Christmas ketchup 242
Christmas lunch
bacon-wrapped chipolatas 127
red beet orzotto 135–6
butternut orzotto 134–5
bread sauce 121–2
countdown 110–12
cranberry sauce 119
Italian roast potatoes with garlic and thyme 163
maple-roast parsnips 130–31
panettone pudding 164
roast goose with pear and cranberry stuffing, and light gravy 149–51
roast potatoes 128–30
roast rib of beef with port and Stilton gravy 155–7
roast stuffed pumpkin with gingery tomato sauce 165–68
rolled stuffed loin of pork with rubied gravy 158–63
spiced and superjuicy roast turkey with allspice gravy 115–18
sprouts 132
stuffings 122–6
vegetarian option 165–6
and vegetarians 107, 108–9
see also Christmas puddings
Christmas morning muffins 214–15
Christmas puddini bonbons 247–8
Christmas puddings ix
Australian Christmas pudding with hot chocolate-chestnut sauce 169
chocolate sponge pudding with hot chocolate sauce 140–42, 143
Christmas puddini bonbons 247–8
ultimate Christmas pudding with eggnog cream 137–40
Christmas rocky road 28
Christmas salad 56
Christmas-spiced chocolate cake 183–4
Christmas-spiced salt 226
Christmas tree decorations, edible 194
Churchill, Sir Winston 219
chutneys ix–x, 221
red beet and ginger chutney 237
Christmas chutney 235
cranberry and apple chutney 239
rich fruit chutney 236
cider, mulled 258
cocktails 3–8
amaretto sour 7
Black Forest martini 6
Cornish champagne cocktail 8
Christmas fizz 4n
espresso martini 249, 250
lychee fizz 5n
lycheeni 5
marteani 249, 250
Moscow mule 8
poinsettia 3
pomegranate martini 4

Santa's little helper 6
Tuscan champagne cocktail 8
Yule mule 8
see also mocktails (non-alcoholic)
coffee
    Christmas-spiced chocolate cake 183–4
    espresso martini 249, 250
    tiramisu layer cake 93–4
Cointreau
    Cointreau cream 183
    marteani 249, 250
coleslaw, Christmas 37
compote
    mixed berry compote 104
cookies
    Christmas chocolate cookies 206
    Christmas cornflake wreaths 210
    cranberry and white chocolate cookies 208
    gold-dust cookies 213
corn
    corn chow-chow 243
    spoon bread 84
corn chow-chow 243
cornflake wreaths, Christmas 210
Cornish hens 94, 96
couscous, festive 97
crab
    crab crostini 17
    wasabi crab cakes 24
Cradock, Fanny and Johnnie: *Coping with Christmas* ix
cranberries/cranberry juice
    Christmas ketchup 242
    cranberry, almond and honey granola 257
    cranberry and apple chutney 239
    cranberry and soy-glazed cocktail sausages 23
    cranberry and white chocolate cookies 208
    cranberry sauce 119
    cranberry-studded mincemeat 189
    poinsettia (cocktail) 3
    rubied gravy 163
    scarlet-speckled loaf cake 202
    seasonal breeze (drink) 11
    yule mule (cocktail) 8
Cromwell, Oliver 138
crostini
    chile cheese crostini 17
    crab crostini 17
    double-blue crostini 15
Cuban cure black bean soup 264
cupcakes, Christmas 216

dates
    lamb and date tagine 72
decorations, edible Christmas tree 194
desserts
    boozy British trifle 42–4
    chestnut chocolate pots 98
    Christmas-spiced chocolate cake 183–4
    eggnog syllabub 27
    girdlebuster pie 87
    gleaming maple cheesecake 70, 74–6
    panettone pudding 164
    pecan-plus pie 205
    prodigious pavlova 45–7
    Prosecco and pomegranate jelly 80–81
    quickly scaled Mont Blancs 94–5
    mixed berry compote 104
    spruced-up vanilla cake 198
    tiramisu layer cake 93–4
    yule log 191–3
    see also cakes; Christmas puddings
double-blue crostini 15
drinks
    amaretto sour 7
    Black Forest martini 6
    blissful blueberry 12
    Cornish champagne cocktail 8
    Christmas fizz 4
    espresso martini 250
    hot honeyed vodka 261–2
    hot schnocolate 262
    lychee fizz 5n
    lycheeni 5
    marteani 250
    mistletoe 13
    Moscow mule 8
    mulled cider 258
    mulled wine (*vin chaud*) 261
    poinsettia 3
    pomegranate martini 4
    pussyfoot 12
    Santa's little helper 6
    seasonal breeze 11
    Tuscan champagne cocktail 8
    Xmas xinger 13
    Yule mule 8
drunken devils on horseback 22

edible Christmas tree decorations 194
edible presents ix–x, 220–21
eggnog cream 140
eggnog syllabub 27
eggs x
    freezing egg whites 42
    espresso martini 249, 250

feta, marinated 228
figs
    honeyed fig vinegar 232
    party Parma ham bundles 20

fish
   crab crostini 17
   parsleyed fish gratin 77–9
   smoked salmon soda breads 18
   wasabi crab cakes 24
freezing ix
   see also Freeze Ahead Tips throughout
fruit
   antioxidant fruit salad 254–5
   mixed berry compote 104
   see also fruit, dried; glacé fruits; *and specific fruits e.g.* cranberries
fruit, dried
   Australian Christmas pudding 169
   chocolate fruitcake 180–82
   cranberry and white chocolate cookies 208
   dried cherries in cherry brandy 227
   golden fruitcake 178
   golden sultanas in Grand Marnier 227
   honeyed fig vinegar 232
   mixed fruits in Pedro Ximénez 227
   rich fruit chutney 236
   scarlet-speckled loaf cake 202
   traditional Christmas cake 172–3
fully loaded potato skins 40–41

gifts, edible ix–x, 220–21
ginger
   red beet and ginger chutney 237
   ginger-glazed ham 100–2
   gingery tomato sauce 168
   gold-dust cookies 213
ginger beer
   mistletoe (mocktail) 13
gingerbread
   gingerbread stuffing 125
   sticky gingerbread 201
gingery tomato sauce 168

girdlebuster pie 87
glazed fruits
   glossy fruit and nut cake topping 177
gleaming maple cheesecake 70, 74–6
glossy fruit and nut cake topping 177
gold-dust cookies 213
goose
   leftovers 152
   light goose gravy 151
   quick cassoulet 152–3
   roast goose with pear and cranberry stuffing 149–50
granola
   cranberry, almond and honey granola 257
grapefruit juice
   pussyfoot (mocktail) 12
gratins
   parsleyed fish gratin 77–9
   potato, parsnip and porcini gratin 64
gravy
   allspice gravy 118
   apple and onion gravy 89, 91
   light goose gravy 151
   port and Stilton gravy 155, 156–7
   rubied gravy 163
guacamole 38

ham
   aromatic Christmas ham 32
   ginger-glazed ham 100–2
   party Parma ham bundles 20
haricot beans
   Boston baked beans 61
herbs x
honey
   cranberry, almond and honey granola 257
   honeyed fig vinegar 232

   hot honeyed vodka 261–2
horseradish, and red beet, sauce 68
hot chocolate-chestnut sauce 169
hot honeyed vodka 261–2
hot schnocolate 262

icing
   smooth hatbox icing 174, 176
   snow scene (instant royal) icing 174, 176
Isis viii

jars, sterilizing 221
jelly
   chile jam 241
   Prosecco and pomegranate jelly 80–81
Julius I, Pope viii

ketchup, Christmas 242
kidney beans
   red salad 58
Klivans, Elinor: *The Essential Chocolate Chip Cookbook* 87

lamb and date tagine 70–72
lasagne, pumpkin and goat's cheese 34–6
leftovers, using up
   beef 157
   goose 152–3
   turkey 143–6
lychees
   lychee fizz (cocktail) 5n
   lycheeni (cocktail) 5
   prodigious pavlova 45–7
loaf cake, scarlet-speckled 202

macaroni cheese deluxe 102–3
mangoes
   antioxidant fruit salad 254–5

274 INDEX

maple syrup
  gleaming maple cheesecake 70, 74–6
  maple-roast parsnips 130–31
marteani 250
mayonnaise
  whole-grain honey mustard mayonnaise 66
meringue 45
mince pies, star-topped 186–8
mincemeat, cranberry-studded 189
mistletoe (mocktail) 13
mocktails (non alcoholic) 10–13
  blissful blueberry 12
  mistletoe 13
  pussyfoot 12
  seasonal breeze 11
  Xmas xinger 13
Mont Blancs, quickly scaled 94–5
Moscow mule 8
muffins, Christmas morning 214–15
mulled cider 258
mulled wine (*vin chaud*) 261
mustard, whole-grain
  red currant and whole-grain mustard sauce 67
  whole-grain honey mustard mayonnaise 66

nuts 69
  Christmas rocky road 28
  panforte 196–7
  pecan-plus pie 205
  pecan Brussels sprouts 132
  seasonally spiced nuts 21
  sticky maple pecans 253, 254
  see also chestnuts

olive oil x
olives 229

onions
  apple and onion gravy 89, 91
  red onion and pomegranate relish 73
orange juice
  pussyfoot (mocktail) 12
  seasonal breeze (mocktail) 11
orzotto
  red beet orzotto 135–6
  butternut orzotto 134–5

pancakes
  pumpkin pancakes with sticky maple pecans 253–4
pancetta
  pancetta Brussels sprouts 132
  peas with pancetta in cream all'italiano 63
  spinach and bacon salad 85
panettone and Italian sausage stuffing 125–6
panettone pudding 164
panforte 196–7
Parma ham bundles 20
parsleyed fish gratin 77–9
parsnips
  maple-roast parsnips 130–31
  potato, parsnip and porcini gratin 64
party Parma ham bundles 20
party Cornish hens 94, 96
passion fruit
  prodigious pavlova 45–7
Passover vi
pavlova, prodigious 45–7
peanut brittle with art and soul 244
peanut butter
  chocolate–peanut butter cups 25
pear and cranberry stuffing 149, 150
peas with pancetta in cream all'italiano 63

pecan nuts
  pecan-plus pie 205
  pecan Brussels sprouts 132
  seasonally spiced nuts 21
  sticky maple pecans 254
  wild rice, turkey, cranberry and pecan salad 144
Pedro Ximénez sherry 137, 172, 227
peppers
  char-grilled peppers with pomegranate 58–9
Picardie, Justine: *Daphne* 8
pickles 229
  see also chutneys
pies
  girdlebuster pie 87
  pecan-plus pie 205
  star-topped mince pies 186–8
pilaff
  turkey pilaff with pomegranate and dill 144
piselli con panna e pancetta 63
poinsettia (cocktail) 3
pomegranate martini 4
pomegranates 49
  antioxidant fruit salad 254–5
  char-grilled peppers with pomegranate 58–9
  Christmas salad 56
  pomegranate vodka 231
  Prosecco and pomegranate jelly 80–81
  red cabbage with pomegranate juice 60
  red onion and pomegranate relish 73
  Xmas xinger 13
pork
  bourbon-glazed ribs 82
  effortless home-cured pork 88–90

INDEX **275**

rolled stuffed loin of pork with rubied gravy 158–63
   see also ham and sausages
port and Stilton gravy 155, 156–7
potatoes
   fully loaded potato skins 40
   Italian roast potatoes with garlic and thyme 163
   perfect roast potatoes 128–30
   potato, parsnip and porcini gratin 64
potatoes, sweet
   roast squash and sweet potato soup with buttermilk blue cheese swirl 53
presents, edible ix–x, 220–21
preserves see chutneys; pickles
prodigious pavlova 45–7
Prosecco
   Christmas fizz 4n
   lychee fizz 5n
   poinsettia 3
   Prosecco and pomegranate gelatin 80–81
   Tuscan champagne cocktail 8
prunes
   chocolate fruitcake 180–82
   drunken devils on horseback 22
puddings, Christmas see Christmas puddings
pumpernickel see soda bread
pumpkin
   pumpkin and goat's cheese lasagne 34–6
   pumpkin pancakes with sticky maple pecans 253–4
   roast stuffed pumpkin with gingery tomato sauce 165–8
pussyfoot (mocktail) 12

quick cassoulet 152–3

quickly scaled Mont Blancs 94–5

raspberries
   prodigious pavlova 45–7
recycling ix
red cabbage
   Christmas coleslaw 37
   red cabbage with pomegranate juice 60
red currant and whole-grain mustard sauce 67
red onion and pomegranate relish 73
red salad 58
rubied gravy 163
rum and brandy butters 190

salads
   antioxidant fruit salad 254–5
   char-grilled peppers with pomegranate 58–9
   Christmas coleslaw 37
   Christmas salad 56
   red salad 58
   spinach and bacon salad 85
   turkey and glass noodle salad 145
   wild rice, turkey, cranberry and pecan salad 144
salmon, smoked
   smoked salmon soda breads 18
salt, Christmas-spiced 226
Santa's little helper (cocktail) 6
Saturn vii
Saturnalia vii
sauces
   apple and onion gravy 91
   red beet and horseradish sauce 68
   bourbon butter 190
   bread sauce 121–2
   Cointreau cream 183
   cranberry sauce 119
   eggnog cream 140

   gingery tomato sauce 168
   hot chocolate-chestnut sauce 169
   red currant and whole-grain mustard sauce 67
   rum and brandy butters 190
   whole-grain honey mustard mayonnaise 66
sausage meat stuffing 115
sausage meat-bosomed turkey 115
sausages
   bacon-wrapped chipolatas 127
   bourbon-glazed sausages 82
   cranberry and soy-glazed cocktail sausages 23
   panettone and Italian sausage stuffing 125–6
   sausage meat-bosomed turkey 115
   see also chorizo sausages
scarlet-speckled loaf cake 202
seasonal breeze (mocktail) 11
seasonally spiced nuts 21
sherry, Pedro Ximénez 137, 172, 227
smoked salmon soda breads 18
smooth hatbox icing 176
snow scene icing 176
soda bread
   smoked salmon soda breads 18
Sol Invictus vi
soups
   chestnut soup with bacon crumbles 50–51
   chicken soup 265
   Cuban cure black bean soup 264
   roast squash and sweet potato soup with buttermilk-blue cheese swirl 53
   tortilla soup 55
spareribs, bourbon-glazed 82
spinach and bacon salad 85
spoon bread 84

sprouts, Brussels
   bean and sprouts 132
   Christmas sprouts 132
   pancetta and sprouts 132
   pecan and sprouts 132
spruced-up spice cake 198
spruced-up vanilla cake 198
squash *see* butternut squash
star-topped mince pies 186–8
steeped Christmas fruits 227
sterilizing jars 221
sticky gingerbread 201
sticky maple pecans 253, 254
stuffing
   chestnut stuffing 122–3
   gingerbread stuffing 124
   panettone and Italian sausage stuffing 125–6
   pear and cranberry stuffing 150
   for rolled stuffed loin of pork 158, 160
   sausage meat stuffing 115
sugar, vanilla 225
sultanas in Grand Marnier 227
syllabub, eggnog 27
syncretism vi

tagine
   lamb and date tagine 70–72
tea
   marteani 249, 250

tiramisu layer cake 88, 93–4
tomatoes
   red salad 58
tomato sauce
   ginger tomato sauce 168
   for lasagne 34
tortilla soup 55
trifle, boozy British 42–4
triple cheese and onion strata 251
turkey
   Christmas roast turkey 115–16, 117
   Ed's victorious turkey hash 146
   leftovers 143–6
   sausage meat-bosomed turkey 115
   spiced and superjuicy roast turkey 115–16
   tortilla soup 55
   turkey and glass noodle salad 145
   turkey pilaff with pomegranate and dill 144
   wild rice, turkey, cranberry and pecan salad 144

vanilla
   spruced-up vanilla cake 198
   vanilla sugar 225
vegetarian Christmas lunch 165–169
   roast stuffed pumpkin with gingery tomato sauce 107, 165–8
vin chaud (mulled wine) 261

vinegar, honeyed fig 232
vodka
   Black Forest martini 6
   espresso martini 250
   hot honeyed vodka 261–2
   lycheeni 5
   marteani 249, 250
   pomegranate martini 4
   pomegranate vodka 231
   winter-spiced vodka 230
   yule mule 8

wasabi crab cakes 24
whole-grain mustard
   red currant and whole-grain mustard sauce 67
   whole-grain honey mustard mayonnaise 66
wine, mulled 261
winter-spiced vodka 230
wreaths, Christmas cornflake 210

Xmas xinger (mocktail) 13

Yule viii
yule log 191–3
yule mule (cocktail) 8
   virgin version 13

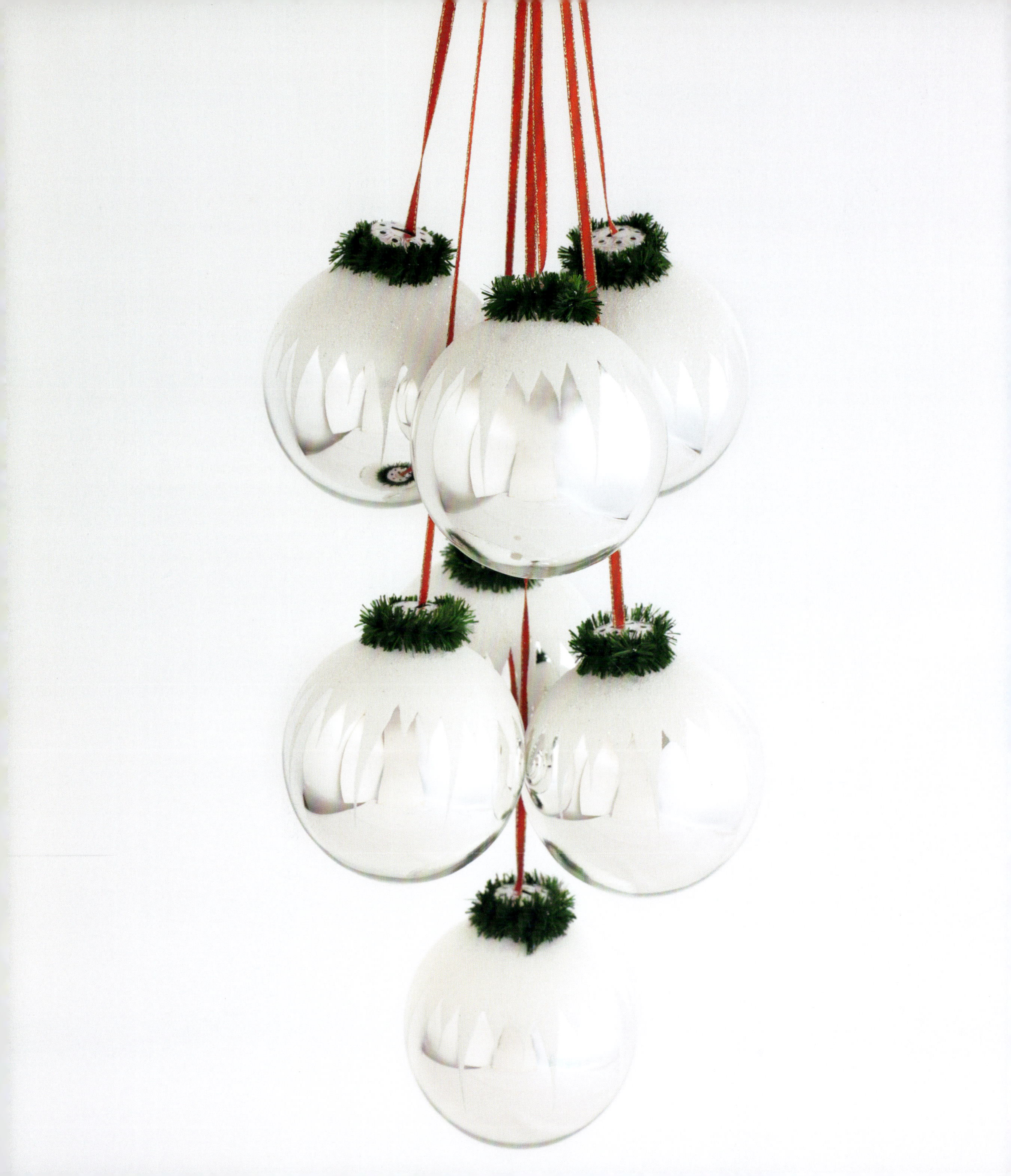

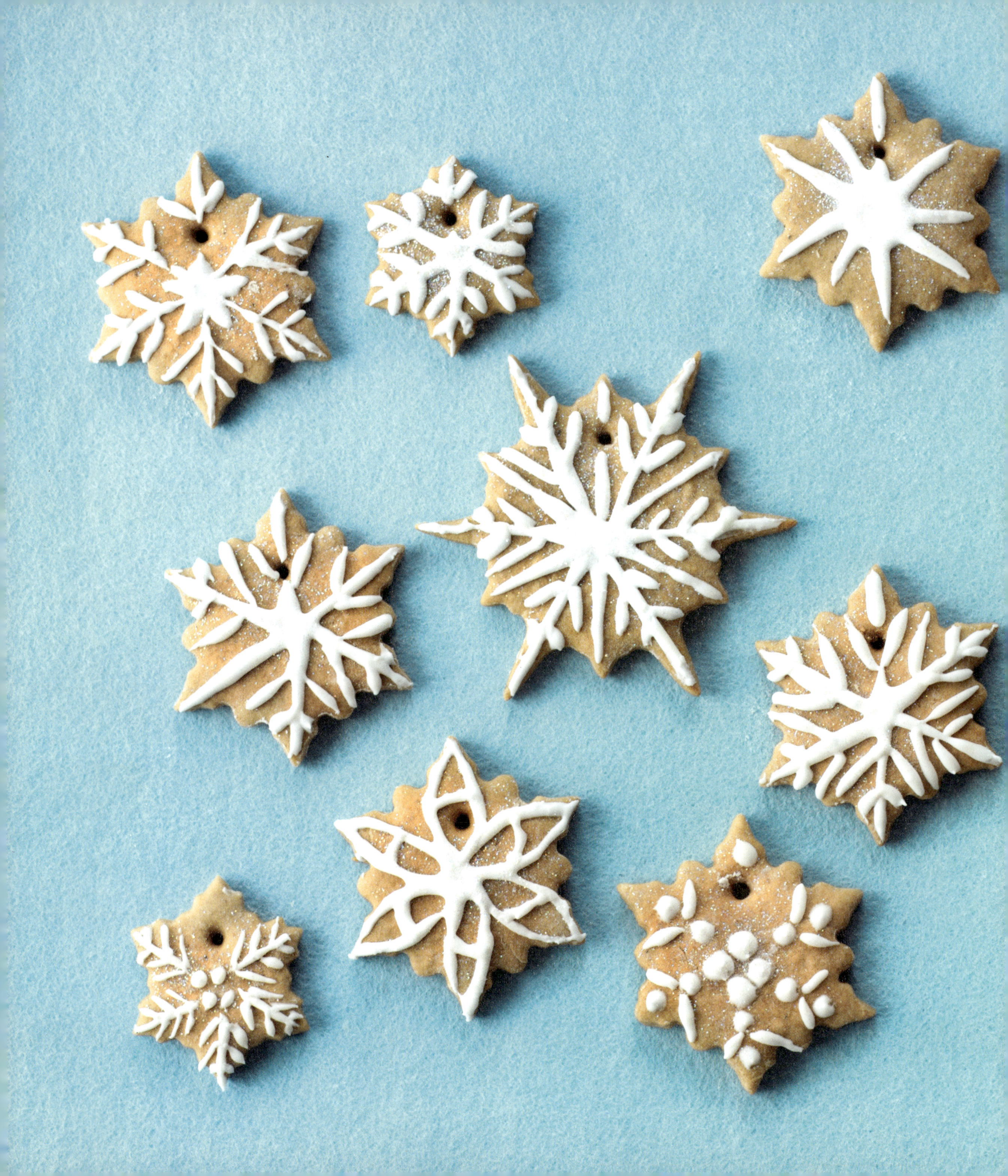